BOYCOTT

Kevin,

Thanks for all your
support with my
efforts and the marathon.

Best,

[signature]

BOYCOTT

STOLEN DREAMS OF THE
1980 MOSCOW OLYMPIC GAMES

Tom Caraccioli and Jerry Caraccioli

Foreword By Vice President Walter F. Mondale

NEW CHAPTER PRESS

BOYCOTT: Stolen Dreams of the 1980 Moscow Olympic Games by Tom Caraccioli and Jerry Caraccioli is published by New Chapter Press (www.newchapterpressmedia.com) and distributed by the Independent Publishers Group (www.ipgbook.com)
ISBN: 978-0942257403
© Tom Caraccioli and Jerry Caraccioli

Cover Photos
Jimmy Carter – Courtesy of Getty Images
Sue Walsh - Courtesy of Sue Walsh
Ron Galimore – Courtesy of Ron Galimore
Gene Mills – Courtesy of Gene Mills
Linda Cornelius Waltman – Courtesy of Linda Cornelius Waltman

Flap Photos
Tom Caraccioli and Jerry Caraccioli – Courtesy of John Filo
Walter F. Mondale – Courtesy of The Office of Walter F. Mondale

Interior Photos
Don Paige – Courtesy of Don Paige and Villanova University
Glenn Mills – Courtesy of Glenn Mills
Gwen Gardner – Courtesy of U.S. Olympic Committee
Gene Mills – Courtesy of Gene Mills
Craig Beardsley – Courtesy of University of Florida
Sue Walsh – Courtesy of Sue Walsh/University of North Carolina
Bill Hanzlik – Courtesy of University of Notre Dame
Amy Koopman – Courtesy of Amy Koopman
Isiah Thomas – Courtesy of Indiana University
Carol Blazejowski – Courtesy of Montclair State University
Luci Collins – Courtesy of USA Gymnastics
David Kimes – Courtesy of David Kimes
Brian Gust – Courtesy of Brian Gust
Lisa Buese – Courtesy of Lisa Buese
Linda Cornelius Waltman – Courtesy of Linda Cornelius Waltman
Thomas Schuler – Courtesy of Thomas Schuler
Ron Galimore – Courtesy of Iowa State University
Debbie Landreth – Courtesy of USA Volleyball

Design by Visible Logic
Special thanks to Chris Nicholson, Irene Tan, Ewing Walker, Emily Brackett and DeAnne McCaslin

Printed in the United States of America

Table of Contents

Foreword

It has oft been said that sports offers the thrill of victory and the agony of defeat. In 1980, the Olympic Games, Winter and Summer, provided both and were bittersweet for me and many of my fellow Americans.

In February, I was thrilled to be in Lake Placid to open the Winter Games and be in the stands when the United States hockey team, which featured many players and the coach from my home state of Minnesota, won the gold medal. Two months later in April, I agonized over addressing the delegates of the United States Olympic Committee in Colorado Springs about the decision to boycott the Summer Games.

I have always been a sports fan, in general, and a fan of the Olympics, in particular. Though I was never quite a good enough athlete to make an Olympic team while growing up in southern Minnesota, I have always marveled at those who were able to accomplish that goal. I have a great sense of loyalty and empathy to the kids who didn't get the chance to live their dream of competing in the 1980 Olympic Summer Games in Moscow. For many, they only had a couple of years in their prime and would never get another chance like that again. They lost a big point in their lives that they weren't going to be able to reclaim. I know this is still a very raw moment in American history, and for that I am sorry.

I will always remember meeting with those athletes in the White House. Like they had been when the announcement was made to boycott the Games in Colorado Springs, they were very respectful and dignified despite the fact that in their hearts I'm sure most disagreed with the decision and just wanted to compete. I also can understand why some of the athletes may have felt as if they were used as political pawns because of what was at stake for them.

Certainly sending a team and going ahead with the Olympics, politically, would've been an easy thing to do. But, I can say unequivocally, boycotting the 1980 Olympic Summer Games was a very painful decision for all involved in making it, but one that we felt was the right thing to do.

The Soviet Union would've loved it if American athletes had made a big issue against our policy. They would've grabbed on to that and said, 'See, America is putting its own athletes down and the athletes are mad about it and want to come to Moscow.'

For the athletes of the 1980 United States Summer Olympic team during this era of American history and the Cold War, it was these men and women who unfortunately, and unwillingly, became the warriors in our country's defense of freedom. These men and women were the ones who were affected the most.

We must remember that America and the world confronted an enormously dangerous new action by the Soviet Union: it had invaded its neighbor Afghanistan without a shred of moral or legal legitimacy, seeking, by brute force, to suppress Afghan independence. Like Nazi Germany, at the infamous 1936 Berlin Olympics, where Hitler tried to use the Olympics to legitimize his hideous government, so, too, Soviet dictators had begun to argue that the world's willingness to hold their Olympics in Moscow demonstrated that world opinion backed the Soviet Union despite widespread international resentment toward their government and its appalling abuse of its neighbor.

Of course, the Soviet Union system later spectacularly collapsed, disappearing forever from the world scene. I believe that our young athletes, who sacrificed so much, deserve great credit for their part in denying respectability to such an odious regime.

BOYCOTT: Stolen Dreams of the 1980 Moscow Olympic Games chronicles this very tragic moment of American and Olympic history and tells the story within its pages about the men and women who were called upon to make an extreme sacrifice because of an international conflict in which they had no control.

—Vice President Walter F. Mondale

Authors' Note

For the scores of athletes who never got the chance to march in the Opening Ceremony of the 1980 Olympic Summer Games, and never competed against the best in the world on an Olympic stage, these pages, ultimately, may be of little comfort. Yet their stories are told so that we may never forget the men and women of the 1980 United States Summer Olympics team who are every bit as worthy and deserving of the moniker "Olympian" as those who came before and after 1980.

To those athletes, the ultimate heroes of that stolen summer, this is their story.

Acknowledgements

One of the first questions we were asked after completing our first book—
Striking Silver: The Untold Story of America's Forgotten Hockey Team—was:
"Do you guys have another book in mind to write?" Our first book was just
released and mere days old. We took that question as a compliment. Truth be
told, we did have another idea or two for a second book. One of those ideas
materialized into this story.

As with any book, it cannot be written without the cooperation, patience,
encouragement, and access of many people. It is with that in mind that we
would like to acknowledge those people.

First and foremost, we would like to thank the athletes of the 1980 United
States Olympic Summer Games team who are featured and graciously told
their stories. They not only represent their Olympic teammates but also our
country, their families and themselves with the utmost dignity—Carol Blazejowski, Craig Beardsley, Lisa Buese-Gani, Luci Collins-Cummings, Ron Galimore, Gwen Gardner, Brian Gust, Bill Hanzlik, David Kimes, Amy Koopman-
Enxing, Debbie Landreth-Brown, Gene Mills, Glenn Mills, Don Paige, Thomas
Schuler, Isiah Thomas, Sue Walsh and Linda Cornelius Waltman.

We would like to extend extra special thanks to Vice President Walter F.
Mondale for his time, insight and writing the foreword for this book. Also,
special thanks to our brother Kevin who continues to inspire, counsel and
protect.

Special thanks to Dick Enberg, Christine Brennan and Anita DeFrantz.

Princeton, N.J. attorney Robert Zagoria proved to be one of the most
valuable contacts we made in this process and we thank him for his time,

energy, exhaustive record-keeping and recollections of his part in this story. Great thanks to Ed Mackiewicz for taking the time to fully explain some of the more complex areas of this part of Olympic history. Cindy Stinger at the United States Olympic Committee was always available and quick with a response to any question or idea we presented.

Thanks to Todd Rucynski, who is more than a trusted friend and confidante.

Thanks to Lynda Pederson in Vice President Walter F. Mondale's office for her friendliness and help which were above and beyond. Thanks to the Minnesota Historical Society staff Molly Tierney and Debbie Miller for their help with research, as well as the LA84 Foundation, Wanda Dowding, Wendy Cook, Cathy Marino-Bradford, Sammy Walker, Otis Davis, John Thomas, Greg Massialas, Dr. Michael Sullivan at Drexel University, Colin Killian at Texas A&M, Tim Stried at Ohio State University, John Heisler at University of Notre Dame, David Berman at Villanova University, Matt Shoultz at Iowa State University, Mike Scala at Montclair State University, Nate Wiechers at Indiana University, Carol Copley at Notre Dame, Tim Gelt of the Denver Nuggets, Jonathan Supranowitz and Raquelle Burnette of the New York Knicks, Luan Peszek at USA Gymnastics, Janey Marks and John George at Getty Images, Graham Seiter, Danielle Perry and Joe Favorito for their help with research and resources.

Thanks to Phil Donahue for helping us track down Soviet journalist Vladimir Pozner. And thanks to Vladimir Pozner for his point of reference in supplying the Soviet perspective to this story.

For their support, thanks to the members of the CBS family including Sean McManus, Tony Petitti, LeslieAnne Wade, Robin Brendle, Jennifer Sabatelle, Gil Schwartz, Dana McClintock, Kelli Raftery, John Filo, Paula Breck and Jim Shefcik

To our mother and father, Barbara and Edward, thanks again for your belief in our abilities and your candid assessments when asked. To our brothers and sisters, Mary Anne, Mike, Paul, John and Kevin, as well as Rudy, Elaine, Jeff and Pam, you've all played a part in shaping our storytelling.

Sincere thanks to Andrew Blauner.

Thanks to our friends and family in Oswego, New York who have supported our efforts in the past and continue to remain interested in our pursuits.

Great thanks to New Chapter Press and Randy Walker for their foresight and commitment to publishing this piece of Olympic history and the stories that symbolize the heartache and disappointment of these Olympic athletes and their 1980 brethren.

A Marcela, *siempre a vos.*

To my wife, Mary, and daugher, Olivia, you make my life exciting, interesting, fun and full of adventures that I can't imagine sharing with anybody else. You inspire me to be the best husband, father, son, brother, and friend to all. My most heartfelt thanks are saved for you both. I dedicate this to you.

Introduction

Politics and the Olympics certainly weren't introduced by President Jimmy Carter when he called for a boycott of the 1980 Olympic Summer Games in Moscow. But for the American athletes who were caught in the middle of a geopolitical chess match between superpowers, understanding the reality of their situation came at different times during their lives.

Some members of the 1980 U.S. team—such as rower Anita DeFrantz (who had competed in the 1976 Summer Games in Montreal and won a bronze medal), water polo player Peter Schnugg, javelin thrower Bruce Kennedy (who was being denied a third time of competing in the Olympics due to politics), weightlifter Philip Grippaldi, long jumper Arnie Robinson, as well as many others—were acutely aware of the gravity of what the boycott meant and the effect it would have on their Olympic dreams and those of their teammates.

As for some of the younger athletes on the team—such as 13-year-old gymnast Amy Koopman, her 16-year-old gymnastics teammate Luci Collins, and 19-year-old track stars Gwen Gardner and Carl Lewis—though disappointed, they figured they would get another chance to compete in the 1984 Olympics in Los Angeles. But many of the other young athletes were trained and conditioned to peak at the right time of their athletic careers, including swimmers Craig Beardsley and Glenn Mills, distance runner Don Paige, and pentathlete Linda Cornelius Waltman; they and others would never realize their dream of competing in the Olympics and would forever see their names alongside an asterisk in press guides and Olympic history books.

Politics and the Olympics will probably never be mutually exclusive, but in 1980 they were tangled in such a way as to strike at the very core of human rights and the Olympic ideal.

What President Carter had described as one of his administration's most painful decisions was summed up by Vice President Walter F. Mondale.

"I am very sorry about it," says Mondale 28 years later. "I know the athletes were asked to pay a price that couldn't be repaid. They lost their one shot at the Olympics. They were good enough to be designated as United States Olympians, so they were at the top of their games. As someone who loves the Olympics and loves the athletes, it was a very painful moment. But I still think it was the right thing to do and America stood tall against a brutal invasion by a dictatorship that was trying to establish a principle that was very dangerous for the future of all us, including the athletes."

Olympian*

The asterisk earned dubious notoriety as a reference mark in 1961. For nearly half a century, the * has continued to dot the landscape of professional and amateur sports with an equally questionable distinction.

In 1961, then-Major League Baseball Commissioner Ford Frick made one of the most controversial rulings ever regarding the history of the game. After watching New York Yankees outfielder and slugger Roger Maris eclipse the immortal Babe Ruth's single-season home run record of 60 on the final day of the 1961 season, Frick convinced baseball historians to list Ruth's and Maris's marks as separate records based on the number of games each player had to accomplish their respective marks.

Frick reasoned, or some say "caved into" his former sportswriter brethren, that Ruth had produced 60 homers in a 154-game season and Maris had recorded 61 in a 162-game season. Therefore, Maris's homer mark should be listed in the record books with an asterisk. From that day on, the * became part of baseball lore and history. And it stayed that way for the next 30 years. Today, the * has become a permanent part of the sports vernacular.

The asterisk in today's sports world continues to denote a questionable achievement and has come into vogue again when talking about baseball's home run records. With the proliferation and accusations of steroids, human growth hormones and other performance-enhancing substances, historians and record keepers continue to be flummoxed when debating the * and its potential use.

For members of the 1980 United States Olympic Summer Games team, the * is a reference mark they would rather not have to invoke when discussing their Olympian status. And though Olympic historians and fans of the Games have never made it an issue, some members of that team feel like that dubious symbol follows them throughout their personal history.

For swimmer Glenn Mills, the * hit him right between the eyes when he was looking through his college alma mater's swimming media guide. "I went to school at the University of Alabama," explains Mills. "In the press guide, Alabama gives its history of all the people that were NCAA champions, Olympians, and things like that. When everything is listed, always next to our names is an asterisk, under the asterisk it reads: 'Made 1980 Olympic team, but country boycotted.' It's very seldom that you see any of our names listed as Olympians without an asterisk. It kind of implies, 'Well, they're Olympians, but maybe not really.' "

Mills suffered further indignity when he traveled to Colorado Springs in the early 1990s to coach at a Select Camp. "We were staying at the Training Center. Some of the coaches were just hanging out, so we decided to go into the gift shop. As we were walking down the hallway into the shop, I saw this kiosk that had a sign that read—'Find Your Favorite Olympian.' I said cool, let me check this out. I love seeing my name on those things. So I punched up

Mills. There were about four or five different Mills on there. I saw my name and clicked on it, and the screen came up. On the top it said, 'Glenn Mills' and under it said, '1980 Swimming.' Where the bio was supposed to be, all it said was, 'Did Not Compete.'

"I just stood there looking at it and actually started laughing. I looked for some of my other friends, like Craig Beardsley, and he had a picture in there, but it said, 'Did Not Compete.' It didn't say anything about being the world-record holder. It was really kind of sad."

Amy Koopman, who was one of the youngest members of the 1980 team at 13 years old, earned her trip to the Olympic Games in Moscow in gymnastics. Even today, though she doesn't dwell on it, Koopman still thinks about being a forgotten part of Olympic history. "I'm disappointed that I never got to compete for the U.S. at the Olympics. Everyone asks, 'Oh… how did you do?' I tell them, 'We didn't go.' Everyone forgets that we didn't go."

Linda Cornelius Waltman, a pentathlete who, in 1980, had one shot at competing in the Olympics, sits quietly in front of the television every time the Olympic Games are staged. She thinks about what she missed. "The worst was four years after when the Olympics were in Los Angeles. I remember sitting in front of the television watching the Opening Ceremony, just crying and thinking I never really got a chance to be a part of that. It just really hit home. Every time watching an Opening Ceremony of an Olympics—I don't think I've missed one—I always shed a tear. Always."

And those tears always accompany the thought that the 1980 team is special. Though, each member of that team also thinks there's little they wouldn't give for a chance not to be so special, not to have an asterisk next to their name. Instead, this team is left with an indelible mark in Olympic history. A mark that is not easily definable. Not easily accepted. And not easily understood.

U.S. volleyball player Debbie Landreth sums up her Olympic experience and how she deals with questions about her past athletic life in a thoughtful and respectful tone. She still feels the pain of not being able to compete, but has not let the * diminish her career and aspirations as the head coach of the women's volleyball team at the University of Notre Dame. "It was definitely a situation where it was much bigger than a match loss," Landreth says. "You had to pick up and move on in life. I wasn't just going to quit. I had to ask myself, 'All right, what am I going to do now?'"

Los Angeles Deputy Sheriff Gwen Gardner, who ran the 400-meter on the U.S. track and field team in 1980, voiced similar displeasure and disappointment when discussing the decision to boycott the Moscow Games. "It was an opportunity that we missed and it didn't change anything by us boycotting that particular competition. It was a great disappointment," she says, her voice trailing off into quiet contemplation that needs no explanation or reference mark.

Don Paige — 1980 U.S. Olympic Track and Field Team

Don Paige
Track and Field

When the 800-meter race at the 1980 Olympic Summer Games in Moscow came on the television screen in Don Paige's family home in Baldwinsville, N.Y., the United States' most celebrated half-miler couldn't bear to watch. Instead, he went outside and sat in the backyard. "My Dad came out and told me Steve Ovett out-kicked Sebastian Coe," remembers Paige more than a quarter century later. "And then he said, 'Boy, I would've loved to have seen you in that race.'"

Don Paige—now president and founder of Paige Design Group, dedicated to building track and field facilities—was, on that day, a six-time NCAA track and field champion at Villanova University, winner of the 800-meter run at the Olympic Trials, and one of the premiere members of the U.S. Summer Games track and field team.

As a tall, skinny kid growing up in a middle-class, blue-collar suburb of Syracuse, N.Y., Paige was one of five siblings who had sports in his blood. "Growing up, we were all pretty athletic. Starting out in ninth grade it seemed like the thing to do, so I took a look at football," Paige recalls with a chuckle. Because of his slender build, he figured football was probably not a healthy option in high school. "I looked at soccer. Soccer wasn't all that popular but it was beginning to grow at our school. So I took up cross-country and found I had a passion for running. That's how I got involved in running in 1971.

"I had a great high school coach in cross-country, Chuck Wiltse," Paige remembers. "Chuck coached JV cross-country and did one of the single most important things that led me to becoming a good runner. He recognized that I could've run varsity after only four or five weeks into the season, but he kept me in ninth-grade cross-country where I ran against ninth-graders. And it taught me one of those deep-down lessons—learning how to win. I could've gone to varsity and probably wouldn't have won. I won a lot of my races in ninth grade and that had an effect on me and was very valuable."

Not only did Wiltse set the young freshman on a path to success, but he also became his lifelong mentor—one of several who helped set a course for Paige's Olympic dream.

Teaching a gifted athlete how to win was only one facet of Wiltse's influence. Wiltse taught the ninth-grade Paige the fundamentals to build a winning attitude and a killer instinct. "You start learning early from a good coach that the basics of a good foundation are important," Paige says. "The other thing ninth-grade cross-country taught me was how to be competitive. Times never really were that important to me. What meant more was to learn to win. I was fortunate that I had a cross-country coach that truly understood that, and understood me."

Paige's success throughout high school landed him at a crossroads about his future. He welcomed the attention from the nation's top college track and field programs. "My top three were Villanova, Kansas and Georgetown," Paige recalls "Tennessee was really up there on my list, too. I was looking for a school where I could get a good education along with good athletics." It looked as if Tennessee coach Stan Huntsman would successfully woo the Central New York phenom to the Volunteer State after a successful recruiting trip left Paige wondering if he might be happy south of the Mason-Dixon line. But, not for the last time in his life, policy altered fate. "Stan had a policy where he usually waited longer in the season before he offered full scholarships," Paige says. "So, he didn't offer me a full scholarship. I then went on to finish my recruiting trips."

One of those trips included a visit to Villanova and a meeting with the inimitable James "Jumbo" Elliott. After several weeks had passed, Paige returned to Philadelphia for the Penn Relays still not having heard from Tennessee. "Getting a scholarship was very important in my family because we were middle-class, the lower end of middle-class, and college would've been a real hardship," explains Paige. After winning the high school division of the Penn Relays, he called Elliott at Villanova and accepted his invitation to attend school in Philadelphia. Within one week, Huntsman finally offered a full scholarship to attend Tennessee, but Paige had to turn it down.

"The funny part of this story is that we now travel around speaking at different engagements across the country and [Hunstman] tells the story of how he could've had Don Paige on his team, but he didn't offer him a scholarship when he was on campus," says Paige with a chuckle. "And he took it one step further and explained that probably wasn't his biggest mistake, because he didn't offer 'Skeets' Nehemiah, Renaldo Nehemiah, one either."

At Villanova, Paige found a mentor and another future lifelong friend in Elliott. "At Villanova, we called Mr. Elliott, 'Mr. Elliott,'" Paige says. "No one called him 'Coach.' Only his closest friends called him 'Jumbo.' And if anyone ever called him 'Coach,' we knew that guy didn't know Mr. Elliott very well."

In track and field, the Olympic dream evolves in stages, if you have talent and desire. "I think a lot of people don't understand the process of becoming an Olympian," explains Paige. "By the time I got to 11th grade, I was a pretty good high school runner. By that time, you're thinking about running in college. You don't start thinking about the Olympics, but you do say to yourself, 'If I run a little better, I may be able to get a scholarship to college.'"

Paige got the scholarship and, in Elliott, a coach who had guided future Olympians (Marty Liquori, Eamon Coughlin) and knew if one of his runners had talent enough to compete on the world's biggest athletic stage. And

Paige saw these same guys—Liquori and Coughlin—and thought it would be great to run in the Olympics someday.

In Paige's freshman season, Elliott inserted the newcomer into a meet at Dartmouth, before which the coach spoke "matter-of-factly" about how he planned to have his 4x1-mile team break the world record. "I was astonished," Paige remembers. "I hadn't even finished a workout and he was putting me on that team. So, Phil Kane speaks up. You almost never challenge Mr. Elliott, but Phil spoke up and said, 'Mr. Elliott, you're putting Don on the team but you're leaving Eamon Coughlin off?' He was one of the premiere milers in college. 'Well,' Mr. Elliott said, 'we're going to break the American record, too.' Eamon, being Irish, would negate the American record. Phil went on and said, 'Don has been struggling here a little bit…' And Mr. Elliott said, 'Yes. I understand, but he'll be fine.'"

The freshman was more than fine. Paige turned in the second fastest mile split in the event and the fastest on the Villanova team. Elliott was always able to sense how well his runners would run, and he had that confidence in Paige from the very beginning. Injuries followed and Paige missed the outdoor seasons of his first two years in college, but he was making progress—not to mention winning NCAA titles—and began to quietly think about the 1980 Summer Games in Moscow.

If Don Paige wasn't on anyone's Olympic radar before the 1979 NCAA Track and Field Championships, he certainly was following the monumental meet in Champaign, Ill. Elliott tapped Paige for an unthinkable feat: winning the 1500-meter and 800-meter races. This was nearly unheard of because of the proximity in which the 1500 and 800 were run.

Paige recalls it with astonishment still in his voice, as if it were yesterday when his coach told the wiry star he had entered him in both races. "I hung up the phone and looked at my teammate Tony Tufariello and he said,

'What's up?' I told him, 'Mr. Elliott has just entered me in the 1500 and 800.' Tony looked at me and said, 'You can't do both.' I said, 'I know.'

"The NCAA has set the trials, semis and finals in such a manner that it is impractical to double. It is physically challenging to say the least. About 30 seconds after I hung up the phone, our assistant coach Jack Pyrah came in. He said, 'The trials, no problem. On Thursday you'll run the trials, have about two hours rest. That will be no problem. On Friday, you'll have to run a semifinal in the 800 and you can cruise through that. You'll be fine. Now, Saturday, you have to run both on the same day and they are about 30 minutes apart. Mr. Elliott thinks because you're running the mile first, you're coming down from that....' And he's making it sound so easy. "

Paige won the 1500-meter. As he sat to bring his heart rate down before the start of the 800-meter run, Elliott tapped him on the bottom of his foot. "Did you bring your sticks [golf clubs]?' " asked the veteran coach.

"It was my senior year and he was teaching me how to play golf," remembers Paige. "He told me, 'Monday we're going to have to go over to the range at the club and hit some balls.' " Elliott then turned away and went back to the stands.

Paige didn't know it then, but later, after winning his second NCAA championship of the day, he realized his coach had just helped him relax enough to take his mind off of what many considered improbable.

The year 1979 was fantastic for Paige as he trained through it injury-free. It was evident to the track and field world that Don Paige was an Olympic contender, and his training verified that notion.

But all that momentum suddenly became irrelevant.

It was in March 1980 that Paige was summoned to the White House to hear a very important announcement: The U.S. had decided to boycott the Moscow Games. "They picked a few athletes in every sport to go down to the White House," recalls Paige. "I still remember the words, the way I heard them. Jimmy Carter said, 'We will not go.' That's the way I heard them. I sat there in shock thinking the United States will not go the Olympic Games in Moscow. I was 23 years old."

Paige had driven from Philadelphia with Elliott, and they climbed back into the car for their trip back to Villanova. As they were leaving Washington, Elliott said, "I'm going to let you cry for five minutes, and you should cry. But when you're done crying, we're going to Plan B.'"

Paige recalls his reaction. "I looked at him and said, 'You've got a Plan B?' He said, 'You've always got to have a Plan B. In life you have a Plan A and Plan B.' So, he let me cry and get it out of my system and then said, 'Do not worry about things you have no control over. You're not going.'"

First, Elliott spelled out Plan A the way he saw it before the White House announcement. Paige would win the indoor nationals in the 1000-meter, and proceed to win the 800 during the outdoor season while foregoing another attempt at a double. That would leave him with six NCAA titles at Villanova entering the Olympic Trials. He would place first, second or third; make the team; march in the Olympic Opening Ceremony; advance to the semifinals of the 800-meter run; and then let the chips fall where they're meant to fall in the finals. An exasperated Paige still remembers, "That was Plan A. Easy, right?"

Elliott's post-boycott Plan B involved proving to the world that Don Paige was the world's best half-miler in 1980 without attending the Olympics. That was not going to be an easy task.

Plan B involved having to win the indoor and outdoor nationals, having to win the U.S. Olympic Trials, running the fastest 800-meter in the world and running undefeated for the entire season—and, to top it off, going to Europe for a post-Olympics race in which he competes against the gold, silver and bronze medal winners, including world record-holder

Sebastian Coe. "Plan B was a four to five-month plan that I had to do to prove to myself how good I really was, since I couldn't go to the Olympics," Paige remembers.

Plan B proceeded as designed, with Paige accomplishing everything he could short of the Olympic gold medal. His final hurdle to a No. 1 world ranking came in the form of an epic race in Viareggio, Italy, versus the legendary Coe.

"I have to thank Marty Liquori, a Villanova alum and friend, for that," admits Paige. "Marty called me in the spring of 1980 at the dorm and told me he entered me in the 800-meter race in Viareggio on the Italian Riviera. I said, 'Great, why?' He said, 'Because Sebastian Coe races the 800 there right after Zurich and this will probably be your only chance to race Coe.' Marty knew the plan. Sure enough, we go to Europe and I can't get in a race with Sebastian Coe."

Paige was not overly surprised at being excluded from the race in Viareggio, so he pleaded his case with the race director. As Paige was deliberating for participation, a quiet voice, and an altogether strange participant, was also in the room listening to the argument—Coe's father.

With Paige's frustration growing after one hour of futile debate, he stood up and issued an ultimatum to both men. "Here's what's going to happen. I'm going to warm up for the 800, take my sweats off, and go to the line," recalls Paige. "You're going to have to remove me from that line. When you do, I'm going to hold a press conference explaining to them how my good friend Marty Liquori entered me in this race months ago and you two wanted me out because you thought I might beat Sebastian Coe."

Paige's perseverance and threat were enough. Because he was not able to compete in the Olympics, this race was his moment in history to prove to himself and to the world who was the best half-miler in 1980. In the final moments before stepping to the starting line, Paige's mind raced back to the words Elliott had offered at Villanova about racing Coe: "If he never gets in front of you, he can't beat you."

When the gun sounded Paige knew it would be a legendary event. "I'm in the race, Sebastian was in the race and there is the designated rabbit," he says. "All year long Mr. Elliott had told me to run closer to the front so I was in third or fourth position. We were at 200 meters, 300 meters, and the rabbit is supposed to take us all the way to 600 meters. Going into bell lap I was in second place, Sebastian in third or fourth. Well, with 300 to go, the rabbit is still on the track, and this was one of the first times in my life that Don Paige would be in the lead with 300 meters to go. We were going down the backstretch and I could feel Sebastian on my shoulder. Mr. Elliott and I had talked about when we thought Sebastian might make his first jump and, sure enough, at 200 meters Sebastian bolted. And I mean bolted. I was thinking, we're in the middle of a career-defining race and Mr. Elliott is right, this son-of-a-gun is fast. He got a step and a half on me instantly. So, I buckled down and held him off on the turn. He took another big jump when we got on the homestretch and got another step-and-a-half on me. Well, when you're a kicker, kickers have this great ability of seeing the finish line and training [their] kick. We were still 80 meters out and we're side by side, and I was thinking—'We're going to tie.' Forty meters to go. Thirty meters to go. I was thinking, 'You've got to be kidding me.' We are exactly almost stride-for-stride, dead even with each other. Again, I'm thinking, 'This can't be, we can't tie.' We crossed the line—photo finish."

Exasperated, Paige clearly remembers, "I'm down the track a bit and I've got my hands on my knees, Sebastian's got his hands on his knees, and he comes over to me and says, 'Thank you,' and pats me on the back. The crowd—they're still waiting. They don't know who's won. I gave some of my teammates, who were sitting in the corner, a little thumbs-up and the crowd roared because I had beaten Sebastian Coe. I won by two one-hundredths of a second.

"That led to me being ranked No. 1 in the world. And at the time, 1980, it was the first time a world record holder and Olympic medallist did not finish No. 1 in the world. It went to a gentleman who didn't race in the Olympic Games."

Glenn Mills – 1980 U.S. Olympic Swim Team

Glenn Mills
Swimming

It was a Friday afternoon in May 1977 at his high school pool in Ridgeville, Ohio, when Glenn Mills took the blocks in Lane 6 for practice. Traditionally Lane 1 was reserved for the slowest swimmers, and Lane 6 for the fastest. Mills was not the team's top swimmer yet, but nobody at the pool that day said a word.

The short, fat kid—whose older brothers Kevin and Kyle had established a swimming pedigree with the Mills name in their small town—had always practiced in Lanes 4 or 5. But that Friday was different.

"They got me out of school and I went home and pretty much knew what had happened when I walked in the door," says Mills as his voice quavers and tears flow freely at the memory from more than 30 years ago. "The cancer had spread into his lungs and he would be sitting there. He couldn't lie down because it was too much weight on him. [So] when I walked in the door and I saw that he was lying down, I knew he was gone. Kyle died on a Thursday. The next day, I went back to practice."

Friday, May 6, 1977, Glenn Mills began a ferocious workout in Lane 6 that would eventually lead him to what he thought would be a spot on the 1980 United States Olympic swim team. "I couldn't work hard enough to where it hurt bad enough," Mills recalls. He never looked back from that point on.

"That was the day I stopped feeling sorry for myself. I went to the pool and I chose that pain. In a very short period of time, within a few months of Kyle dying, I went to a regional event in Louisville, Ky., and ended up qualifying for Senior Nationals by two-tenths of a second as a freshman in high school. I had barely made Junior Nationals in one event and I just made this huge jump. From there, good things started to happen."

The faster Mills swam, the harder he worked. Within one year there was no one in the Cleveland area who was strong enough, yet alone competitive enough, for Mills to train with in the 100 breaststroke. "My Mom and Dad asked if I would want to try and train in Cincinnati the summer of my sophomore year," Mills remembers. "So I went down and spent the summer with Dave Wilson, who ended up getting a silver medal in 1984 in the 100 backstroke."

Mills' parents had told him that if things worked out well and he was making progress, they'd think about buying a townhouse in Cincinnati so he could train there more often. "I was thrown into this environment of obvious greatness," Mills says. "I remember when I got in there the first day, I was the sixth fastest guy in the lane that I was going to be training. By the end of the summer, with the attitude that I was still going to work as hard as I could, I jumped up to the sixth fastest guy in the nation. I got sixth in the Senior Nationals."

Though Mills' progress was attracting attention from the coaches in Cincinnati who foresaw a potential future Olympian before them, his motivation was steeped in a promise he had made several years before to his brother Kyle. "My freshman year in high school, I got ninth in the state. At that point I said to him that someday I would win the high school state meet for him, since he wasn't going to be able to do it." And as the younger Mills continued to train and excel in Cincinnati, his focus remained steadfast to achieving that goal.

"All I was trying to do was over-prepare myself so much by my senior year in high school that there would be no doubt I was going to win that state meet for my brother Kyle," remembers Mills. "The people in Cincinnati didn't know about that. They thought I was there, just like everybody else, training for the

Olympics. Here my goal was to win the state meet, and my coaches' goals were to put me on the Olympic team. I didn't even know it."

Mills was progressing well enough for his parents to make good on their townhouse promise. With his mother by his side, Mills moved to the "Queen City" in the summer of 1978. "Dad drove down there every weekend for two years—540 miles round trip. He'd hop in the car Friday afternoon, drive down, and then [get] back in the car on Sunday night to drive back up."

Cincinnati had a policy that no parents were allowed to watch practices. Mills' Dad was the exception and the only parent allowed to watch practice on Saturday mornings. "He'd always have to sit back in the shadows so he couldn't be seen," Mills recalls, laughing at the memory. "At the same time, I always knew he was there, so my best practices were Saturday mornings. I would kill myself on Saturday mornings."

In the next Senior Nationals meet, Mills placed sixth in the 100 breast-stroke. In the summer following his junior year in high school, he placed fifth, but the difference between his time and the winning time was shortening. The next high school season was close at hand and it was clear to Mills that his focus would be firmly on the State Championship meet.

Mills remembers that meet like it was yesterday. "My oldest brother Kevin had flown up from Alabama for the meet. He had told me that [I'd see] the guy next to me turning for the last 25 meters. I remember hitting the last wall and I didn't see him. So, I was like, 'Oh man.' I had never felt that good in a race. I was going so much faster than I had ever imagined. I remember the pool was set up in such a way that when you finished you couldn't see the clock—you had to swim back out to see the clock. When I finished, the noise was so loud, I didn't know what had happened.

"I swam back out," Mills tearfully remembers, "and I looked up and I had swam 55.4 [seconds]. I had broken the national record by almost a full second and just crushed anything I thought I could ever do. I had won the race by almost three seconds and that record stood for 20 years.

"I remember going up to the awards ceremony, and I had Kyle's hat that he had worn when he lost his hair during chemotherapy, and everybody knew the story [of my promise] at that point. When I walked up, there was this huge roar that went through the building. I always said I would have had to win the gold medal at the Olympics, break the world record by a few seconds and be met by 10 supermodels at the end of the lane to come close to that feeling. This was the culmination of everything. I was 18 years old, the top recruit in the United States, and it was February 1980. I hit my peak right then."

Two weeks later, the teenage Mills went to the Senior Nationals as the second seed in the 200 breaststroke despite having never finished higher than fifth. Mills swam his way into the finals, where he stood next to one of his heroes growing up—John Hencken. Hencken already had four gold and two silver medals from the 1972 Summer Games in Munich and 1976 Games in Montreal. "We went into the last turn of the 200 breaststroke dead even," Mills recalls, "and I won the race by almost two seconds. From there I broke David Wilke's national record." (Wilke had won the 1976 Olympics and set the world record.)

The way Mills figured it, he had done the 100 for his brother. Then he thought Kyle was looking down at him saying, "Okay, you did what you did for me. Thank you very much, but you're going to start swimming the event you're really good at and you're going to learn how to swim fast just in time for the Olympics." Everything was coming together and Mills was winning every race no matter what anybody threw at him.

Then, on March 21, 1980, President Jimmy Carter squelched the dreams of Mills and hundreds more of America's Summer Olympic athletes when he fulfilled his threat to boycott the 1980 Summer Games in Moscow after

Soviet leaders failed to withdraw Russian troops from Afghanistan by 12:01 a.m. on February 20, 1980.

Since the boycott was enacted in March, USA Swimming postponed its Olympic Trials. The governing body of swimming in the U.S. figured it would send the world a message by holding its Trials *after* the Moscow Games. "What we were supposed to do," Mills says, "was go in and beat their records, swim faster than the guys at the Olympics. I remember going to the meet. It was a very strange environment. People still wanted to win. We were the only sport to hold trials after the Olympics."

Mills, still a teenager at the time, didn't fully appreciate the magnitude of Carter's decision until years later. "I was 18 and concerned with much bigger and more important things, like whether or not I was going to have a date Friday night and where I was going to school the next year," says Mills, smiling. "I look back at some of my older friends who put so much hard work in trying to petition to having us go. I really thank them for that. Being so young and everything, I hadn't really figured it all out yet. The thing is, the rapid improvement over three and four years, going from somebody who was ninth in the state [of Ohio] to a few years later one of the top swimmers in the world, I just figured I'll make it in '84. Even when [the boycott] was going on, I was just going to improve and make it again in '84. No big deal."

When 1984 rolled around and the Olympic Summer Games returned to Los Angeles, the spirits of the summer athletes from the U.S. were renewed with optimism that would, hopefully, erase the pain and disappointment of 1980. Mills, then 22, figured his Olympic dreams would finally come true. So the defending U.S. Olympic Trials champ in the 200 breaststroke climbed onto the blocks at the '84 Trials.

"I went out 3.5 seconds slower than my buddy John Moffet and another guy, Richard Schroeder, and I ran out of pool. I couldn't run them down. They swam a really smart race. I was pleased with how I competed and sad at how I finished. I finished my career on an emotional…," his voice trails off. "I knew I was respectable, but I didn't do what I set out to do."

Just like that, Mills' Olympic dreams were unrealized forever.

When he went to college following the disappointment of 1980, his father gave him a plaque with a quote from Jesse Owens that read: "It's not the Olympics that make the Olympian, it's the preparation." Mills sustains that belief today and, though disappointed he did not have the chance to compete in the Olympics, he is not bitter. "There is pride that goes along with being an Olympian," Mills says. "We are pretty much fully accepted by our peers. They know what we did. We are respected and that's really what means the most to us."

In 2000, USA Swimming honored the members of the 1980 U.S. Olympic swim team in Indianapolis. "We were invited to go back for a reunion at the Olympic Trials," Mills recalls. "They had gotten us all together and decided to march us out. We were all standing there on the bulkhead and they told the story of the boycott, read each one of our names, and we got to do a little wave. At the end of the thing, there were about 5,000 people there, and they all stood up and just started clapping. It was probably the first time, in a long time, we really felt that we were what we thought we were. We were Olympians. And here we were getting respect from the people watching the current crop. It was like they remembered, and there was a lot of vindication that came along with that day."

Twenty-eight years later, Mills doesn't dwell on the negative of his Olympic experience in 1980. Quite the contrary. "Craig Beardsley, John Moffet, we became lifelong friends there. And a family was created," says Mills, with a smile on his face.

CHAPTER **11**

Afghanistan

Following days of troop build-up of tens of thousands of Soviet ground forces along the northern border of Afghanistan and thousands more in Kabul, Bagram and Shindand air bases under the pretext of a field exercise, the Soviet Union launched a major military intervention on December 27, 1979—Day 54 of the American hostage crisis in Iran.

Intelligence reports had initially described the troop movements as "security enhancement" for Soviet personnel in Afghanistan and assistance for the ailing Afghan regime.

But then Soviet Army tanks, along with ground force divisions of between 30,000 and 50,000 troops, rolled into Afghanistan from the north across the Amudarya River, the border with what was then Soviet Uzbekistan, and into the rugged Afghan countryside. Simultaneously the forces in Kabul attacked the Tajbeg Presidential Palace compound where the nominal president of Afghanistan, Hafizullah Amin, had taken refuge, and assassinated him.

A nearly 10-year war, often referred to as the equivalent of the United States' Vietnam War, had begun. In the end it would haunt both the former Soviet Union with defeat and eventual demise, and the United States by setting the beginning stages for the most devastating attacks the U.S. had ever suffered.

* * * * *

The Soviet war in Afghanistan was a conflict that involved Soviet forces supporting Afghanistan's communist-led Marxist People's Democratic Party of Afghanistan (PDPA) government against the largely Islamic fundamentalist mujahideen insurgents who were fighting to overthrow Soviet rule. Muslims from all over the world flocked to Afghanistan to join the rebels in the jihad, the "holy war," against the infidel Soviets. Among those foreign rebels—who found support from the U.S., Pakistan and other Muslim nations in the context of the Cold War—was a scion from a wealthy family from Saudi Arabia, Osama bin Laden. He would remain unknown for many years while using the Afghanistan conflict to learn the ways of warfare and radical Islam that later would be used against the United States.

* * * * *

The PDPA was founded in 1965 by a group of 30 Afghans in Kabul.[1] Rooted in Marxism, many of its members, who studied and received military training in the USSR, looked to Moscow for guidance and inspiration.

During its early years, PDPA members' allegiances were divided between its two leaders, Nur Mohammad Taraki and Babrak Karmal. Taraki and Karmal agreed on the basic objectives of the party, including socialist political and economic reforms, as well as complaints about the backward nature of Afghanistan's underdeveloped infrastructure and poor distribution of wealth and land perpetuated by traditional tribal and religious customs. However, Taraki and Karmal disagreed on how to solve these problems.

Taraki and his followers argued for radical socialist reforms using whatever means necessary to institute them. Karmal and his faction advocated gradual socialist change by working within the state system and converting different elements of Afghan society along the way.

In 1967, the PDPA split into two rival factions: the Khalq (Masses) led by Taraki, and Hafizullah Amin, supported by elements within the military; and the Parcham (Banner) faction, led by Karmal. The split reflected ethnic, class and ideological divisions within Afghan society. Karmal and Parcham continued to strive for the same kind of socialist reforms pursued by Taraki, but the two factions competed for power nonetheless.

Political discontent rose among many Afghans toward the country's leader, King Zahir Shah, who had ruled since the age of 19 when his father was assassinated in 1933. The PDPA was leading the way in expressing the people's disillusionment and frustration with the social and economic conditions and the unwillingness of the leadership to take control in fixing the nation's problems.

By the early 1970s, Zahir's administration had shut down the Parcham newspaper, quashed Parcham demonstrations, and thrown party members in jail. In response, Karmal and Parcham now voiced the same anti-monarchy opposition as the Khalqis.

Parcham and Khalq were not the only groups opposed to Zahir Shah's administration. The king's cousin, Sardar Mohammad Daoud, who had served as prime minister from 1953 to '63, also was eyeing the royal palace, as were several other former officials and relatives of the king.

Amid poor economic conditions (caused in part by a severe drought from 1971 to '72) and charges of corruption and malfeasance against the royal family, Daoud realized a race was on to replace the king. So he sprinted ahead. On July 17, 1973, along with key military officers and the minister of the interior, who was a Parcham sympathizer, Daoud seized power in a near-bloodless military coup. He promptly abolished the monarchy, formally repealed the 1964 constitution, and declared Afghanistan a republic with himself as its first president and prime minister. Zahir eventually found refuge in Italy.

* * * * *

The seizure of the government had been viewed favorably both in Moscow and Washington, D.C. It was seen as a revitalization of a long-standing Soviet investment of a client-state relationship with Afghanistan. As prime minister, Daoud had established close ties with Moscow that resulted in the Afghan military being equipped with Soviet weapons, large numbers of Soviet military advisors assigned to Afghanistan, and the training of Afghan military officers in the Soviet Union, as well as economic aid and other actions that affected the Afghan political landscape. [2]

The exact nature of Daoud's relationship with Parcham was unclear— whether the two agreed on political objectives for Afghanistan, or if theirs was just a political marriage of convenience. Either way, after the ousting of the royal family, Daoud initiated some of the progressive reforms demanded by his leftist supporters. But his marriage to the reformist program proposed by his early backers was soon divorced, and over time Daoud became a political liability for Moscow's aspirations in Afghanistan. He consolidated his personal power by purging the government of leftists. He replaced them with his own powerful clan, and sought more economic independence from the Soviet Union by exploring closer ties with Iran and the U.S. Still, he was careful never to fully shun the Soviets. The CIA noted that Daoud "was happiest when he could light his American cigarettes with Soviet matches."

Because Daoud leaned neither left nor right in his policies for change, he failed to quell the political instability that continued to plague his country and managed to alienate Afghanistan's socialists, moderates and religious fundamentalists. His pursuit of personal power by purging the leftists from the government and banning political opposition (including the Communist Party faction that supported his coup), as well as fostering a more independent foreign policy by strengthening his ties with Iran and the U.S., led to intense opposition sparked by the factions of the PDPA. Islamic fundamentalists also started to rebel against Daoud's "atheistic" reforms, as he failed in his attempts to carry out badly needed economic and social reforms through the promotion of a new constitution.

* * * * *

In 1977, the U.S. State Department remarked that Daoud's closer ties to Iran had "made significant contributions to the improvement of regional stability—thereby helping to fulfill another principal U.S. objective."[3] But despite U.S. approval, Daoud's authoritarian rule was not as well received by those who had to live under it.

PDPA members, Parchamis and Khalqis alike, had grown increasingly impatient with Daoud and were anxious to see him removed from power. Despite Khalq criticism toward their Parcham rivals for having thought they could work with Daoud after supporting his takeover, the two sides formally reunified in 1977 to form the People's Democratic Party of Afghanistan.

However, some believed that Soviet pressure played a role in the unification. With the PDPA's strong infiltration of the military, they were now positioned to influence events if and when Daoud lost his grip on power.

★ ★ ★ ★ ★

That time came on April 17, 1978, when Mir Akbar Khaibar, a leading member of the PDPA and vocal critic of Daoud, was mysteriously assassinated, possibly by Daoud's minister of the interior. Public outrage of Khaibar's death turned his funeral into an anti-government rally as thousands of mourners demonstrated against the Daoud administration. In response, Daoud clamped down further on the PDPA by arresting several of its party members. That in turn provoked PDPA supporters in the military to take action.

Ten days later, the military, collaborating with the PDPA, the very group that had supported his coup nearly five years earlier, overthrew and executed Daoud and members of his family. Daoud's republican government was replaced with a socialist one. The new coup was proclaimed as the beginning of the "Saur [April] Revolution."

Soon after, the takeover triggered a larger-scale rural rebellion against the new government, leading to a major insurgency by the end of 1978. This, according to some historians, would be the impetus of the Soviet invasion of Afghanistan 10 months later.

★ ★ ★ ★ ★

A pro-Soviet communist government was established, and Nur Mohammad Taraki, secretary general of the PDPA, became president of the Revolutionary Council and prime minister of the Democratic Republic of Afghanistan (DRA).

The Soviets took immediate steps to solidify the new communist regime by dispatching teams of political and military advisors to Afghanistan, as well as signing a new agreement for $250 million in military assistance.

The new government caused U.S. officials some initial concern, as they wondered whether Moscow had played a secret role in the PDPA takeover. But U.S. intelligence officials in Kabul detected no Soviet hand in the coup and advised caution in dealing with the new regime. They reasoned that while Daoud had been consolidating his personal power and pursuing new foreign ties, he had neglected the domestic issues that were straining his country. In turn, he had alienated many Afghans, including the progressive intellectuals who were demanding reforms and the religious leaders and intellectuals—or "Islamists"—who had already taken up arms against Daoud and been neglected and repressed. U.S. officials further reasoned that because it had stronger influence over the military and within the capital city of Kabul, the PDPA was in a stronger position than the Islamists to seize power.

Despite having reunified to overthrow Daoud, the Khalq-Parcham unity was not strong. Opposition to the Marxist government emerged almost immediately. The internal conflicts within the PDPA resulted in exiles, purges, imprisonment and executions. The new DRA government consisted mostly of Khalqis, due to the Khalq's control of the military. Not long after the April takeover, Khalq's two main leaders, Nur Mohammad Taraki and Hafizullah Amin, quickly consolidated Khalq rule by dispatching members of the Parcham faction, led by Babrak Karmal and Mohammed Najibullah, to foreign diplomatic posts and throwing others into jail.

With their Parcham rivals out of the way, the Khalqis moved quickly to impose radical secular reforms that ran counter to the beliefs of a population deeply rooted in Afghan traditions and Islam. Among the reforms that ignited such strong opposition were new marriage laws that threatened the security of rural women by significantly reducing the size of their dowry, and land reform laws. This measure was meant to help small farmers. In fact, many opposed the land reform for having alienated them from landowners who had helped in the growing and selling of crops.

Many of the disenfranchised landowners, along with religious leaders, began taking up arms against the Taraki-Amin government. By the latter half of 1978, a revolt began in the Nuristan region of eastern Afghanistan among the tribes of the Kunar Valley. Civil war quickly spread throughout the country among other ethnic groups, including the Pashtun majority. The government responded to the unrest with violent force, as an estimated 20,000 prisoners were sent to Pul-e-Charkhi prison outside of Kabul, and from there were executed by firing squad. An estimated 27,000 political prisoners, including village mullahs and headmen, were killed between April 1978 and the Soviet invasion in December 1979. Others—such as the traditional elite, the religious establishment and intellectuals—fled to Pakistan to join Islamic Afghan dissidents.

★ ★ ★ ★ ★

During this time, the United States found itself in a bit of a policy dilemma with the PDPA's ascension to power. In a secret memorandum to Secretary of State Cyrus Vance following the April takeover, the administration's early concerns were stated:

"We need to take into account the mix of nationalism and communism in the new leadership and seek to avoid driving the regime into a closer embrace with the Soviet Union than it might wish."

At the same time, the memo also pointed out factors embracing a hardline approach to the new government:

"Anti-regime elements in Afghanistan will be watching us carefully to see if we acquiesce in or accept the communist takeover.... Pakistan, Iran, Saudi

Arabia, and others of our friends in the area will see the situation clearly as a Soviet coup. On the domestic front, many Americans will see this as an extension of Soviet power and draw the parallel with Angola, Ethiopia, etc."[4]

The U.S. compromised by maintaining a relationship with the government while keeping channels open to the opposition. However, as dissent grew within Afghanistan toward the PDPA's radical reforms, the U.S. also grew increasingly uncomfortable.

By the end of the year, U.S. intelligence reports showed that at least 1,000 Soviet advisors were in Afghanistan, three times the number that were present at the time of the most recent coup. The reports also revealed that Moscow had signed another agreement of "cooperation and friendship" with the Afghan regime, which was described by U.S. intelligence analysts as allowing the Afghan government to summon military assistance from the Soviet Union.

* * * * *

That provision raised the antennae of U.S. intelligence analysts because of the growing insurrection. The violent resistance fueled by the dictatorial methods of the regime led to large numbers of insurgents receiving arms and assistance from ethnically allied guerilla organizations in Pakistan. The Afghan army was eroding and plagued by low morale and desertion to the insurgency.

* * * * *

In March 1979, a mutiny of Afghan soldiers joined tens of thousands of insurgents dressed in Afghan military garb to stage a violent uprising in the town of Herat. Over a thousand people were killed, including many Soviet military advisors, as the situation spun out of the PDPA's control. In urgent response, the Afghan leadership requested Soviet military assistance.

On March 17, the Politburo of the Central Committee of the Communist Party of the Soviet Union (CC CPSU) called an emergency meeting. Earlier in the day, the Soviets had spoken with Hafizullah Amin and with their military advisors in Herat. According to since-declassified transcripts of the meeting, Minister of Foreign Affairs Andrei Gromyko explained to his comrades the Soviets' understanding of what had happened in the uprising:

> *An artillery regiment and one infantry regiment comprising that division [17th division of the Afghan army numbering about 9,000 men] have gone over to the side of the insurgents. Bands of saboteurs and terrorists, having infiltrated from the territory of Pakistan, trained and armed not only with the participation of Pakistani forces but also of China, the United States of America and Iran, are committing atrocities in Herat. The insurgents infiltrating into the territory of Herat Province from Pakistan and Iran have joined forces with a domestic counter-revolution. The latter is especially comprised by religious fanatics. The leaders of the reactionary masses are also linked in large part with the religious figures.*
>
> *The number of insurgents is difficult to determine, but our comrades tell us that they are thousands, literally thousands.*
>
> *Significantly, it should be noted that I had a conversation this morning at 11:00 with Amin—Taraki's deputy who is minister of foreign affairs—and he did not express the slightest alarm about the situation in Afghanistan. And on the contrary, with olympian tranquility, he said that the situation was not all that complicated, that the army was in control of everything, and so forth. In a word, he expressed the opinion that their position was under control.*

Amin even said that the situation in Afghanistan is just fine. He said that not a single incident of insubordination by a governor had been reported, that is, that all the governors were on the side of the lawful government. Whereas in reality, according to the reports of our comrades, the situation in Herat and in a number of other places is alarming, and the insurgents are in control there.

Gromyko further reported:

I asked Amin, 'What kind of actions do you consider necessary from our side?' I told him what kind of aid we might be able to render. But he had on other requests, he simply responded that he had a very optimistic appraisal of the circumstances in Afghanistan, that the help you have given will stand us in good stead, and that all of the provinces are safely under the control of lawful forces. I asked him, 'Don't you expect any problems from neighboring governments or a domestic counter-revolution, and so forth?' Amin answered firmly that no, there are no threats to the regime. In conclusion, he conveyed his greetings to the members of the Politburo, and personally to Leonid Brezhnev.

Gromyko went on to explain that two-to-three hours following his discussion with Amin, he received news that chaos had erupted in Herat:

About a half hour later, we again received news from our comrades that Comrade Taraki had summoned the chief military advisor Comrade Gorelov and Charge d'affaires *Alekseev. And what did they discuss with Taraki? First of all, he appealed to the Soviet Union for help in the form of military equipment, ammunition and rations, that which is envisioned in the documents which we have presented for consideration by the Politburo. As far as military equipment is concerned, Taraki said, almost in passing, that perhaps ground and air support would be required. This must be understood to mean that the deployment of our forces is required, both land and air forces.*

With that passing comment from Taraki, the Soviet leadership knew what the Afghanistan government expected from their ally. But questions within the Soviet leadership arose about what enemy they would be engaging if they decided to respond to the request. Would they be fighting the insurgents, or would it be a combination of insurgents, religious fundamentalists, Muslims and ordinary citizens? And thus, would they be waging a war, in part, against the people of Afghanistan?

As members of the Politburo meeting discussed their policy options for dealing with the growing problems in Afghanistan, Aleksey Kosygin spoke up in proposing the immediate policy concerns:

First of all, we must not delay the supply of armaments until April but must give everything now, without delay, in March. That is the first thing.

Secondly, we must somehow give moral support to the leadership of Afghanistan, and I would suggest implementation of the following measures: Inform Taraki that we are raising the price of gas from 15 to 25 rubles [$21 to $37] per thousand cubic meters. That will make it possible to cover the expenses that they will incur in connection with the acquisition of arms and other materials by a rise in prices. It is necessary in my opinion to give Afghanistan these arms free of charge and not require any 25 percent assessment.

And third, we are slated to supply 75,000 tons of bread. I think we should re-examine that and supply Afghanistan with 100,000 tons. These are the measures that it seems to me ought to be added to the draft of the decision and, in that fashion, we would lend moral assistance to the Afghan leadership. We must put up a struggle for Afghanistan; after all, we have lived side by side for 60 years. Of course, while there is a difficult struggle with the Iranians, Pakistanis and Chinese, nevertheless Iran will lend assistance to Afghanistan—it has the means to do so, all the more so since they are like-minded religiously. This must be borne in mind. Pakistan will also take such measures. There is nothing you can say about the Chinese. Consequently, I believe that we must adopt the fraternal decision to seriously assist the Afghan leadership.

Kosygin went on to further question and warn his comrades about the Afghan leadership of Taraki and Amin:

Whatever you may say, Amin and Taraki alike are concealing from us the true state of affairs. We still don't know exactly what is happening in Afghanistan. What is their assessment of the situation? After all, they continue to paint the picture in a cheerful light, whereas in reality, we can see what is happening there. They are good people, that is apparent, but all the same they are concealing a great deal from us. What is the reason for this, that is hard to say…

In addition, I would consider it necessary to send an additional number of qualified military specialists, and let them find out what is happening with the army.

Moreover, I would consider it necessary to adopt a more comprehensive political decision. Perhaps the draft of such a political decision can be prepared by our comrades in the Ministry of Foreign Affairs, the Ministry of Defense, or the Foreign Department of the KGB. It is clear that Iran, China and Pakistan will come out against Afghanistan, and do everything within their power and means to contravene the lawful government and discredit its actions. It is exactly here that our political support of Taraki and his government is necessary. And of course, Carter will also come out against the leadership of Afghanistan….

It seems to me that we must speak to Taraki and Amin about the mistakes that they have permitted to occur during this time. In reality, even up to the present time, they have continued to execute people that do not agree with them; they have killed almost all of the leaders—not only the top leaders, but also those of the middle ranks—of the 'Parcham' party.[5]

With all of the opinions and policy being discussed about what to do if the situation worsened, one part of the Soviet policy was crystal clear: The Soviets could not surrender Afghanistan to the enemy. It also was clear to Gromyko, based on the conversations with Taraki and Amin, that the Afghan leadership had incorrectly assessed the state of affairs in the army and in the country, and was concealing information.

* * * * *

The following day, Taraki informed Kosygin that if the Soviet Union didn't lend its support, the Afghan army would not be able to hold off the insurgents in Herat, and the revolution would be doomed. In his next breath, Taraki surmised that if the army *was* able to hold out, survival of the revolution would be assured. Despite the Afghan's 100,000-man army, not all of which was in Herat, Taraki was asking to receive reinforcements in the form of tanks and armored cars for the infantry. Soviet leadership worried that their military involvement would be uncovered, that the whole world would learn that Soviet tanks were engaged in a military conflict in Afghanistan.

Because the Afghan situation was an internal revolutionary conflict, there was no legal justification under the United Nations Charter that would allow the Soviets to send troops for aid. According to the charter, a country can appeal for assistance, and troops can be sent, only if the state is subject to external aggression.

Sensing a tide of negative world opinion if they did deploy troops into Afghanistan, the Soviet leadership, though they supported the Afghan government's actions, decided not to involve their military. They reasoned that deploying troops would mean waging war against the people. They would be looked upon as aggressors.

Though they denied the request for troops, the Soviets knew they could not lose Afghanistan. As an acceptable medium, Soviet General Secretary Leonid I. Brezhnev agreed to provide Afghanistan with economic and military assistance in the form of equipment and advisors, but not with military manpower.[6]

* * * * *

After the Herat uprising, U.S. intelligence began to report a significant increase in Soviet military activity in and around Afghanistan. As promised by the Soviet leadership, more weapons and artillery were shipped into Afghanistan, including tanks, small arms, fighter aircraft and helicopter gunships. It also was observed that two Soviet divisions were conducting training exercises north of the Afghan border, an area that in the past had been virtually dormant.

In July 1979, the Soviets deployed an airborne battalion combat unit to Bagram airbase north of Kabul. There were now 2,500 to 3,000 Soviet military personnel advisors in Afghanistan, not counting the airborne battalion; some were attached to the Afghan army engaging in combat, including piloting helicopters.

As history would later reveal, U.S. involvement began after the Soviet invasion of Afghanistan in late December 1979, with CIA aid to the mujahideen in 1980. But in 1998, Zbigniew Brzezinski, President Carter's national security advisor, told the French magazine *Le Nouvel Observatur* that the decision to fund, arm and train the Afghan insurgents was made much earlier. The policy that Brzezinski helped craft was—unbeknownst even to the mujahideen—part of a larger U.S. strategy. "It was July 3, 1979, that President Carter signed the first directive for secret aid to the opponents of the pro-Soviet regime in Kabul," said Brzezinski in the article. "And that very day, I wrote a note to the president in which I explained to him that in my opinion this aid was going to induce a Soviet military intervention." As Brzezinski further explained in the article, "We didn't push the Russians to intervene, but we knowingly increased the probability that they would."[7]

Six months later, when the Soviets did indeed intervene, they tried to justify their actions by stating they were fighting against a secret involvement of the U.S. in Afghanistan. World opinion was against them. "The day that the Soviets officially crossed the border, I wrote to President Carter, we now have the opportunity of giving to the USSR its Vietnam war," Brzezinski predicted. "Indeed, for almost 10 years, Moscow had to carry on a war unsupportable by the government, a conflict that brought about the demoralization and finally the breakup of the Soviet empire."

★ ★ ★ ★ ★

By August, a group of Afghan army officers made an attempt to seize the Presidential Palace, but the move was thwarted. The event demonstrated a dramatic deterioration of the loyalty of the Afghan army units. The Soviets were now facing the possibility that the army they were providing support for might come apart. U.S. intelligence was reporting that Soviet divisions were in a heightened state of readiness.

As a September 14 intelligence community "Alert Memorandum" stated, Soviet leaders seemed to be on the threshold of committing "their own forces to prevent the collapse of the regime and protect their sizable stakes in Afghanistan." This hypothesis was qualified by stating that if the Soviet Union did ultimately increase its military role, it would likely do so incrementally by raising the number of military advisors to increase assistance to the Afghan army in combat operations, as well as possibly bringing in small units to protect key cities.[8]

Hafizullah Amin, who as the Afghan defense minister was in charge of the failed counter-insurgency operations, was becoming the focus of Soviet frustration. Despite the Soviet's aid, the Khalqis, particularly Amin, had little use for the Soviet counsel that accompanied the economic and military aid. Correspondingly, U.S. State Department intelligence soon learned that Moscow had little use in Afghanistan for the rule of either Taraki or Amin—but had more tolerance for the moderate Taraki.

By mid-September Amin was sensing a coup, and took action. Taraki attended a Non-Alignment Movement conference in Havana, Cuba, and then a meeting in Moscow where he and Soviet officials reportedly discussed Amin's future. When Taraki returned to Afghanistan, Amin had him removed from power, arrested and executed.

In October, following a grim report from Soviet military advisors that the Khalqi government had lost control of 23 of Afghanistan's 28 provinces to rebel forces, the Politburo drew up plans for military action.

* * * * *

As Amin asserted his power, Soviet leaders continued to be wary of him and what they perceived as a political shift in alliance with the West. According to an early-December 1979 personal memorandum from Yuri Andropov to Leonid Brezhnev, Andropov warned of secret activities by Amin that included contact with an American agent, and promises to tribal leaders to shift away from the USSR and to adopt a "policy of neutrality." Other signs included closed meetings disparaging Soviet policy and their advisors, and removal of Soviet headquarters in Kabul.

Amin's secret activity made the Soviets worry about losing the gains that had been made by the April Revolution, in addition to Afghanistan's perceived growing alliance with the West. To offset their concerns, the Soviets continued to work closely with Amin and with the leadership of the PDPA and DRA in order to alleviate any worries Amin had that the Soviets did not trust him nor wish to deal with him. At the same time, Soviet leadership began to make contingency plans to handle Amin and what they felt was growing anti-Soviet sentiments within the population.

* * * * *

Following a meeting on December 8 with Brezhnev and a small circle of the CC CPSU Politburo members, discussion of the situation in Afghanistan rendered a preliminary plan with two options: 1) removing Hafizullah Amin by the hands of KGB special agents and replacing him with Babrak Karmal; and 2) sending Soviet troops into Afghanistan for the same purposes.

Two days later, they chose the latter. Soviet Defense Minister D.F. Ustinov informed Chief of General Staff Nikolai Ogarkov that the Politburo decided on a preliminary plan to temporarily deploy 75,000 to 80,000 Soviet troops to Afghanistan. Despite Ogarkov's objections about using military force and his pleas to deal with the situation through political means, he was told that troops should start preparing.

On December 12, at the session of the CC CPSU Politburo elite members, the final decision to send Soviet troops into Afghanistan was made unanimously. The Soviet leaders believed that introduction of troops, which was secretly referred to as "the measures," was intended to promote the interests of strengthening the state, and pursued no other goals.[9]

* * * * *

At a December 17 White House meeting of top national security cabinet officials, intelligence reports revealed a Soviet airborne battalion build-up at Bagram, bringing the number of Soviet troops in Afghanistan to over 5,000. There also were reports that Soviet military command posts had set up along the northern border of Afghanistan, that combat divisions were deploying, and that aircraft build-up was continuing.

A week later, on December 24 and 25, waves of military aircraft were detected flying into Afghanistan, and it became clear the airborne divisions were now being mobilized.

* * * * *

On December 27, an explosion in the center of Kabul knocked out the general communications system. The Soviet invasion of Afghanistan had begun. Armored units made their way from Kabul International Airport and headed to various strategic centers on the outskirts of the city, where Afghan army divisions had been stationed. A special KGB force of 700 troops dressed in Afghan uniforms stormed the Tajbeg Presidential Palace and assassinated Amin.

A broadcast that was allegedly made from the Kabul radio station announced that Amin's repressive, dictatorial rule had come to an end, and that former Deputy Prime Minister Babrak Karmal, one of the leaders of the Parcham faction who had been in exile in Eastern Europe, was heading a new government.

* * * * *

The White House had been monitoring these developments, and since November had been meeting with top national security officials about methods for aiding anti-Soviet Afghan insurgents. Nevertheless, President Carter publicly expressed his shock and surprise at the news of the invasion.

At a White House meeting on December 29, U.S. National Security Advisor Zbigniew Brzezinski commented, "All knew that a major watershed had been crossed."[10]

★ ★ ★ ★ ★

The invasion of Afghanistan was the largest single military action taken by the Soviet Union since 1945, and was a major turning point in the history of the Cold War. Furthermore, it became a defining event that helped delegitimize Soviet policy, along with marring the global opinion of communism in general.

The Afghan crisis also had a major influence on U.S. foreign policy, shifting it away from the somewhat restrained 1970s policies of detente and toward a more forceful philosophy. Among the many facets of the new strategy was the covert operation that ultimately armed and supported the mujahideen guerillas in their fight against the Soviets. This operation evolved into the largest in the history of the Central Intelligence Agency.

Gwen Gardner – 1980 U.S. Olympic Track and Field Team

Gwen Gardner
Track and Field

So far in Gwen Gardner's life following the 1980 Olympics, the 400-meter runner has not been forced to divulge her past to a certain population she deals with on a regular basis.

In Los Angeles, where Gardner grew up and still resides, high-speed chases are a part of everyday life. And so, when criminals decide to escape the scene of a crime on foot, the question that begs an answer is: If those criminals knew the background of the officer they were trying to out-run, Deputy Sheriff of Los Angeles County Gwen Gardner, would they decide they're better off putting their hands in the air and surrendering before succumbing to the inevitable?

Criminals in Los Angeles County would find themselves out of breath, out of energy and out of luck after trying to compete with the world-class deputy sheriff. Gardner, who has worked in law enforcement since 1988, has 20 years of experience dealing with bad guys. And she knows a thing or two about the psychology of dealing with them, because of her athletic career.

"The mental toughness that is created gives you the discipline to go through the [police] academy and the whole process," Gardner explains. "Athletics gives you a mental toughness. When you're tired, it changes your perspective. When you're used to being tired because of running and competing, you find a way to get through it. Like situations where you work in a jail environment where criminals are arrested and housed. Or the way some of them may or may not talk to you. Some of them may challenge you to fight."

45

Gardner has never been one to be shy about a fight or a challenge. As a youngster, she dreamed of competing in the Olympics after watching her idol Barbara Ferrell win a silver medal in the 200-meter run at the 1968 Summer Games in Mexico City and a gold in the 100-meter at the '72 Games in Munich. "I remember watching the 1968 Olympics on television. In my mind I said, I want to do that. I was eight at the time and didn't voice it to anyone until I was in junior high. When I was 14, I told my parents I wanted to run track when I got into high school."

The halls of Gardner's Crenshaw High School were not absent of big dreamers and talented athletes who would dot the playing fields and athletic landscapes of the U.S. in the 1980s and beyond. Darryl Strawberry, a top Major League Baseball draft pick and multiple Word Series champion, attended Crenshaw, as did other future professional athletes.

"Darryl came out two years after I did," remembers Gardner. "Johnny Gray was a four-time Olympian [1984, '88, '92, '96] and ran the 800-meter. He stills holds the American record in the 800. A basketball player that went to the NBA was Marques Johnson. Baseball player Chris Brown and football player Wendell Tyler of the 49ers and Rams all went to Crenshaw."

While in high school, Gardner finally told her parents about her aspirations of someday making an Olympic team. "I didn't act upon that thought process until I turned 15," she says. "That's when I joined the track team at Crenshaw."

After her math teacher, Mos Benmosche, suggested as much, Gardner decided the 400-meter would be the event that would take her toward her goal. "I started running and training for the 400 as a 16-year-old junior."

Following her junior season, Gardner's progress was attracting attention. "As a junior in high school I made the Five Nations international competition," Gardner recalls. "It was the United States, Japan, New Zealand, Australia and Canada. I ran the 400-meter on that team in 1977." It was her first taste of international competition and she knew she wanted more.

As a senior in high school, Gardner finished second in the 400 at the California State Championships. Her coach, Fred Jones, who also coached Gardner's club team—Los Angeles Mercurettes—was renowned for sending his athletes to the Olympics. His runners have competed in the Olympic Games from 1960 to 1980 and again in 2000. Jones was no stranger to Olympic-caliber talent. And in Gardner, he saw that talent.

Gardner's focus was on making the Olympic team in 1980. Two-a-day workouts, hills, beach work, running in the sand, intervals, weight training, diet regime and competing in meets across the country and around the world prepared her for getting to the 1980 Olympic Trials in Eugene, Ore.

Her quest began with a series of races in which the track athletes had to run a qualifying standard in their respective events. Next came four rounds of competition to get to the finals. After the finals, if they qualified, they were invited to the Olympic Trials.

Gardner was invited. And then the 19-year-old toed the blocks and exploded to a second-place finish and a berth on the 1980 U.S. Olympic Summer Games track and field team. But when she crossed the finish line, it was already with the knowledge of the boycott. "It was bittersweet," Gardner says with a snicker. "By then I knew, even though I obtained the goal I had strived for as a child—I would always be an Olympian just like all the other athletes who competed—[that] it would have an asterisk because we didn't actually go over to Moscow and compete."

Like her 1980 Olympic teammates, Gardner set her sights on the 1984 Summer Games. Those would be held in her backyard of Los Angeles, and Gardner wanted to be a part of them. But before that could happen, she would have to earn a living during the four-year Olympic cycle. Earning that living would change the course of her Olympic destiny.

"I was playing a halfback stunt-double for a movie about women playing against male football players—'Oklahoma City Dolls'—and I broke my leg in October 1980," Gardner recalls unemotionally. "It took me, because the injury and the way it healed altered the way I ran and walked, about two years to get back. I got better in 1984. I was right there. They took the top four in the final round, and I was fifth." And just like that, in the land where make-believe comes true, Gardner's Olympic dream was finished.

Today, Gardner sometimes quietly competes in the California Police and Fire Games. Without fanfare, she runs. When she is complimented on her athletic prowess, the deputy sheriff is polite. When people learn she was an Olympian in 1980, they are awed.

"It's still, in my mind, a great accomplishment," Gardner says about making the team. "It was a great personal goal and something that a lot of people try for and don't make. I was eight years old when I thought about making the Olympics."

Nearly 30 years later, she still tastes the bittersweet of realizing her dream when she ponders what might have been. "You never really know what could've happened," Gardner says. "There were world-record holders that should've won but didn't."

Gardner still carries the disappointment of 1980 with her. But, just like the way the soft-spoken deputy sheriff goes about her business as a law enforcement officer in Los Angeles, her disappointment seldom shows. Her life is about correcting the wrongs others have written. Unfortunately, history cannot rewrite the wrong her eyes see when she recalls the 1980 Olympic Summer Games.

Gene Mills – 1980 U.S. Olympic Wrestling Team

Gene Mills
Wrestling

Looking at Gene Mills in his heyday of the late 1970s, you can't help but notice his resemblance to Robert DeNiro's Vito Corleone in "Godfather II." If you slicked back Mills' hair, wiped away the ubiquitous grin on his face from amassing 1,356 career wins as the most feared wrestler in the world and replaced it with the ever-present snarl his face had before he went on to destroy an opponent on the wrestling mat, you'd swear Mills was the young Godfather himself.

The native of Pompton Lakes, N.J., and the first four-time All-American athlete at Syracuse University devoted his life to becoming not only an Olympian but an Olympic champion who would not be satisfied with just a gold medal hanging from his neck. "When I was a senior in high school I went to watch the Olympics in Montreal, and that is when I decided that I was not only going to win the Olympics in 1980 but pin my way through it," remembers the still-cocksure Mills. "I wanted to be the first guy to beat everyone so bad and pin my way through it. I just thought no one had ever done it and it would be fun to do."

Mills was so sure of his ability to compete and win, after garnering the New Jersey State Championship and the high school national championship in his senior year, he told Syracuse University, which was offering him a full scholarship to wrestle and go to school, that he needed to redshirt his senior season because he intended to be wrestling as a member of the U.S. Olympic team in Moscow. "They thought it was a joke but it wasn't," Mills says, laughing at the memory.

Mills didn't joke then and he doesn't joke today when he discusses the dedication and hard work he endured to become the greatest 114 1/2-pound wrestler of his day, maybe of all time. "I was training eight-to-10 hours a day. That year [1980] I had gone to the hardest wrestling match in the world, called the Tbilisi Tournament," Mills recalls. "We would take world and Olympic champions over there and a lot of them would never win a match, yet alone place. In a 22-year history, from 1958 to 1980, there were only four Americans that had ever won the Tbilisi Tournament. At Tbilisi, you had to go through the best of the best. We had Olympic champs go over there and have zero wins and seven losses. That's how tough the competition was. I went through that pinning everybody. And I won it, becoming the fifth American to ever win it. I crushed everyone at the World Tournament that year, too."

Not only did Mills win the fabled Russian tournament, he was named Most Outstanding Wrestler. He had pinned guys that would go on to win gold, silver and bronze in Moscow. There was no one who could touch the bantam-weight dynamo—no one on the wrestling mat, that is.

For Mills, becoming an Olympian was just a means to reach his ultimate goal: Olympic champion. "I know there was nobody on this planet that could come close to me," says Mills. "I was on a mission and I proved it. It's not like I just won. I dominated like nobody had ever done before. So, I joined the biggest club in the world—The Shoulda, Woulda, Coulda Club. And it sucks!"

But it's not like Mills was taken out by injury or even another wrestler who might have gotten lucky and caught him on a bad day in the most important meet of his life. That is what still bothers Mills to this day. "The Olympics was always something that was supposed to be a separate thing from politics," Mills says. "It was always said this was a time for everyone to come together to separate politics from sport. President Carter chose not to live up to what the Olympics represents."

The politics that invaded the life of Mills, as well as his Olympic brethren, cast shadows on any thoughts of celebrating the accomplishment of being an Olympian when he and his teammates were invited to Washington for a gala celebration in their honor.

"I said stuff in the paper prior to going to Washington," Mills says, laughing. "If I said that stuff now I'd probably be in prison. I had quotes that made it into the *Philadelphia Inquirer*, *New York Times*, *Washington Post*, saying how I would love to be locked in a room with President Carter and wrestle him and put him into intense pain.

"You can't make those kind of statements anymore, but that is how I honestly felt. I worked my whole life for a dream and he took it away. And he wasn't even a wrestler. It's not like I got beat by a wrestler—I got beat by a peanut farmer. At the time, I really couldn't see it. I couldn't believe in it. I couldn't back it. I still don't. I still believe we should've went, but…"

Mills remembers spending a lot of time alone soul-searching. And even crying. Something the two-time NCAA champion and 1980 U.S. Olympic Athlete of the Year has a hard time admitting or believing is that he was broken to a degree that no opponent on a wrestling mat ever came close to doing. "Everything I worked for all those years was taken away by a peanut farmer they called the president," Mills says.

Mills was 21 years old in 1980, so it was not out of the question that he could reset his sights on the 1984 Summer Games in Los Angeles. In a 1981 interview for the *Syracuse Post-Standard*, Olympic coach Stan Dziedzic described Mills as "the smartest wrestler in the nation, whose mental capacity is his greatest attribute." But his body didn't hold up. After surgery to reconstruct his rotator cuff and the ligaments, tendons and nerves in his shoulder,

Mills wanted to wrestle in the 1984 U.S. Olympic Trials. "But I wasn't cleared yet and my doctors said it was a stupid thing to try. I know I could've walked away with ease, but…"

Solace is hard to come by when discussing Gene Mills' Olympic experience because the "what if" is palpable with the Phoenix, N.Y., high school wrestling coach. Barring injury or accident, Mills was prepared to go to Moscow and triumph—arms uplifted, gold medal around his neck—just like the picture he had of 1976 U.S. Olympic wrestler and gold medalist John Peterson. Instead, 1980 turned out to be the most disappointing year of his life and the beginning of a bitterness and resentment that still consumes him.

"I see all these other guys that won the Olympics," Mills says. "People getting recognized. I'm not on the all-decade teams. I don't know if I would be doing what I am today. Of course, I don't know what other opportunities would've come my way."

For Mills, the one thing he doesn't doubt is that he would still be working with young athletes. Mills offers a two-week wrestling camp, has traveled all over the country teaching his craft to would-be champions, and for the past 25 years has owned and maintained two wrestling clubs—Mohawk Valley Wrestling Club and Pin-to-Win Wrestling Club.

In the end, his thoughts always return to his unfulfilled dream and disillusionment about what happened to his Olympic dream. "I was probably the most dominant wrestler in the world for years, and I can't even get recognized for it because I don't have an Olympic gold medal under my belt. I think about it a lot."

New Jersey High School State Champion. High School National Champion. All-American. NCAA Champion. Three-time World Cup Champion. 1980 World Super Champion. 1980 Tbilisi Champion. 1980 U.S. Olympic Athlete of the Year. National Wrestling Hall of Fame Enshrinee.

While Robert DeNiro took his snarl to the podium to accept the 1974 Academy Award as the Best Supporting Actor in "Godfather II," Gene Mills lives unfulfilled with his athletic career and accomplishments after being denied the opportunity to finish off the last line of his résumé with the one title he coveted more than anything—Olympic champion.

III

Carter Doctrine

The international diplomatic response to the Soviet invasion of Afghanistan was severe. United States officials called it one of grossest displays of international behavior that had occurred in a long time. President Jimmy Carter demanded immediate withdrawal and levied severe trade restrictions against the Soviet Union, including curtailing delivery of 17 million tons of grain for livestock feed. He also declared in a televised speech shortly after the invasion, "History teaches, perhaps, very few clear lessons. But surely one such lesson learned by the world at great cost is that aggression, unopposed, becomes a contagious disease. The response of the international community to the Soviet attempt to crush Afghanistan must match the gravity of the Soviet action."[11]

Two-and-a-half weeks later, in his State of the Union address on January 21, 1980, President Carter reiterated his worries of the Soviet Union's threat to create instability and upset peace in the region by using Afghanistan as a stepping-stone to possibly control much of the world's oil supply.

He explained to the American people that despite our country's sometimes cooperative, competitive and confrontational relationship with the Soviets during the previous three-and-a-half decades, because of the Soviet Union's use of its great military force against a relatively defenseless nation, our relationship with them had come to a crossroads whereby peace or global conflict were at stake.

The president traced the U.S.-Soviet relationship since World War II: from the 1940s, when they created the Atlantic Alliance; to the 1950s, when the U.S. contained Soviet challenges in Korea and the Middle East; to the 1960s, when the U.S. met Soviet threats in Berlin and Cuba; to the 1970s, when three presidents negotiated with Soviet leaders in attempts to halt the growth of the nuclear arms race. And now he was denouncing the world's other superpower by stating:

> *The vast majority of nations on Earth have condemned this latest Soviet attempt to extend its colonial domination of others and have demanded the immediate withdrawal of Soviet troops. The Moslem world is especially and justifiably outraged by this aggression against an Islamic people. No action of world power has ever been so quickly and so overwhelmingly condemned. But verbal condemnation is not enough. The Soviet Union must pay a concrete price for their aggression.*
>
> *While this invasion continues, we and other nations of the world cannot conduct business as usual with the Soviet Union. That's why the United States has imposed stiff economic penalties on the Soviet Union. I will not issue any permits for Soviet ships to fish in the coastal waters of the United States. I've cut Soviet access to high-technology equipment and to agricultural products. I've limited other commerce with the Soviet Union, and I've asked our allies and friends to join with us in*

*restraining their own trade with the Soviets and not to replace our own
embargoed items. And I have notified the Olympic Committee that
with the Soviet invading forces in Afghanistan, neither the American
people nor I will support sending an Olympic team to Moscow.*

The president further explained his administration's feelings toward the
Soviet invasion, what it could mean for world peace, and what the position
of the United States would be.

*The Soviet Union is going to have to answer some basic questions:
Will it help promote a more stable international environment in
which its own legitimate, peaceful concerns can be pursued? Or will it
continue to expand its military power far beyond its genuine security
needs, and use that power for colonial conquest? The Soviet Union
must realize that its decision to use military force in Afghanistan will
be costly to every political and economic relationship it values.*

*The region which is now threatened by Soviet troops in Afghanistan
is of great strategic importance: It contains more than two-thirds of
the world's exportable oil. The Soviet effort to dominate Afghanistan
has brought Soviet military forces to within 300 miles of the Indian
Ocean and close to the Straits of Hormuz, a waterway through which
most of the world's oil must flow. The Soviet Union is now attempting
to consolidate a strategic position, therefore, that poses a grave threat
to the free movement of Middle East oil.*

*This situation demands careful thought, steady nerves, and
resolute action, not only for this year but for many years to come. It
demands collective efforts to meet this new threat to security in the
Persian Gulf and in Southwest Asia. It demands the participation of
all those who rely on oil from the Middle East and who are concerned
with global peace and stability. And it demands consultation and close
cooperation with countries in the area which might be threatened.*

Meeting this challenge will take national will, diplomatic and po-litical wisdom, economic sacrifice, and, of course, military capability. We must call on the best that is in us to preserve the security of this crucial region.

Let our position be absolutely clear: An attempt by any outside force to gain control of the Persian Gulf region will be regarded as an assault on the vital interests of the United States of America, and such an assault will be repelled by any means necessary, including military force.[12]

This powerful warning was labeled the "Carter Doctrine."

* * * * *

As the Cold War got colder by the day, the Carter administration's response to the invasion of Afghanistan put the world on alert. The U.S. was neither interested in, nor prepared for, a war with the Soviet Union in Afghanistan or the Persian Gulf region, but President Carter did call for an increase in the defense budget. Congress re-instituted draft registration. And the president asked the world to join the U.S. in boycotting the Summer Olympics in Moscow unless Soviet troops began to withdraw from Afghanistan by 12:01 a.m. Eastern Standard Time on February 20.

* * * * *

Though not all agreed about the purpose of the invasion, Carter's reaction to the Soviet Union was met with widespread approval among U.S. policy makers. Hard-liners, such as Ronald Reagan, who would be Carter's opponent in the 1980 presidential election, had warned numerous times that the Soviet Union was "on a roll" in the Third World and needed to be dealt with, while moderates thought the intervention was an egregious act and the Soviets should pay a price. All agreed that the Soviet Union should withdraw from Afghanistan.

How to convince Moscow became the question, since the Soviet government had quite a different view.

"The war in Afghanistan was a response, if you will, on the part of the Soviet Union to what it saw as an intractable position taken by the United States on the issue of medium-range missiles in Europe," says Vladimir Pozner, Russian television host of *Vremena* ("These Times"), the Russian political-show version of *Meet the Press*.

"The Soviet Union mounted a huge campaign against those missiles being located in Europe," Pozner continues. "There were huge demonstrations in Western Europe against that. Nevertheless, the United States held firm and went ahead and did that. At that point, the hawk faction in the Soviet government probably said; 'Look, here's proof-positive that no matter how we try to reach an agreement with the United States, they will not meet us halfway. They will do whatever they want to do. It's time that we show some muscle.' I believe the decision to go into Afghanistan had to do with that kind of reasoning—'All right, we're going to show them a thing or two. They don't want to understand our desires, our needs. They don't really want to negotiate with us. Well, we'll go ahead and do what we want to do.' That's what I think really was the reason for the decision to go into Afghanistan."

American congressional conservatives also were wary of dealing through negotiations because, like the Soviet contempt for U.S. policy makers, they in turn did not trust the Soviet Union's willingness to negotiate in good faith. Most U.S. moderates and liberals fell in line with their conservative colleagues supporting covert aid to the Afghan rebels, and virtually no one supported diplomacy as a means of resolution.

After minimal deliberation at the White House, President Carter decided on a two-pronged approach: contribute modest levels of covert aid while seeking a forum for settlement through negotiations.[13]

* * * * *

While the administration was dealing with how to handle the situation in Afghanistan and the U.S. hostage crisis in Iran, Vice President Walter F. Mondale became the point person for dealing with the threat of a U.S. Olympic boycott. Putting the administration's stance in context, Mondale explains, "We had to tell the Soviet Union, 'We're putting the squeeze on you and this is the price you're going to pay if you don't change course.' If we said, 'We're going to keep an eye on you for two months,' they would've laughed at us.

"We were trying to put pressure on the Soviet Union [so] that it would hurt so much that they would stop their invasion of Afghanistan. We tried to, short of war, because we weren't able to deploy forces and we knew we wouldn't be effective with that. So we had to find other means of putting the pressure on. We embargoed the sale of grain, a very painful step, but one we thought would hurt them. We restored registration for the draft. I used to go on the campuses [and] that was not popular at all—but we had to show the Soviet Union that we were for real. We cut off a lot of technical assistance and credits and other things that we could do, and tried to get the rest of the world to join with us."

The administration's next step to further make their point to the Soviet Union concerned the upcoming Olympic Summer Games in Moscow. "The thing that stood out there, that we really debated about because we knew it could have such serious consequences to our best young athletes, was whether we should try to spoil the Moscow Olympics," Mondale says. "[The Soviet government was] using the Moscow Olympics very similar to the way in which Hitler used the 1936 Olympics, trying to show the world that they were a credible, acceptable and a normal nation with nothing wrong. They wanted to do that in the process of trying to destroy Afghan independence. So, we thought that history showed us that this could be used in that way."

Mondale further explains, "I was personally very aware of the '36 Olympics, not because I had been there, but because I had read the history. I knew about Jesse Owens and how Hitler dealt with it. I also knew because I had traveled to the Soviet Union a couple times. I saw how they were using the upcoming Moscow Olympics to flaunt their legitimacy in the eyes of their citizens and around the world. It was not just another event, another good movie that came to town. It was central to the Soviet political strategy at home and abroad. So, I may have brought [the boycott] up. Others may have brought it up as well, but I know I brought it up with the president and said, 'I think this is something we ought to consider.' From a legal standpoint, we consulted with the IOC and USOC. We had people in the White House who had friends and relatives in the USOC. I was very aware of how painful this was to American athletes. They only have a certain couple of years in their prime and that's it. They'll never have another chance to show their stuff at the Olympics."

* * * * *

At the same time, the administration was working on alternatives to a boycott, proposing the 1980 Summer Games be transferred from Moscow to another site or multiple sites, postponed, or cancelled altogether. That resolution was proposed at a day-long meeting of the USOC in Colorado Springs on January 26 and was supported by a vote of 68-0. Despite the unanimity, USOC President Robert Kane said the committee did not take a definite stand on whether it would support a boycott. "We are not finessing the issue," said Kane in a story in the *Newark Star-Ledger* on January 27, 1980. "[Discussions of a boycott are] simply not timely until after the International Olympic Committee meets and deals with this resolution." Kane went on to further say, "Subsequent to action by the International Olympic Committee on the U.S. proposal, the USOC shall meet to consider appropriate action to be taken by the USOC under such circumstances as may exist at that time."[14]

The day prior to the USOC meeting, a group of 50 athletes training at the Olympic facilities held a news conference and issued a statement that denounced "the use of athletes as a 'political lever'" and recommended a "total economic boycott of the Soviet Union." The athletes went on to say, "We must use actions which will achieve results, not symbolic gestures which only vent emotions."[15]

★ ★ ★ ★ ★

Despite speculation that the Soviet government might call for its own Olympic boycott of the Winter Games in Lake Placid, N.Y. that were just days away, the 1980 Winter Olympics began as scheduled—with all expected participants—on February 12. It was, incidentally, Day 100 of the U.S. hostage crisis in Iran. As the Soviet Union's athletes marched in the Opening Ceremony, the Soviet army continued its march through Afghanistan, and a looming cloud of international tension hung over the small Adirondack village as Carter's February 20 deadline approached.

* * * * *

During a February 13 news conference, President Carter continued to assert the seriousness of the Soviet's actions in Afghanistan by explaining how crucial this area was to the world. He also noted the volatility of the region, and reiterated that the Soviets had been indulging in a steady military buildup over a number of years and had taken that military force beyond its own borders.

Answering a question about the gravity of the crisis in Afghanistan, the president said, "Everything we've done has been to contribute stability, moderation, consistency, persistence and peace. We have taken actions on our own, and we have asked our allies and others to join in with us in the condemnation of the Soviet Union and [to] demand that the Soviets withdraw from Afghanistan and to convince them that any further adventurism on their part would cause grave consequences to the Soviet Union."[16]

Later during the news conference, President Carter was asked to differentiate between his administration's position of making the Soviets "pay a price" and not having the boycott "intend to be punitive." He explained:

"We have no desire to use the Olympics to punish, except the Soviets attach a major degree of importance to the holding of the Olympics in the Soviet Union. In their own propaganda material they claim that the willingness of the International Olympic Committee to let the Games be held in Moscow is an endorsement of the foreign policy and the peace-loving nature of the Soviet Union.

"To me it's unconscionable for any nation to send athletes to the capital of [another] nation under the aegis of the Olympics when that host nation is actively involved in the invasion of and the subjugation of innocent people. And so, for that reason, I don't believe that we are obligated to send our athletes to Moscow.

"And I would like to repeat, if the Soviet Union does not withdraw its troops from Afghanistan by the 20th of this month, then neither I nor the American people nor the Congress will support the sending of an Olympic team to Moscow this summer."[17]

* * * * *

One week later, when the February 20 deadline came, news from Washington regarding the 1980 Summer Olympics was in stark contrast to the news from Lake Placid at the Winter Olympics.

U.S. speedskater Eric Heiden won his third of five gold medals, while the U.S. hockey team remained unbeaten in five games by defeating West Germany 4-2 and advancing to the semifinals to play the mighty and heavily-favored Soviet Union.

Despite the anxiety of whether they would get their chance to compete, many of the U.S. Summer Olympians watched their winter brethren's success and became even more inspired to fulfill their own Olympic dreams. "We used it for motivation," recalls swimmer Glenn Mills.

Mills says their coach would come to practice and ask, "Do you have any idea what the Russians are doing today?"

"We had no idea, but figured that he must," Mills says. "We would come in the next morning after the hockey team won and he would say, 'Look what's happening—you can do that. You can make this affective change on America.' It was really cool to think that. Eric Heiden was unbelievable. It was a great, great Winter Olympics for us and we weren't even supposed to be that good in the Winter Olympics. We were thinking, 'Wait until we get to do our thing in the summer.' It was such an emotional high. We were so happy for all of them and we couldn't wait to do it ourselves."

* * * * *

There was still hope after the deadline passed. But in the coming months that hope faded, and the dream of competing in the 1980 Olympic Summer Games in Moscow vanished.

Craig Beardsley — 1980 U.S. Olympic Swim Team

Craig Beardsley
Swimming

The vestiges of Craig Beardsley's political connections branch back in his family tree to another political maelstrom: a life-and-death struggle in the Far East. Beardsley's maternal grandfather, who fought alongside Chiang Kai-shek in the early 20th century, was a key figure in the generalissimo's political maneuvers in China.

It's almost as if Beardsley was destined to be a part of an immortal political story. In fact, because of his involvement on the 1980 Summer Olympic team, Beardsley had the unlikely opportunity to reconnect with his Chinese heritage in Shanghai and to learn the extent of his family's political roots.

When Chiang's Nationalist Party ultimately fell to the Chinese Red Army, Beardsley's grandparents were forced to leave China for good. Beardsley's political ties to American politics took deeper root as his grandfather served as the consulate general for a pre-communist China. Little did anyone know that his future grandson would one day become an Olympic swimmer entangled in his own political battle.

The politics of the Olympic boycott surrounded Beardsley like a haze, but he didn't actively voice his opinion to the Carter administration. "I had tunnel vision," Beardsley says. "I knew my job was to swim as fast as I could and I didn't want anything to get in my way. I was aware of what was going on around the world and that's why I took that original stance. It bothered me most for the people who I thought really, really got screwed [by] the '80 boycott. On top of that, coming off the Winter Olympics in which it was the exact opposite, where everyone was, 'This is the greatest sporting thing ever.' You see what happened in 1980 during the Winter Olympics and you see the void of the Summer Olympics and it was just unbelievable… it was unbelievable that that could happen. They are the exact polar opposite."

Beardsley's unique status as an '80 Olympian often leads him to pontificate about how life might be different if he had been able to compete, and about how the Games have changed since he first dreamed the Olympic dream. "To this day I still have people ask me about it. I realize the younger people have no idea what happened. It was a big sacrifice for a lot of people to train, and the fact that the Olympics only came once every four years, it took your complete life commitment to perform at that level. And you only really had one shot, maybe two shots. Today, you really can financially afford to stay around, train and make a living. It has changed the whole dynamic of the sport. Back then it was an opportunity that was totally… not right. I don't take it personally, but I always feel bad for the people who really could have made their mark in Olympic world history. I was just a small part of it.

"I always compare myself to someone like Tracy Caulkins when I talk about being in the Olympics. Tracy had everything. At that time Tracy was, and probably still is today, one of the greatest swimmers of all-time. She had an American record in every single event, something like 53 national titles. The only one who has ever been that close is Michael Phelps. I felt, at that point, more disturbed about the boycott for people like that. I was still an up-and-coming name. I was ranked up there near the top of the world but I really hadn't broken through yet. Tracy could've won seven gold medals in 1980 and gone down in the history books forever, but she was denied that opportunity. For me, I was still a nobody. I approached the trials in 1980 with the attitude [that] I still had something to prove. I didn't know what I was capable of doing."

Beardsley showed what he was capable of doing by setting a world record in the 200 butterfly at the Olympic Trials. A similar feat in Moscow would have set him atop the swimming world listening to the "Star Spangled Banner" with his hand over his heart, clutching a gold medal and watching the Stars and Stripes rising to the rafters a little higher than two other flags.

Oddly, at the time, even though Beardsley would have won gold and could have become a poster child and cashed in financially from his exploits, he had mixed feelings about the politics that created the boycott. "At that time, I don't want to say that I supported the boycott, but I wasn't against it either," he admits. "I tried to think there was some good in it. We were doing the right thing. I supported everything at that time."

As the years went on, Beardsley better understood the role politics played, and still play, in the world of sports. "I began to realize that it was just another political movement. I became strongly opinionated about trying to separate sports and politics. It will never happen. Sports, like music, is one of those great things that bind people together."

As Beardsley's political views changed and his outlook became more cynical, his perspective did not. "In retrospect, it was a small price to pay when you look at what's going on today," Beardsley says, referring to the wars in Iraq and Afghanistan. "People are dying and risking their lives. What I had to do was a small sacrifice."

Besides, Beardsley knew he could probably swim in the Olympics in 1984 if he wanted to commit to four more years of training and hard work. He returned to the University of Florida and resumed his college swimming career. In 1982, after toppling his own world record and winning his second consecutive NCAA title in the 200 butterfly, he graduated college and decided to target the Olympics one more time. "I had a lot of mixed emotions. I was already burnt out on the sport but felt like I owed it to everyone else—my parents, coach. The last person I really felt I owed it to was myself. In hindsight, maybe I should've taken some time off and come back fresh to the sport. I didn't because I wanted to keep my momentum going."

That momentum was thwarted at the 1984 U.S. Olympic Trials. Beardsley was battling a cold, and performed under potential. "I was considered a shoe-in for the 200 fly, [but] I had a horrible swim," Beardsley recalls with disgust. "I was two seconds slower than my best time and I finished third."

With only the top two finishers qualifying, Beardsley's Olympic dream ended. "It was then I really started to reflect on my swimming and the what-if. I realized the boycott affected a lot of people's lives. And, of course, back then we didn't have million-dollar contracts riding on our performances. We were just doing it because we wanted to do it. We weren't affected financially one way or the other at that point. Sure there could've been endorsements, but who knows?"

Missing the Olympic Games in Los Angeles re-ignited the political spark that had been festering in Beardsley since 1980. "I was completely frustrated. I was very fed up with politics in general, the whole organized structure of sports. I needed to walk away for a bit. It bothered me."

What Beardsley did, along with teammate Glenn Mills, is go to South Africa and conduct swimming clinics. In the 1970s and '80s, athletes were frowned upon for traveling to the apartheid-ridden sections of the Dark Continent. But with the noblest of intentions, the pair ignored the warnings of international banishment and made their own political statement. "People walked miles to come see us swimming and talk about swimming," Beardsley remembers. "We crossed boundaries and borders. I felt like what we were doing was a great humanitarian thing and we were banned for it. I was to- tally disgusted with the governing body of our sport federation, politics and everything. It turned me off. Maybe for other people it would've turned a switch on to become more active politically. At that point I was burned out on the sport and burned out on the politics."

Yet, the past politics of that previous life still follow the New York City kid who learned to swim at the 92nd Street YMCA when he was four years old. "When it comes to the word 'Olympics,' it's not an easy answer and I'm not really sure how to spell it out," Beardsley says, laughing. "I have no regrets for not going in 1980. The only thing is that it is very vague. I look at my swimming and I was a world-record holder. My most vivid memory of the 1980 Olympics, still to this day, is not being able to describe what my Olympic experience was, because I really don't know."

Politics aside, what Beardsley has been able to take from his experience as a 1980 U.S. Olympian are the friendships he made with the hundreds of other athletes who shared part of his journey. "The people who were on [the U.S. team], in every sport, I have a closer bond to them because we all went through the same experience in history together. I talk to a lot of other swimmers who have been to other Olympics and I think our group is probably much closer because of what we didn't get to do. My friendships with these guys are what's most important now. I have no regrets from my swimming career."

The unexpected perk of traveling to China as a consolation from the boycott led Beardsley to Shanghai. It was a chance to reconnect with, and learn about, his family, as well as the politics that have affected their multiple generations.

Today, Beardsley is happy with his life. He serves as an unofficial ambassador for swimming and exudes enthusiasm when talking about his sport. And, ultimately, his unofficial title seems only fitting—while making complete political sense.

Sue Walsh — 1980 U.S. Olympic Swim Team

Sue Walsh
Swimming

"The times are what say who was the best," Sue Walsh says.

That sentiment still resounds with the former world record holder and 1980 U.S. Summer Olympian swimmer. In 1979, Walsh swam the fastest time in the world in the 100 backstroke and the second fastest in the 200 backstroke. Undoubtedly, Walsh would have been a gold medal contender in those events if she had been allowed to compete in the Moscow Games in 1980.

Nearly 30 years later, Walsh still checks the times of Olympic swimmers during the summer quadrennial of events featuring the world's best athletes united in sport. She thinks back, but doesn't dwell, on the day she should have been in that position.

Walsh was 18 years old and had been swimming for 10 years when her Olympic dream nearly came to fruition. After a less-than-enthusiastic start as a kid, Walsh took to the sport of swimming and never looked back. She usually didn't have to. "I hated it at first," Walsh admits. "I came home crying after the first few practices. I was eight and learned something that I use today. My parents said, 'Do it for two weeks and if at that point you don't enjoy it, then you don't have to do it.' I began to really enjoy it and made a lot of good friends."

As her talent evolved, Walsh and her parents continued to look for a more competitive program with more of a commitment. Though Walsh was not living in a hotbed for breeding world-class swimmers—Hamburg, N.Y., a suburb of Buffalo—she was proving to herself and to the rest of the national swimming community that her talent should be taken seriously. "By the time

I turned 13, I was reaching national qualifying times, and at that point it hit my parents, 'Well gosh, maybe Sue has some potential,'" Walsh recalls. "That was in 1975, the year before the 1976 Olympics when the women did really well. I remember sitting in my living room and watching the women swim."

Those women, led by U.S. Olympic swimming legend Shirley Babashoff, ignited a fire in Walsh that wouldn't soon extinguish. "I remember specific relays—in fact, I get goose bumps right now thinking about it," Walsh says. "I don't know that the television coverage was great, but what we did see was so awesome to watch and it felt like you were a part of it. If I remember correctly, their bathing suits were stars and stripes and you felt very patriotic wanting to be the one standing up on the awards platform and hopefully receiving some medal. It really was very motivational watching them perform against swimmers whom we found out later had an advantage otherwise."

Walsh is the youngest of five siblings, and as her swimming career began to blossom, so did her distinction within the community and beyond. Her father, Bob, was well-known in the little town of Hamburg, and Sue was referred to as one of "Bob Walsh's kids." But as she continued to make a name for herself, Bob became "Sue Walsh's dad." Having never been singled out as a "special member" of the Walsh family, Sue's siblings let her know when it was her turn to take out the trash or to do the dishes. "I think that was wonderful, because it kept me grounded and I didn't think I was better than anybody else," she says. She also recalls when her brothers and sisters made a T-shirt for Bob that read on the front, "I'm Sue Walsh's Dad" and on the back, "I have four other kids too!"

"They were supportive and did whatever I needed but were never, ever the type of parents to pressure me or criticize me when I would swim a race that I didn't swim to my potential," Walsh says. "That was unique. I've seen a lot of parents who don't handle that area particularly well. They were great. They loved me unconditionally and swimming was not who I was—it was what I did. We didn't really chart any course or revel in anything. It was part of our lives that we enjoyed and they did whatever they needed to do to help me become successful."

Part of that love involved picking on their little sister to make sure she knew not to get a swelled head. It worked.

Upon graduating high school in January 1980 (she finished her studies at Mount Mercy Academy in Buffalo, N.Y., half a year early), Walsh dedicated the next six months to training. It was also during that time President Carter and his administration were making decisions that would affect her athletic career forever. "There was a period, probably in January, when the announcement was made, and I was sitting in front of the TV as the president announced we would not be participating," Walsh recalls. "The devastation you feel, disappointment," she says, her voice trailing off. "It was really difficult to focus and put forth the effort because you're thinking, Why? If I can make a team on paper only, is that really worth it? I came to the conclusion that it was."

With that frame of mind, Walsh continued with her workouts despite how the politics of the situation might play out. "At the time, I was very, very disappointed. I was 18 years old and didn't understand the politics," she admits. "I don't know that I understand the politics today either, because it certainly didn't encourage the Soviets to get out of Afghanistan. What I tried to focus on was that I was 18; I was going to college on scholarship; I could train for another four years and have another opportunity."

As the spring of 1980 approached and her workouts intensified, Walsh developed mononucleosis. "I remember laying in bed so tearful with my ever-faithful dog laying beside me thinking, that's it—I have spent all this time, energy and focus for that one event and I'm probably not going to have the chance to try."

It was during her convalescence that she became an even better swimmer without taking one stroke in a pool. "I think at that point I really developed some great skills of visualization and mental preparation," she says. "I would lay in bed and go through my races—100 back in particular—and I really developed in that period." Cultivating that talent proved to be a blessing, as her mental preparation became a key element in her athletic prosperity.

Walsh made the U.S. Olympic team in the 100 backstroke and probably would have raced in the 400 medley relay. Each event, again, likely would have resulted in Walsh standing on a podium with a medal draped around her neck.

Following the disappointment of 1980, Walsh rebounded and attended the University of North Carolina on an athletic scholarship. She had four years to earn her college degree and swim competitively in the NCAA ranks, while also keeping her focus on 1984 and Los Angeles.

At the '84 Olympic Trials, Walsh found herself sick again, this time with a sinus infection. As the reigning American record-holder in the 100 back-stroke, a berth on the '84 team seemed like a sure thing going into the race. She touched the wall and turned to the clock to see where she had placed, and saw her name in the third position by .01 seconds. Three years earlier, that was good enough to assure her a spot on the team. But due to a rule change, it meant she would be relegated to sitting home and watching the Olympic Games on her television. "That probably hurt even more, because I thought I was at the end of what I felt like I could do as far as training," Walsh says, still disappointed. "I knew that was the last chance and I was totally deflated."

Despite Walsh's disappointments in her Olympic quest, today she sees that time of her life with much different eyes. Instead of competing at the Olympics in 1980, the U.S. swim team was given the opportunity to travel to China and compete there. Walsh, along with her teammates, used this trip to forge a special bond with one another that exists to this day. And, oddly, that experience resounds every bit as much, if not more, than if they had traveled to Moscow.

"That was sort of our consolation prize," Walsh says. "That trip really opened my eyes to see how other people lived and what they didn't have and to bond with the people on the team—Glenn Mills or Craig Beardsley, Tracy Caulkins, and the list goes on of the people I know and am still friends with or correspond. I wouldn't have had that opportunity if we had gone to the Olympics. The focus would've been different. There would've been a lot of stress in the Olympic Village. A lot of what I got to experience in China wouldn't have happened. Having had that opportunity was tremendous and something I cherish."

Ultimately, time does not stand still. As hairs gray and the once invincible body of an Olympic athlete begins to show the signs of age, Walsh hearkens back to one of her original thoughts on her experience as a world-class athlete. "The great thing about swimming compared to other sports is that your time tells all. You don't have to be in the lane competing against that other person to tell who was better on that specific day. If you've got the times, and you've both swum in 50-meter pools, then you knew who was the best."

Time may not stand still, but *times* do.

CHAPTER IV

"Ours Will Not Go"

The Carter administration was resolute in its initial declaration: Without a total withdrawal of Soviet troops from Afghanistan, the United States would not participate in the 1980 Olympic Summer Games to be held in Moscow in July.

After having explained his policy to the American people in his State of the Union address, and continually stressing that the Soviet incursion was "the most serious threat to the peace since the Second World War" in subsequent news conferences, by mid-March President Carter had a solid majority of Americans supporting the proposed boycott.

A Gallup poll asked the nation, "Do you think the U.S. should or should not participate in the Olympic Games this summer?" Sixty-three percent of the population agreed with the president's sentiments, while 29 percent disagreed, and eight percent had no opinion. Feelings on the issue did not deviate across politically partisan lines; 66 percent of Republicans, 65 percent of Democrats and 59 percent of independents responded against participating in the Games. The poll also showed no gender gap, as 64 percent of men and 62 percent of women were against sending the team. And even the majority of younger adults (18-to-29 years old), who were thought more likely not to favor a boycott, responded 58-percent in favor of Carter's proposal.[18]

Opinion in Great Britain was not as disproportionate as in the U.S., but a good percentage of Brits did sympathize with President Carter's plan. In a similar poll, 1,200 British adults were asked: "Would you approve or disapprove if Britain were to withdraw from the Moscow Olympic Games this summer?" Results showed that 44 percent disapproved, 41 percent approved, 11 percent didn't know, and four percent wasn't aware of the proposed boycott.[19]

As days went by, a U.S. boycott of the Olympic Games in Moscow seemed imminent.

That inkling was confirmed on March 21 when President Carter met with a group of U.S. Olympic athletes and their representatives at the White House and announced that the country would not be participating in the 1980 Olympic Summer Games. Without equivocation, the president declared that no matter what other nations decided, "Ours will not go. ... The decision has been made."

Though President Carter did not have the statutory power to prevent an American team from participating in the Moscow Games, he and his administration made, in no uncertain terms, their position known to those who did have the authority: the members of the United States Olympic Committee.

* * * * *

The Olympic Games had been thrust into world politics as never before. By the end of March, on top of the trade embargoes the administration had already imposed, what had been a voluntary ban on exports to the Soviet Union of sporting goods and other products relating to the Olympic Games in Moscow had become mandatory. The volume of exports effected by the embargo, which included products ranging from chewing gum and soft drinks to soccer balls and landing pits for pole vaulters, was estimated to be worth $20 million to $30 million. The order also applied to payments made to the Soviet Union for Olympic rights, including the television broadcast rights for which NBC had paid $87 million. NBC had announced previously that it would not exercise those rights if the U.S. did not partake in the Games.

* * * * *

Despite many of the world's governments remaining outraged at the Soviet Union's continued aggression and occupation in Afghanistan, their Olympic governing bodies were not sold on the advantages of keeping their athletes from participating in the Games.

In England, Prime Minister Margaret Thatcher declared that the country should not compete in Moscow, and the House of Commons echoed her stance by passing a resolution 315 to 147 to support the boycott. But the public disagreed, and a week later the British Olympic Association voted to participate anyway. This decision represented a serious blow to President Carter's call for a boycott, since Thatcher was the only Western European leader who had wholeheartedly allied herself with U.S. policy.

Both sides of the British argument further campaigned their cases. The British Foreign Office appealed to athletes to decide on their own whether to forgo Moscow, while members of the opposition Labor Party welcomed the Olympic Association's decision by commending British athletes' determination to "maintain their integrity and to safeguard the future of international sports competition."[20]

★ ★ ★ ★ ★

In Canada, the newly-elected liberal government of Prime Minister Pierre Trudeau did not immediately disclose a position, but during the election campaign in February, Trudeau supported acting in concert with other nations. The Canadian Olympic Association executive committee mulled the issue, then recommended that Canada also not boycott the Summer Olympics.

★ ★ ★ ★ ★

Though President Carter had made it quite clear in his meeting with the athletes that they would not be competing in Moscow, the U.S. Olympic Committee had to vote to make it official. That vote was scheduled for April 12.

Under the rules of the International Olympic Committee, the decision whether to participate must be made by the country's national Olympic committee—the USOC—and not the government. Any political interference by the government could lead to expulsion from the Olympics.

The USOC's cooperation was no sure thing.

Several days after the president's meeting with the athletes, representatives of 32 groups that governed America's amateur athletes—which composed the controlling bloc of the vote to boycott—held a meeting in Colorado Springs, Colo. Afterward they presented a clear counter-message to the Carter administration, opposing the boycott. Headlines across the country mirrored the March 31 front page of *The Washington Post*: "Carter Gets Word: 'Try and Stop Us.' "[21]

USOC Executive Director F. Don Miller tried to temper the emotion from that meeting by emphasizing that the committee had not yet made a decision, even if President Carter already had, and that official acceptance of the invitation to attend the 1980 Olympic Summer Games was not due until May 24. "If the president determines at the time Olympic entries are due that our participation would be detrimental to the national interest and security, I'm certain that as good Americans we would respect that," Miller told *The Washington Post* for an April 4 article. "I think we all recognize that the president of the United States is the one who must make that decision."[22]

* * * * *

With the USOC's official vote still more than a week away and opposition to the boycott intensifying after the meeting in Colorado Springs, the Carter administration invited the representatives of the governing bodies of the Olympic sports, plus members of the Athletes' Advisory Council, to meet with State Department officials at the White House. The contingency attended the meeting armed with the athletes' counterproposal—for the U.S. to participate in the Games but not in the opening, closing or medal ceremonies as a visible protest, as well as having the athletes stay in the Soviet Union only on the days of their events and be restricted to the competition venues, training facilities and the Olympic Village. But the athletes' suggestion had already been unofficially rejected. A White House aide, who had reviewed the proposal previously, said such plans had been considered and discarded before the president called for a boycott.

Still, rower Anita DeFrantz, who was chosen as the Athletes' Advisory Council spokesperson, had hoped they would not be flat-out rejected before the meeting. "I had alternatives to suggest, because I knew what it was like to be at the Olympic Games," says DeFrantz, who had won a bronze medal at the 1976 Summer Olympics. "There were other ways. If Carter wanted to make a statement, what more significant statement could be made than to have [only] one athlete walk into the stadium with the Olympic flag during the Opening Ceremony?"

On the day of the meeting, instead of discussing the White House agenda of alternative games for U.S. and foreign athletes to participate in after the Olympics, the USOC contingent turned the discussion into an emotional rally in support of participating in Moscow.

That left administration officials at the meeting (including Deputy Secretary of State Warren Christopher, Defense Secretary Harold Brown and White House Counsel Lloyd Cutler) just trying to quell the emotion. Christopher explained the administration's argument by stressing three points: the brutal war being waged by the Soviets in Afghanistan; deterrents to the Soviet aggression called for sacrifices; and if the United States decided to participate in the Olympic Games, it would be a tacit approval of Soviet actions. Following the meeting, Christopher told reporters that no threats had been made to the sports officials, but reiterated what the president had said previously—that the administration would take strong measures to see that the United States was not represented at the Games.

What those "strong measures" would be were not mentioned directly, but there were whispers of revocation of athletes' passports and/or withholding visas should they try to go to Moscow on their own, changing the USOC's tax-exempt status, and changing the national sports statutes under which the USOC was organized.

In an *Associated Press* article, Harmon Hawkins, president of the U.S. Yacht Racing Union and a proponent of the boycott, detailed the administration's blunt position by quoting Cutler, who also had spoken at the meeting. "Cutler made it clear that the bottom line is, 'If you vote not to support the president, you are doing the worse thing you can possibly do.' "[23]

Jim Hawkins, head of the U.S. Speedskating Association, projected the same sentiment in *The New York Times* on April 4: "[The administration] said it was in the interest of national security. They were saying, in effect: 'If you decide to go, you're unpatriotic.' And perhaps that would be so, in terms of the way it was put."[24]

At the end of the two-day meeting, the athletes' proposal was not embraced or accepted by the Carter administration, and the USOC still had not resolved whether to support the boycott.

* * * * *

The administration was wielding considerable clout in assuring that the USOC made its decision in accordance with the president's wishes, and that it decided sooner, during the USOC meetings in Colorado Springs from April 11 to 13, rather than later, at the May 23 deadline.

With the backing of near-unanimous resolutions in both houses of Congress, as well as the support of the majority of the American public, members of the USOC knew that defiance of a presidential directive could result in extreme consequences. The USOC also knew that it would have to seek subsidies from the federal government to cover the projected financial shortfall they faced—a projected budget deficit of nearly $7 million for the four-year period ending December 31, mostly due to the loss of revenue caused by the prospect of a boycott. They also could not afford the reduction or loss of private and corporate contributions that would be inevitable should they go against the president.

At the same time, implicitly or otherwise, heat was being felt by official Olympic sponsors, and cold was being felt by the USOC's fund-raisers. Levi Strauss & Co., the makers of Levi's jeans, decided that it would not send uniforms to Moscow for Olympic stadium workers, and nixed plans to be a television sponsor for the Games. Sears, Roebuck & Company decided to withhold a $25,000 pledge to the USOC unless the committee agreed to boycott the Games. And five other companies were "delinquent" in pledge payments to the committee.

Prior to the Afghanistan invasion and the call for a boycott, the USOC was exceeding its budget projections, which called for it to raise $43 million between the 1976 and 1980 Olympics. But in the first three months of 1980, $4.2 million in expected contributions fell $1.6 million short. Most of the falloff occurred due to state Olympic committee fund-raising events that had been cancelled or postponed pending a decision on the boycott.[25]

F. Don Miller alleged that the White House played a part in Sears' actions, which he called "sheer blackmail." The administration denied charges that they had asked corporations to withhold funds; and Sears, while acknowledging that the White House did ask them to back the boycott, seconded that sentiment and denied Miller's accusation.[26]

"This is not something Carter and I would've done," explains Vice President Walter F. Mondale. "We didn't deal that way."

Of course, one couldn't be certain what was being done by others in Washington.

★ ★ ★ ★ ★

With the USOC vote just days away, other countries were waiting to see what the U.S. would decide. The administration worried that if the growing revolt among athletes and others within the committees led to a vote against the president's wishes, then the call to other allied countries for a boycott would crumble. The governments of at least 25 countries had supported President Carter's appeal, including Great Britain, Canada, Japan, Norway, the Netherlands, the Philippines, Kenya, Malaysia, Saudi Arabia and most of the other Islamic countries.

Despite their worries, the administration felt they had a commitment from leaders of the Olympic committees to support a boycott—thus their request for the vote to take place so quickly. With the cooperation of the USOC, the administration could then campaign for favorable responses from other European nations—including Germany, France and Italy—which was considered essential to persuading other countries in Asia, Latin America and Africa to go along with the boycott.

* * * * *

Meetings continued between administration officials and some of the USOC delegates who would be voting in the coming days. Lloyd Cutler, Secretary of State Cyrus Vance and General David Jones, chairman of the Joint Chiefs of Staff, made their final appeals. Vance was particularly clear in stating that no other peaceful action could be a more forceful message to the world and the Soviet Union than to support the call for a boycott.

"I had the opportunity during that time to ask the chairman of the Joint Chiefs of Staff if he could tell me that one life would be saved," DeFrantz remembers. "He said no, he could not. It took me awhile to decide to ask that question because if he had said yes, then I really would have had to deal with my ethical compass. It was very disappointing that by staying home, not even one life would be saved."

Following the meetings, some members of the delegation were still not swayed but declined to predict how the vote might go. They would either accept the president's plan for a boycott, deny it, or vote to delay the final decision until mid-May. If they postponed the verdict, they would confer the right to decide to a smaller group of Olympic officials, based on whatever the president determined at that time.

* * * * *

On April 10, just hours before the USOC delegates were to convene in Colorado Springs, President Carter spoke at the annual convention of the American Society of Newspaper Editors. In the speech the president declared that he was prepared to take "legal action" to keep U.S. athletes from competing at the Moscow Olympics. His comments all but secured the likelihood of the delegates voting to support the boycott.

There was still fleeting hope that the USOC would vote to delay the decision. But the president's steadfast stance, as evidenced in his address, told committee members in no uncertain terms that any vote to participate would be futile.

As a further sign of the administration's commitment to a boycott, President Carter sent Vice President Mondale to Colorado Springs to address the house of delegates before they cast their votes.

Bill Hanzlik —1980 U.S. Olympic Basketball Team

Bill Hanzlik
Basketball

For former Seattle Supersonic first-round draft pick and 10-year National Basketball Association veteran Bill Hanzlik, playing in the 1980 Olympic Summer Games in Moscow was more about preparing himself for the next step in his basketball career than worrying about the possible color of the medal he would bring home or whether he would even get the chance to compete.

"The thing I remember most about that time is that I felt so bad for the volleyballers, the weightlifters, the gymnastics people," recalls the native of Middletown, Ohio. "That was their one opportunity, their one moment to reach their pinnacle. With basketball, playing in the NBA was the epitome of playing the sport. You didn't feel as bad not going to the Olympics as those other people. That was their one shot."

Hanzlik, who grew to 6-foot-7 in high school, spent time in three different high schools, in three different states and three different regions of the United States. During his sophomore year, Hanzlik played in Mobile, Ala. He spent his junior year on the West Coast in Lake Oswego, Ore., and graduated from high school in Beloit, Wisc., where he played his senior season. Hanzlik is the youngest of five children who all cherished playing basketball. It was only natural that baby brother would follow in his siblings' footsteps.

"We had a hoop in the backyard and I just enjoyed going out and playing," remembers Hanzlik. "As I grew I decided it would be really neat if I could help my parents by getting a basketball scholarship. In the summer, I worked my way in the gym and I would shoot and play. My junior year, I started to be recruited a lot. My dad sent a tape to [the University of] Notre Dame and they became very interested and recruited me. I took a visit down there and really liked it, and chose Notre Dame."

By becoming a scholarship player, Hanzlik realized one of his goals from when he had first begun playing the sport. As he matured at Notre Dame, Hanzlik caught the eyes of USA Basketball coaches and became a player they tracked and followed. He played on teams that traveled to South America and China prior to his senior season in college. At that point he was no stranger to the USA Basketball family, but still thought it would be a long shot for him to make the 1980 Olympic team that was assured to include the likes of Isiah Thomas, Rolando Blackman and Mark Aguirre.

"I was probably a bubble guy," Hanzlik admits. "But because they had voted to boycott the Olympics, there were some guys who decided not to even try out. That opened an opportunity for me and I made the '80 Olympic team."

Whereas other athletes in other sports coveted the honor of representing the U.S. at an Olympic Games, Hanzlik didn't see it that way. Instead he looked at it as "a great opportunity to work on my game and peak my abilities for the NBA." That was his motivating factor when he went to practice each day.

Hanzlik also was under no illusion there would be a stunning development that would somehow overturn the boycott. The disappointment for him, as a basketball player, was not acute. It barely rated a blip on his emotional radar when all was said and done.

"I was a realist," reasons Hanzlik "I knew we weren't going to go and it didn't do any good to cry over spilled milk. At the time, it wasn't that big a disappointment for me personally. I got drafted by the Sonics and was going to the NBA. That was the key thing and I knew it wouldn't make any difference if we weren't going. I was the 20th pick overall in the first round. That is the other thing that helped me when I made that Olympic team—it vaulted me up in the draft a little bit."

And the realist in Hanzlik also figured any attempt by other athletes to somehow sue their way to the Olympic Games in Moscow was improbable as well. "I knew there was a movement of athletes that were trying to switch it," Hanzlik says. "It was a bunch of crock."

Though Hanzlik never thought he would go, he also had other thoughts on how the issue was handled. "The other thing I thought was poorly done was that none of the athletes were ever consulted. It was a decision made. Not that the athletes could've changed anything, but I thought they should've talked to them beforehand."

And while many members of the U.S. team felt disheartened by the festivities and gala in Washington, D.C., designed to appease the disappointment of not going to Moscow, Hanzlik, again, had a different view of the events. "I remember going to the White House and getting some private tours," he recalls. "They did a lot of nice things for the athletes. That was fun. We had a great time for a weekend."

Hanzlik was 22 years old and riding high toward a career in the NBA—his dream. A trip to Moscow would have been a nice way to cap off a summer in which he graduated from Notre Dame as an engineering major, received job offers at General Electric and Eaton Corporation, was drafted in the first round of the NBA and was named to the 1980 U.S. Olympic Basketball team. Not going to the Summer Games in Moscow hardly damped his spirit.

"If I look at it now, I think, golly that would've been really cool to go," admits Hanzlik, who was named to the second team of the NBA's 1986 All-Defensive Team. "I think I was so young at the time that it was beyond me. It wasn't until I got a little maturity later on that I began to understand what makes sense and what doesn't make sense. Unfortunately, I was too into sports and training and I didn't worry about political things at that time."

Today, pondering a theoretical conversation with President Carter, Hanzlik says a series of questions comes to mind: "Do you think you made the right decision? Do you think it was a mistake? And how would that have changed if we had gone? What would've happened differently?"

Those questions would probably be the tip of the iceberg for many other Olympic athletes from the 1980 Summer team who didn't have the chance to fulfill their dreams. For Hanzlik, getting answers would be nice but, ultimately, not necessary to complete the chapter that was his 1980.

Amy Koopman – 1980 U.S. Olympic Gymnastic Team

Amy Koopman
Gymnastics

Imagine yourself at 13 years old.

For most, it was an age when maybe you started to part your hair a little differently. Or you started to wear certain clothes that made you look and feel older. Maybe you started to wear makeup. Or maybe you experienced your first boy-girl party. Maybe you got to hang out a little later on Friday night at the local gathering place. Or maybe you got to ride the subway all by yourself for the several blocks to your friend's house in the city.

For Amy Koopman, 13 years old meant she was an Olympian.

"I started when I was 7 1/2," Koopman recalls. "I was just a kid who was always jumping on the bed, climbing on the counters, climbing in the trees, hanging upside down by my knees. I had babysitters who were cheerleaders and they were teaching me certain things—walkovers, splits, cartwheels. And then they started teaching me back handsprings. When they'd leave I'd try it myself. Needless to say I landed on my head more often than not."

Landing on her head didn't sit well with Koopman's parents, so they enrolled her in a more organized gymnastics class in Arlington Heights, Ill. When she first entered the class, the instructors performed the traditional test of the student's skill level. "They had asked can I do a front handspring and I said, 'I don't know. What is it?' So, somebody would show me and I would just do it," says Koopman, laughing at the memory. "I had never done it before. It was just one of those things. Within two months I was put on their competitive team. Training to compete."

By the time she was eight years old, Koopman was twisting, turning, flipping and tumbling in the gym for 20 to 25 hours per week. She started as a Class 3 gymnast, the lowest level. She competed in Class 3 for one year and finished within the top three in the state competitions. A year later, she competed in Class 2 with the same results. At 11 years old, the pre-teen competed as a Class 1 gymnast and finished 15th in the state.

As Koopman was entering the seventh grade at 12, her gymnastics career continued to prosper despite changes to her routine. "My gym was falling apart," Koopman says. "My coach sold his Addison Gym and moved to the Schaumburg Gym for a while and trained us there for the next year. Then my coach left and I had to find another gym."

The other gym Koopman found was located in Northbrook, Ill., where the Mid-America Twisters were located and coached by Bill Sands. "I didn't know much about him before I went to his gym," she admits. "He used to coach at the American Academy in Des Plaines, Ill., and had broken off and formed his own gym two-to-three years prior to when I started. He was a very intense individual who would've loved to have trained the entire Olympic team."

At first Koopman didn't like training with Sands and the Twisters. "There was a night-and-day difference in the programs," Koopman recalls. "I was not happy there. I was training for the AAU Junior Nationals and went to Bill Sands' gym for three weeks. They were changing everything and it was frustrating me, so I left. I went back to my old gym run by someone else. I trained on my own for the next three weeks until after the competition. Needless to say, I didn't do all that great in the competition."

Koopman tried again at Sands' gym in the summer months, when most gymnasts start to learn new skills. The transition proved to be a lot smoother the second time around, and she continued her progress. Changing her entire routine meant Sands and Koopman would put in 28 hours a week at the gym. And the grind of training was excruciating. "At times, I think you were more afraid of the coach than not doing the skill," she admits. "Unfortunately, that type of training only works for a while until you're not afraid of them. I'm not saying he was a bad guy. He wasn't. I'm saying in any sport most kids are willing to give you 90 percent effort, but to give you that extra 10 percent is not comfortable. And he definitely came after the last 10 percent."

The extra effort Sands wanted, and eventually Koopman gave him, resulted in her advancing to Class 1 status before turning 13. After finishing 25th at the Class 1 Nationals in 1979, Koopman advanced one whole level to Elite status and found herself finishing fifth at the Olympic Trials in Jacksonville, Fla., one year later. She stood amongst the best female gymnasts in the country and was introduced as a member of the 1980 U.S. Summer Olympic team at age 13—the *second* youngest on the team.

Though she knew the boycott had been announced, the young gymnast held out hope that somehow she would be able to travel to the Soviet Union, home of one of her childhood idols, Olga Korbut, and compete against another idol, Nadia Comaneci. Instead, she got to go to Washington, D.C., and meet the president.

Though meeting any president of the United States would be considered a high point in one's life, Koopman recalls her trip to Washington this way: "I remember a lot of athletes not even going up to shake his hand or to receive the commemorative medal they were handing out," Koopman stills recalls with amazement. "Obviously, there were very, very many who were upset and didn't feel politics should have entered the sports arena."

For Koopman, though, she was a 13-year-old kid being tossed in the air by burly weightlifters and water polo players while completing double backflips before splashing into the hotel pool. "I remember having a blast. I remember doing a lot of sightseeing and getting to meet the other athletes." Koopman also remembers that at age 13, four more years until another shot at Olympic glory didn't seem like an eternity. At least she thought.

"At that time, I can't say that I was disappointed, because I couldn't grasp the concept of what the Olympics was other than what I had seen on TV. I don't think I ever really thought about it. Now I do. Now I realize what I missed. Back then I thought, I have another shot. I'll be around for '84. Unfortunately, four years is a long time."

Koopman finally made it to Moscow in 1981 as a member of the U.S. team that competed at the World Championships. "I at least got to see where I would've competed had I gotten to go in '80," she says.

In 1982, again Koopman competed at the World Championships and was starting to make a name for herself on the international stage, when her routine was disrupted once more. Her coach, Bill Sands, announced that he would be leaving in the summer of 1983 to pursue a graduate degree at the University of Utah. Sands wanted some of his star gymnasts, including Koopman, to work toward finishing high school one year early in order to continue training with him at Utah. "I knew that was not going to happen," Koopman remembers. "There was huge amounts of tension in the gym and everything just fell apart. For me, it was a combination of the growth spurt and being tired all the time. I think I went through a depression. There were mornings when I didn't want to get out of bed and go to school. I was too tired. I think I was burned out. If I had had a more stable situation, maybe I could've gotten through it. Maybe not. I actually ended up quitting [my gym] in October of '82."

Koopman's parents couldn't believe it. They didn't understand the mental turmoil she had experienced and the lack of an outlet to alleviate that stress. So, in December of 1982, Koopman packed her bags and headed west to train with SCAT Gymnastics and 1984 Olympic gymnastics coach Don Peters. "Luckily, I had an aunt and uncle who lived out there and was able to stay with them at first," she says. "Here I was, a kid of 16, one thousand miles from home, new high school and a new gym. I was still having some of the same issues. I don't know if some of my heart went out of it or… I just remember skills that used to be easy were now scary because I didn't know where I was."

Koopman's center of gravity at 16 years old, 5-foot-2 and 105 pounds, was far different than it had been at 13 years old, 4-foot-9 and 77 pounds. "I knew they considered me overweight and too big, which was ridiculous," Koopman says. "It was a combination of that, me and a lot of different factors. One day the coach, Don Peters, came to me and told me, 'Go home. You're wasting your time and money. You'll never make the 1984 Olympic team.' To this day, I'm not sure if he did me a favor or I should be upset."

As Koopman sat and watched the story of the 1984 U.S. women's gymnastics team unfold, there was part of her that wondered what it would have been like if she could have endured the turmoil of the previous years. The payoff? Standing on the medal platform in Los Angeles and listening to the U.S. national anthem while watching her country's flag rising a little higher than the others.

More than two decades later, Koopman, no longer a wide-eyed teenager, fully understands the magnitude of what she missed out on and the events that precipitated such a drastic measure by the Carter administration. "I'm not disillusioned by the Olympics at all," admits the 41-year-old mother. "The Olympics are a fabulous venue to display the top athletes of the world. If anything, I'm disillusioned with politics. I still love the United States of America. It's the best country there is, but, again, it goes back to years and years and how many boycotts of the Olympics have there been? Two. I don't think politics has a place in this particular venue. I don't think it did any good."

These days Koopman has trouble explaining her participation, or lack of, in an Olympic Games that went on without her or the rest of her teammates. "I guess what is hard for me today is: Okay, I made the Olympic Team but we never got to go. I don't ever really feel like I was an Olympian. I think it was during the 2005 [U.S. Olympic] Hall of Fame induction in Chicago—we were a part of it, but you just didn't feel like you quite were. It was cool to go and be included as someone who was an Olympian, but to have been able to be a part of an Olympic Village and be able to watch all the different sports, to go to the Opening and Closing Ceremonies, that is the part that you miss. I think what upset me more was when the Olympics were on our own soil in 1984, we didn't even get a ticket to our own event. It would've been nice to be recognized somehow. It was all just swept under the carpet."

Ultimately, Koopman knows her rise to the Olympic team in 1980 was meteoric. "I still think back and wonder if that was another person," Koopman says, smiling at the thought. "It seems so long ago now. To be able to say I was one of the best gymnasts in the United States is pretty cool."

And like the light that flashes across the nighttime sky, as children wish upon that star for their dreams to come true, the realization that light is fleeting doesn't resonate until much later in life. It is only then that you have the opportunity to fully understand and appreciate the spectacle that unfolded before your very eyes as a child.

CHAPTER **V**

The Vote

After a week of ongoing meetings, briefings and discussions between President Jimmy Carter's administration and United States Olympic Committee leaders, the 341 voting members of the USOC House of Delegates convened in Colorado Springs, Colo., to vote on whether to accept or reject the call to boycott the 1980 Olympic Summer Games in Moscow.

Despite strong sentiment for voting against the boycott, the meetings had apparently persuaded many of the delegates to instead vote in favor. Still, many other delegates were resentful and felt they had been strong-armed by the administration with, among other things, threats of legal action to prevent American athletes from competing in Moscow. Ultimately, the delegates knew that if they voted against the president, the future of the USOC could be irrevocably damaged.

Resigned toward their leanings on the vote, influential USOC leaders and delegates centered last-minute discussions on how they could best leverage a pro-boycott decision with the president. The USOC was looking for assurances of federal assistance for a $4 million appropriation that the White House had requested in its 1980 budget, promise of tax-exempt status for non-profit sports organizations within the USOC, as well as the administration's assistance in reviving the organization's fund-raising efforts that had fallen since the president's call for the boycott in January.

On the day before the vote, far more consequential international issues were being addressed in the White House. Most prominently, President Carter and his cabinet were deciding a course of action to attempt rescuing the 52 Americans that had been held hostage in Iran for 159 days.

At the same time, a group of athletes held a press conference indicating that a legal challenge was virtually certain if the USOC voted to reject the invitation to compete in Moscow. Admittedly, the athletes knew their legal action would, in all likelihood, be futile, since Congress could amend the Amateur Sports Act of 1978 and the president probably could invoke authority under the Emergency Powers Act to preclude them from traveling to Moscow. Nevertheless, the band of athletes, with the support of the American Civil Liberties Union and other groups, was set to test President Carter's authority over their fate.

Earlier in the week, the USOC agreed to allow a member of the administration to address their delegates one more time before the vote, as a final effort to present President Carter's viewpoint and sway opinion. It was believed that the person to give that address would be Lloyd Cutler. But after an escalation in discussion within the administration, Vice President Walter F. Mondale decided that he wanted to attend the meeting. The USOC's Executive Committee didn't like that idea, until President Carter personally asked USOC Executive Director F. Don Miller for permission to send Mondale instead.

★ ★ ★ ★ ★

On Saturday, April 12, 1980, in the Antlers Plaza Hotel in Colorado Springs, amidst a packed ballroom that included nearly 300 athletes, sports leaders and business officials who made up the USOC House of Delegates, and nearly 200 reporters and cameras, Vice President Mondale addressed the delegates before they were to cast one of the most important votes in the history of the United States Olympic movement.

* * * * *

President Kane, Members of the House of Delegates, Friends:

I appreciate the opportunity to speak to you on behalf of the honorary president of the U.S. Olympic Committee—the president of the United States. And I am delighted to be in the lovely community of Colorado Springs—the home of the U.S. Olympic Committee.

I speak to you as leaders dedicated to amateur sport, and as citizens dedicated to America's best interests. I know that everyone in this room loves our country. And I want to express the nation's gratitude for your efforts at Lake Placid to persuade the International Olympic Committee to move or postpone the Moscow Games. I thank your leaders as well for stating that the committee would be guided by the president's decision on the best interest of the nation.

As we meet today, the lesson of the Soviet invasion of Afghanistan still waits to be drawn.

History holds its breath—for what is at stake is no less than the future security of the civilized world.

If one nation can be subjugated by Soviet aggression, is any sovereign nation truly safe from that fate? If 100,000 Russian troops, and the barbaric use of lethal gas, and the specter of nightly assassinations—if these fail to alarm us, what will? If the Soviet lunge toward the most strategic oil-rich spot on Earth fails to unite us, what will?

And if we and our allies and friends fail to use every single peaceful means available to preserve the peace, what hope is there that peace will long be preserved?

While history holds its breath, America has moved decisively to show the Soviet Union that it cannot invade another nation and still conduct business as usual with the United States. Our country has:

- *embargoed 17 million tons of grain,*
- *tightened control on high technology trade,*
- *limited Soviet fishing in our waters,*
- *raised our defense budget to upgrade all aspects of our forces,*
- *strengthened our naval presence in the Indian Ocean,*
- *intensified development of our Rapid Deployment Forces,*
- *and offered to help other sovereign states in the region to maintain their own security.*

In the U.N. General Assembly, the United States joined more than a hundred other nations in an unprecedented majority—calling for the immediate, unconditional and total withdrawal of Soviet troops from Afghanistan. But the president, the Congress, and the American people understand that a world which travels to the Moscow Games devalues its condemnation and offers its complicity to Soviet propaganda.

I am convinced the American people do not want their athletes cast as pawns in that tawdry propaganda charade. And I urge you to respect that undeniable consensus.

Your decision today is not a question of denying our Olympic team the honor they deserve—for the American people, as you know, deeply respect the sacrifice we are asking our athletes to make.

It is no longer a question of whether participation in the Moscow Olympics confers legitimacy on Soviet aggression. When the Communist Party prints a million handbooks to tell its top activists that the Summer Games mean world respect for Soviet foreign policy, surely that issue is behind us.

Nor is it a question of drawing a line between sports and politics. That line the Soviets long ago erased. When billions of rubles are diverted to the Games from Soviet domestic needs; when Moscow and other Olympic cities are purged of dissidents who might speak out; when Soviet children who might meet Western people and ideas on the streets are packed off to internal exile; when Soviet emissaries roam the globe offering athletes expense-paid trips to Moscow; when Soviet sports officials distort the number of teams committed to participating—surely the issue of Soviet politics in Soviet sports is behind us.

Above all, the decision you will make today is not a choice between a sports issue and a national security issue. For the president and Congress have made it clear that the Olympic boycott is a genuine element of America's response to the invasion of Afghanistan. It is an unambiguous statement of our national resolve. It is a keystone in our call to our allies for solidarity.

We must not—and cannot—break that link between America's power to check aggression and America's call for an Olympic boycott. Your vote is a test of your will, our confidence, our values, and our power to keep peace through peaceful means.

It is not a partisan issue—for both political parties resoundingly supported the president's action in Congress. It is not a parochial issue—for the American people overwhelmingly agree that we must not go to Moscow.

And it is not a national issue—for citizens and governments throughout the world share our judgment.

From his exile in Gorky, Andrei Sakharov—the unsilenceable voice of human rights, and the father of the Russian H-bomb—calls on America, saying that, "A united position of the Moscow Olympic Games must obviously be a basic part" of the world's response. This morning, as many as 50 nations—leading political and sports powers—await your signal to join us.

Athletes and sports organizations and national bodies around the world await your lead to mobilize their commitment. They do so for good reason. Today virtually every industrial nation on Earth is dangerously dependent on Persian Gulf oil. How could we convince the Soviets not to threaten the Gulf, if a blow was dealt to our deterrent? How could our government send a message to Moscow, if tomorrow's Pravda *brags that our policies have been repudiated?*

It is fitting that the same ancient nation that gave us the Olympics also gave us democracy—for your decision here is truly a referendum on freedom.

And thus it is also a referendum on America's character and fundamental values. The athletes here, and the athletes you represent, may have been born a full generation after the Berlin Olympics. But as their advisors and trustees, you bear the responsibility of linking that history to their duty. For the story of Hitler's rise is more than an unspeakable tragedy, more than a study in tyranny. It is also a chronicle of the free world's failure—of opportunities seized, aggression not opposed, appeasement not condemned.

By the Fall of 1935, the Nazis had passed the notorious Nuremberg Laws reducing Jews to the status of non-persons, and were flexing their military muscle. For a hopeful moment, American opinion was galvanized—and editorials and amateur athletic unions across the country urged a boycott of the Berlin Olympics.

An American member of the International Olympic Committee, Ernest Jahncke, made the plea most eloquently when he wrote the President of the IOC:

"If our committee permits the Games to be held in Germany, there will be nothing left to distinguish the Olympic idea from the Nazi ideal.... It will take years to re-establish the prestige of the Games and the confidence of the peoples of the world. Sport will lose its beauty and its nobility and become, as it has already become in Nazi Germany, an ugly, ignoble affair."

The call for a boycott was rejected. And the reasons for rejection are bone-chilling—even across all these decades.

Don't drag sports into the arena of politics, they were told. It will destroy the Olympic movement, they were told. It will only penalize our American athletes, they were told. Solutions to political problems are not the responsibility of sporting bodies, they were told. Let us take our Jews and blacks to Berlin and beat the Nazis, they were told. If America refuses to go, we will be the only ones left out in the cold, there were told.

Such reasons prevailed. Only weeks after American attendance was assured, Nazi troops took the Rhineland—and Hitler readied Germany for the Games. His preparations cast uncanny foreshadows. For he expelled foreign journalists who told the truth about persecution. He ordered his vicious propaganda concealed from foreign visitors. And he, too, looked forward to legitimacy. As Joseph Goebbels boasted on the eve of the Olympics, the Reich expected the Games "to turn the trick and create a friendly world attitude toward Nazi political, economic and racial aims."

It worked. Not even Jesse Owens' magnificent personal triumph diminished Hitler's international propaganda success—a coup he linked directly to his Master Race Doctrine. We revere Jesse in death as in life—for he was an exemplary American, an inspiration to millions everywhere, and a personal friend loved by many of you here today. But neither Jesse's achievement in Berlin, nor any words spoken at the Games, prevented the Reich from exploiting the Olympics toward their own brutal ends.

Listen to Nazi War Minister Albert Speer's report on the Führer's mood as the happy spectators left Berlin: "Hitler was exulting over the harmonious atmosphere that prevailed.... International animosity toward Nazi Germany was plainly a thing of the past, he thought."

Before long, the Nazi war machine scarred the face of Europe—and soon the night closed in.

We are far from that time—but not far from that script.

Like you, I understand the ideals of sport—for sportsmanship is synonymous with fair play. Like you, I am in awe of the Olympic tradition—stretching over centuries, reaching out across cultures.

And like every American, I know the exhilaration of Olympic victory. Few moments in my life match the electricity I felt at Lake Placid. And few human experiences can compare to the years of sacrifice, pain, and yearning that you and our athletes have invested in this summer.

But I also know, as you know, that some goals surpass even personal achievement. To any young athletes who feel singled out for suffering, I say, it is war above all that singles out our young for suffering. And it is war that our peaceful resolve can prevent. Everyone is being asked to sacrifice. We need only ask the farmers of the midlands if they have sacrificed—or ask the workers in our export industries if they have sacrificed. Or ask the computer companies whose products have been embargoed. Or ask the businesses whose years of planning have come undone. Or ask the young sailors in the Indian Ocean Task Force. Or ask the American families whose taxes support our defense budget. Or ask the Afghan athlete who faces the Soviets not on a field in Moscow, but as a resistance fighter in Kabul.

We recognize the enormous price we are asking our athletes to pay. We recognize the tremendous sacrifice we are asking of sports officials. But on behalf of the president of the United States I assure you that our nation will do everything within its power to ensure the success of the Los Angeles Games, to help the Olympic Committee restore its finances, to provide even greater assistance to the development of amateur sport, and above all, to recognize the true heroism of our athletes who do not go to Moscow.

I believe all Americans will thank you—both for the contribution you make to our national security, and to the further integrity you confer on amateur sport.

For I believe that the Olympic movement will be forever strengthened by your courage. You will have restored to the Modern Olympics the ancient "truce of the gods." No nation may serve as the Olympic host while invading and subjugating another—that was the rule for the Greek city-states, and that must be the rule again today.

Forty-five years ago, when an American Olympic official took his stand against Berlin, he said this: "Place your great talents and influence in the service of the spirit of fair play and chivalry—instead of the service of brutality, force, and power. Take your rightful place in the history of the Olympics. The Olympic Idea has been rescued from the remote past. You have the opportunity to rescue it from the immediate present—and to safeguard it for posterity."

His words reach out to us across the decades. History rarely offers a second chance. If we fail to seize this one, history itself may fail us. Thank you. [27]

★ ★ ★ ★ ★

Hours after hearing the vice president's emotional address—and an even more impassioned speech calling for the boycott by William E. Simon, a 16-year USOC veteran who was a former secretary of the Treasury and an otherwise outspoken Republican critic of President Carter—the United States Olympic Committee delegates voted to endorse the president's call for an American boycott of the 1980 Olympic Summer Games in Moscow.

For the first time in its history, by a 2-to-1 margin—1,604 to 797 with two abstentions—the USOC delegates, most of whom cast multiple votes apportioned according to the sports organizations they represented, elected to reject the invitation to participate in an Olympic Games.

The U.S. team would have been entered in archery, basketball, biathlon, boxing, canoeing/kayaking, cycling, diving, equestrian, fencing, field hockey, gymnastics, judo, pentathlon, rowing, shooting, soccer, swimming, team handball, track and field, volleyball, water polo, weightlifting, wrestling and yachting.

★ ★ ★ ★ ★

The next day headlines from the nation's newspapers, including *The New York Times* and *The Washington Post*, heralded: "U.S. OLYMPIC GROUP VOTES TO BOYCOTT THE MOSCOW GAMES" and "A Major Victory for Carter: USOC Votes to Boycott Games."

Because of the vote, momentum for a widespread boycott among other nations was expected to build during the following month. The Carter administration's hope that other countries would follow the United States' lead was beginning to come to fruition. The day after the USOC vote, West Germany Chancellor Helmut Schmidt declared that the Soviet occupation in Afghanistan would make his country's Olympic participation impossible. It was generally believed that if the West German Olympic Committee, which was set to meet on May 15, decided to vote for a boycott, most of the rest of Western Europe, Japan and several Third World nations would do the same. Many other countries that had opposed a boycott—including Canada, Australia, New Zealand, the Netherlands and Italy—were expecting their Olympic committees in the coming weeks to change their positions now that the USOC had made its decision. In the days following the vote, Egypt, Saudi Arabia and Iran prominently joined the U.S. in deciding to boycott the Games.

Though it was highly unlikely, talk of a widespread boycott leading to the cancellation of the Moscow Games was being heard. Still, plenty felt that no matter how many countries decided not to go, the Games would go on.

* * * * *

Reaction from the host country to the news of the American vote was met with angry cries of "blackmail" and claims by Soviet officials that President Carter had used the American athletes as part of his re-election campaign. In their efforts to ramp up their own propaganda, Soviet news agencies were quoting disappointed U.S. athletes and officials who were against the boycott.

The decision by the U.S. not to participate in the Games was a clear message to the Soviet Union that their actions in Afghanistan were not acceptable to at least part of the world. At the same time, Soviet officials construed that the Carter administration knew the boycott would likely be taken in stride by Moscow, and would not lead to a withdrawal of their forces from Afghanistan.

The Soviets further surmised that Carter also likely knew the United States' action toward these Olympic Games would most certainly result in the Soviet Union boycotting the next Games that were scheduled for the United States—Los Angeles, in 1984. "Though it would never be said tit-for-tat," suggests Russian television news journalist Vladimir Pozner, "[the Soviet Union] would find a reason not to go, under a different pretext, of course, which is exactly what happened, along with several countries of the Soviet bloc."

* * * * *

While the vote's outcome was deemed a victory for the Carter administration, both sides had mixed feelings of patriotism, as well as sorrow for the ones who ultimately were caught in the middle of it all—the athletes.

"It was a terrible feeling," remembers Mondale. "I was in athletics when I was a kid. I know what it meant. That meeting in Colorado was about as painful as could be. That's why I went out to Colorado, personally, to the USOC, [to] talk to the athletes and committee to make the personal case on why we were doing this. We didn't want to do this from a distance. What I'll never forget was, here were these athletes—most of them were there—careers were going to be affected and all of them were respectful. They listened carefully. I don't know if in their hearts they accepted it, but there was a dignified vote. I have a lot of regrets for the athletes. But did we have to do it? Would it have been wrong to go along as if things were fine? I don't have any doubts about that."

USOC President Robert Kane also expressed his support for the administration and similar sorrow for the athletes by stating to reporters in a news conference, "More than anything else, the preservation of our patriotism and support of the president of the United States had to be re-affirmed. I'm completely satisfied that it was a right decision, at the same time feeling desperately sorry for the athletes who have to live by it."[28]

* * * * *

Some of the athletes present were visibly emotional and deeply disappointed, but also philosophical about the position they were in. Naturally, feelings of disappointment about the boycott were prevalent. But many also harbored disappointment toward the governing body, which they felt had sold out its own people by violating its constitution and capitulating to the president. At the same time, there were feelings that if the vote had gone the other way, the athletes would have been used as a vehicle for foreign policy and would have had to accept being part of a bigger cause.

Other athletes who were not present were equally disappointed. "There was always this hope that somehow the decision was going to be reversed and the boycott really wasn't going to happen," says volleyball player Debbie Landreth. "It was crushing, devastating. We were on tour with the East Germans at the time. We had just finished playing a match and we found out about the decision. It was just so disappointing. Even though we knew there was a good likelihood of it, it's one of those things where we couldn't really prepare ourselves for it because we wanted to believe."

Lest there be any doubt the actions taken by the administration and the decision rendered was a political or foreign-policy decision, Vice President Mondale remains adamant to the contrary to this day. "It was a security position," he says. "The idea that the Soviet Union could invade another country was not just an interesting fact but a very, very destabilizing, dangerous new step, with a lot of serious international consequences. The Soviet Union had just invaded another country and were killing people left and right. We had to deal with it. Otherwise, it would have encouraged them and others to do more of this sort of thing. Regardless of the politics, we couldn't let them get away with that without paying a price. There is always politics. In other words, this is played out in a democracy, played out in international affairs. But, this decision that we took, and the steps that we took, were all taken to try and impose a price. None of them would've made sense if you were just talking domestic policy. Certainly going ahead with the Olympics, politically, would have been an easy thing to do. Certainly canceling grain service to the Soviet Union is not a very good idea if you want to carry Iowa [in the presidential election]. Having [draft] registration for all 20-year-olds across the country was not a very good idea domestically. At least we could say that, unlike 1936 when we went to the Berlin Olympics and Hitler used it for his purposes, we did not do that in 1980. We did a lot of things that were painful, but we felt like we had to stand up to them."

* * * * *

For a group of 25 other disappointed U.S. athletes, they too were about to stand up.

Isiah Thomas — 1980 U.S. Olympic Basketball Team

Isiah Thomas
Basketball

While 19-year-old Indiana University freshman Isiah Thomas and most of his family were reveling in the prospect of his potential summer date in Moscow for the XXII Olympiad as a member of Team USA, not everybody shared the same enthusiasm.

"Everyone was really excited with the exception of my Mom," admits Thomas, now president of Basketball Operations and head coach of the NBA's New York Knickerbockers. "My Mom wasn't too excited about us going to Moscow for the Olympics."

For Thomas' mother Mary, who fought to keep her son disciplined and alive in their drug and violence-addled Chicago neighborhood, the Olympics may have been okay if it didn't involve travel to the capital of communism. "There was a lot of fear and tension around the Olympics," Thomas remembers. "Right before that, there was the hostage situation. That was always being talked about along with the terrorist situation. That was on everyone's mind even back then." Plus, Mary didn't want any part of something that might disturb either the progress her son was making in school or his dream of a career in the NBA.

Before talk of a boycott, those following the prospects of which players might make Head Coach Dave Gavitt's Olympic team were not surprised when the young Hoosier standout was mentioned as a shoe-in. Despite the fact basketball tryouts occurred after the boycott announcement, Thomas was elated to be chosen. And his mother, though surely disappointed her son would not be able to compete in the Olympics, was most likely relieved that he would not have to travel to Moscow.

"It was more than anything you could've imagined or dreamed," says Thomas, smiling at the memory. "As a kid, I don't think anyone could dream at that young age… to one day say I was going to be representing our country in the Olympics."

For Thomas, the happy-go-lucky star of one of college basketball's powerhouse programs, the prospect of traveling and competing in the Olympics far out-weighed any fears he may have had. "I remember we had these Levi's sweat suits," Thomas recalls, laughing. "They were red, white and blue and were velour. They had USA on them and I remember just being so proud to wear it and to have it. The fact that you had the chance and opportunity to represent your country on the global stage was quite an honor."

Thomas' rise to Olympian, like his rise to the NBA, was a steady evolution. Unlike his NBA dream to one day play amongst the greatest players in the world, Thomas hadn't given much thought to the possibility of representing his country. "Every time I watched the Olympics as a kid," he recalls, "you always cried watching those guys on the stand when they put the gold medal around their neck. You never in a million years thought you would be one of those guys that were picked to be on an Olympic team. I would say it evolved as I got further in high school and college."

The fact that Thomas even decided to participate in the Olympic tryouts was newsworthy. Since tryouts followed the announcement of the boycott, many of the country's best collegians opted not to even bother playing for a spot on the team. As a sophomore the following year, Thomas would lead the Hoosiers to the 1981 NCAA Championship as a *Sporting News* first-team All-America selection; and even then, he already looked back at his Olympic experience with pride. "I just thought it was an honor to represent my country even though we weren't going abroad," Thomas says. "I wanted to represent at home and be proud of the honor that I was selected to participate. And even though there was a boycott, I was still proud to represent."

Despite the boycott, the United States Olympic Committee and NBA organized what they called the "Gold Medal Games," in which the Olympic men's basketball team traveled to various American cities for a few weeks and played pro teams in exhibition games. "It was a disappointment," Thomas says. "At that time it was made clear to us by the president of the stance he was taking and the country was taking. We wanted to do what was right by our country, so we understood and we all followed through."

The disappointment was present, but not all-consuming. Thomas' future following his sophomore year in college was vastly different compared to his fellow Olympic teammates'. And Thomas knew it and appreciated that fact. "I heard about the disappointment of some of the athletes who had trained and worked so hard in different sports, and this was their once-in-lifetime opportunity to fulfill their dream and to cash in on endorsements and everything else," Thomas says. "From a monetary standpoint you sympathize with those athletes but, at the same time, you understood the delicate situation our country was in.

"Unfortunately, sports and politics have always gone hand-in-hand, whether it be a civil action or political action. Each arena always flows into the other. Changes that are made, or demonstrations that are made in the sports arena, somehow always seem to impact the political arena. Sports has always been used as a tool to bring people together, and also as a tool to advance different causes."

For Thomas, his Olympic experience had no bearing on his future prospects as a professional basketball player. The 12-time All-Star played 13 seasons with the Detroit Pistons before retiring following the 1993-'94 season. He helped lead his team to back-to-back NBA titles in 1989 and 1990 while earning Finals MVP honors in the latter. Thomas' playing career culminated by being recognized in 1996 as one of the Top 50 Greatest Players of All-Time in NBA history, as well as his induction into the Naismith Memorial Hall of Fame four years later.

Thomas averaged 9.3 assists and 19.2 points over his NBA career, and ranks fifth all-time with 9,061 assists, and 46th with 18,822 points.

While his Olympic experience may seem like no more than a footnote to a career that has brought him fame and fortune, Thomas doesn't see it that way. "I was just trying to be a good basketball player, and to be selected for the Olympic team was a great honor. I cherished it."

Carol Blazejowski — 1980 U.S. Olympic Basketball Team

Carol Blazejowski
Basketball

In 1980, Carol Blazejowski was a member of the U.S. Summer Olympics contingent invited to Washington, D.C. by President Jimmy Carter for a gala celebration to celebrate their accomplishment—making the Olympic team—despite not having been allowed to compete in Moscow.

"I invited my parents," Blazejowski recalls. "It was lovely and we were respectful. And, okay, it was after the fact and it really wasn't that meaningful, but there is a photo that hangs on the wall in my office at home with me shaking President Carter's hand. Rosalyn is next to him, his daughter Amy was a little kid next to him, too. And I'm looking at him with respect but, knowing how I am, it's kind of a smirk."

That smirk tells a lot about the feisty character of the former tomboy who grew up playing every sport there was to play—stickball, baseball, tackle football, to name a few—in her Cranford, N.J. neighborhood. That was before she ever thought about dribbling a basketball. That was pre-Title IX, when little girls didn't have the same athletic opportunities as boys. Blazejowski would eventually do something about it, and her attitude would help blaze a pioneering trail for girls to follow in future generations.

Blazejowski's athletic biography is earmarked with chapters of historic firsts, hardships and sacrifices that led to her ultimate success. When her grade school teacher and junior high school gym teachers encouraged the lanky pre-teen in her basketball pursuits, they lit a fire that still burns brightly today. "I was in uncharted waters and it was very difficult to be the exception rather than the rule when you got the quizzical looks from the boys all the time," Blazejowski says. "I wanted to play sports and it was uncomfortable at times and people didn't understand, because it wasn't the norm. [But those teachers] made me feel that it was okay."

So when it came time to test the boundaries of society, Blazejowski did not shy away.

"I was taller than most of the boys in my class, and the gym teacher saw that I had a little bit of talent and introduced me to the roundball, and thought I could be pretty good at this, too," Blazejowski says. "At that point it was really love at first sight. I really, really, enjoyed the game, but there were no recreation leagues for girls. There were no organized school programs for girls and it wasn't until high school that I said to the athletic director, 'Look, we don't have a girls' team here and if you don't get a girls' team here by the time I'm a senior, I'm going to try out for the boys' team.' I had been playing with them in the streets, on the corner, all the time playing with the guys, and I finally wanted to see if I could be competitive at the girls' level. All the parochial schools in the area had it but the public schools didn't have a girls' team. Sure enough, by my senior year, we had a girls' team—I guess the athletic director didn't want me trying out for the boys' team that he coached—and we went 35-1 and lost in the state finals."

Following her senior year in high school, where Blazejowski averaged 25 points per game and was an All-State selection, she didn't have to look far from Cranford to find her next basketball home: Montclair State College. It was at Montclair that Blazejowski would become a three-time All-America player, lead her team to the first women's Final Four in 1976, be named the first Wade Trophy winner as women basketball's player of the year in 1978, hold NCAA single-season scoring records with 38.6 points per game (1,235 total points), finish her career with 3,199 points (31.7 points per game, second only to Pete Maravich in all-time scoring among male and female college players), and gain her reputation as a force in women's basketball.

"I really hit my stride during my sophomore year," remembers Blazejowski. "I had aspirations. I had played and people had seen me. I knew '76 was the first time women's basketball was going to be introduced into the Olympics. Men had been there forever, but this was the inaugural year for the women and I had aspirations to try out for that team. And I did. I went to Missouri. And I was young. I was a sophomore, about 20 at that point, and went there feeling that based on my college history and my game, I really had a legitimate shot at this. I didn't think that anybody could shoot as well as I did. I went there and performed very well—only to be cut."

Dumbfounded that she didn't make the team, Blazejowski asked for a post-tryout meeting with Billie Moore, head coach both at the University of California, Los Angeles, and of the 1976 U.S. Olympic women's basketball team. Moore told Blazejowski her defense wasn't good enough to make the team. Reeling with disappointment but remaining cocksure, she reasoned with the coach. "Every night that we scrimmage and I average double-figures in scoring, who was playing defense on me? Because the person playing defense on me is on this team." That person happened to be Pat Summit, now the legendary women's basketball coach at the University of Tennessee.

Disillusioned and devastated, Blazejowski returned to Montclair State for her junior season and led the nation in scoring while vowing never to participate or try out for any more USA teams. Blazejowski believed that 1976 was her only shot and she should have made the team.

Her reputation grew even more on March 1, 1977, when she scorched Queens College for 52 points in the first women's basketball doubleheader at Madison Square Garden, still a record at the New York City landmark.

Following her junior season in 1977, Blazejowski received a call from Lucille Kyvallos, the coach at Queens College who would be heading the U.S. team at the World University Games in Bulgaria later that summer. Still upset about the Olympics, Blazejowski told Kyvallos, "I've been to these tryouts. I don't like it and I'm not going to do it."

But Blazejowski says Kyvallos persisted. "She kept calling and calling and said, 'You have to play for me, okay?' And I guess the message there was that I was on the team, so don't worry about it. So I went and played in my first international experience in Bulgaria and we won the silver medal. I really enjoyed it.

"In '79 we played at the World University Games in Mexico City, where the team became the first U.S. women's basketball team to win a gold medal. I said, 'Geez, maybe this isn't so bad.' Then there was the Pan Am Games in '79 and it was [for] another World Championship [the team would win a silver medal], and I went to the tryout and made that team. I had reversed fields now and I was entrenched in USA Basketball. These two experiences made me more motivated and hungry so that they could never deny me a second time. My biggest goal in life at that point was to make the 1980 Olympic team and compete in Russia."

Playing for the 1980 U.S. team would prove a daunting task for the 1978 graduate. Blazejowski had two years to fill with sacrifice and training before trying to realize her Olympic dream. "I didn't have college ball anymore," she says. "I went to graduate school, held part-time jobs, worked out with my college team, played against the men. I scrambled for two years to make ends meet to train very hard for one thing: to make the Olympic team. That was the two years that set up 1980."

The dedication was rewarded. Blazejowski made the 1980 team, and based on her international experience, was named captain.

"You're finally on the team, but I've always lived under the reservation of doubt," Blazejowski says. "We had our whole summer planned as far as competition and what-not. We were at Colorado Springs at the training center, back in the day before they had that beautiful gym now. We were going around to local high schools with none of the amenities they have now. It was a real feeling of camaraderie, one goal. We knew the Russians were the best, but it was a thrill and honor. I felt very proud, that not only had I made the team but, given the circumstances in the past, overcome all that and achieved that goal. It was very rewarding. And when we all came together as a unit, it was like a big family."

But Blazejowski's intuition and doubt became a reality that clouded her entire experience, and the uneasy feeling of a boycott never abated. "There was always hope that we would go," Blazejowski admits. "We had to go to a qualifying tournament in Bulgaria before we went to Russia, so we were training for that. We would talk amongst ourselves and think, 'There is no way [the boycott] is going to happen.' You know, wishful thinking."

Alas, she was bitterly disappointed again, and found herself at yet another crossroads. Blazejowski was 23 years old and the 1984 Olympic Games in Los Angeles were four years away. It had been such a personal struggle for the two years leading up to '80 that she couldn't imagine another four years of sacrifice. "I was an amateur and couldn't play professional ball for a living, and that was upsetting to me. I sacrificed all of that and I'm finally on a team and I can't go because of political issues of the world. I was not only bitter but I got physically ill over it in terms of anxiety and nerves. I lost a whole lot of weight and was just so troubled by 'Now what? What am I going to do?' And it was very upsetting."

Like many of her 1980 Summer Olympic brethren, a run toward 1984 never materialized. For Blazejowski, her Olympic dream and will still burned, but a short stint in the Women's Basketball League squelched that ambition. Despite never being paid the full amount of her contract, USA Basketball stripped Blazejowski of her amateur status. Her Olympic dream died that day for good.

As the bitterness subsided and years passed, Blazejowski had time to reflect on her experience. Still very much outspoken, the general manager of the WBNA's New York Liberty continues to make a name for herself in the world of basketball.

Still, her Team USA years remain important. Blazejowski's most vivid memory is of the team's fortitude. "We went to the qualifying tournament knowing we weren't going to Moscow, but our team stuck together in Bulgaria and won," she recalls. "We had nothing to play for, nothing to go to, we had no reason. We could've all just lied down. But we all had such great pride in ourselves, our team and country, and we went there and won the qualifying tournament. That for me was a bit of vindication. It was very rewarding because that was our Olympics."

In 1994, Blazejowski was inducted into the Naismith Memorial Basketball Hall of Fame in Springfield, Mass. Today, she views her role in basketball as someone who has seen the game from all sides, and she is absorbed with the desire to help cultivate the sport she loves. "My dreams were blown up in smoke temporarily, but I let it motivate me to move in a different direction and maybe help build the sport of basketball. I think I've done that as a player in USA Basketball and now in the WNBA as a general manager. I'm perpetuating a new dream to really grow the sport and contribute as best as I can."

CHAPTER VI

The Lawsuit

Anita DeFRANTZ et al., Plaintiffs,

v.

UNITED STATES OLYMPIC COMMITTEE, Defendant.

Civil Action No. 80-1013.

To the United States District Court, District of Columbia, it was simply "Civil Action No. 80-1013." But to hundreds of 1980 United States Summer Olympic athletes, *Anita DeFRANTZ et al. v. UNITED STATES OLYMPIC COMMITTEE* was one final chance for them to attain the dream that many had trained their whole lives for—to compete in the Olympic Games.

* * * * *

Prior to 1980, deciding whether to participate in the Olympics had never been an issue. Acceptance was seen as a formality that was simply assumed and accepted.

Now, if there was to be *any* chance of U.S. athletes participating in the 1980 Olympic Summer Games in Moscow, it was going to have to be by virtue of a ruling in a court of law.

★ ★ ★ ★ ★ ★

With understandable fear amongst the athletes and lots of support—including the quiet backing of people within the United States Olympic Committee—rower Anita DeFrantz, who had become the athletes' spokesperson during the run-up to the boycott announcement, led a group of 25 athletes and one USOC executive in an unprecedented class-action lawsuit filed on behalf of their teammates against the USOC.

On April 23, William H. Allen and Edward R. Mackiewicz from the Washington, D.C., law firm of Covington & Burling, along with Robert Zagoria, an attorney located in Princeton, N.J., and attorneys from the American Civil Liberties Union (ACLU), represented the athletes in seeking the court to issue an injunction ordering the USOC to withdraw its boycott of the 1980 Olympic Summer Games. The suit contended that the USOC's actions violated a constitutional right to compete in the Olympics, citing the Amateur Sports Act of 1978, which they argued specifically barred anyone from denying another the opportunity to compete in the Olympics for anything other than sports-related reasons.

Though the athletes were hardly confident that they would overturn the USOC's vote to boycott, it was their last-ditch effort to participate in the Games.

* * * * *

Anita DeFrantz's name may have been the first of the 25 athletes who filed the suit, but she represented hundreds more. The impact of the suit was incalculable.

"I was scared," DeFrantz remembers 28 years later. "I was scared for my family. I had to talk with them to make sure that they understood that I thought this was an important thing to do."

She also made sure that the 24 teammates who agreed to put their names next to hers as plaintiffs knew there might be repercussions. There was no way to know what might happen, and her concern for them was deep and genuine.

"It was tough because as athletes we had agreed to listen to our head coach, who ultimately was the commander in chief," DeFrantz says. "It was the head coach's decision to stay home, and yet he hadn't trained. He hadn't played or tried out."

The 24 other athletes, who *had* trained and played, were: rowing teammates Carol Brown, Carlie Geer, Judy Geer, Jan Harville, Patricia Brink, Patricia Spratlen, Robert Espeseth, Jan Palchikoff, Holly Hatton, Tom Woodman and Cosema Crawford; weightlifters Robert Giordano, Louis Mucardo, Philip Grippaldi, Terry Manton, Jim Curry and Arthur Drechsler; discus thrower Mac Wilkins; shot-putter Allan Feuerbach; long jumper Arnie Robinson; pole vaulter Jeff Taylor; fencer Bruce Jugan; water polo player Peter Schnugg; and canoeist Blaise Stanek; as well as one member of the executive board, Burton William Shaw.

* * * * *

THE PLAINTIFFS

Anita DeFrantz—was a member of the 1976 U.S. Olympic team and won a bronze medal as a member of the women's eight-oared shell. She had been training since 1974, exercising and practicing for her event an average of 30 hours per week.

Robert Giordano—was a weightlifter with extensive experience in international competition, finishing first in competitions against Canada and Australia. He had been training for the Games since 1970 and was exercising and practicing for his event 20-to-25 hours per week.

Louis Mucardo—was a weightlifter who had competed on the U.S. Amateur team in the Junior World Championships in 1975, 1976 and 1977. In the U.S. Senior Championships in 1978, he placed 11th. In the Pan American Games in 1979, he won a silver medal. At the time of the lawsuit, he was ranked second in the U.S. and had been practicing 20-to-25 hours per week for three years in preparation for the 1980 Olympic Summer Games.

Philip Grippaldi—was a weightlifter who had participated on the 1968, 1972 and 1976 U.S. Olympic teams, placing fifth in Mexico City, fourth in Munich and fourth in Montreal, respectively. He had been training for the Olympics for 20 years.

Terry Manton—was a weightlifter and a National Collegiate champion in 1974, 1975 and 1977. He placed third in the 1978 U.S. Senior Championships. He had been training 20-to-25 hours per week for eight years in preparation for the 1980 Olympic Summer Games.

Carol Brown—was a member of the 1976 U.S. Olympic team and won a bronze medal as a rower. She also won silver medals in the 1975 and 1978 World Championships.

Mac Wilkins—was a discus thrower and won a gold medal as a member of the 1976 U.S. Olympic team. He had been a national champion in the discus throw for the previous four years, and for five of the previous seven years. He won a gold medal at the 1979 Pan American Games. He had been training since 1970 and was preparing for the 1980 Olympic Summer Games by training 18-to-28 hours per week.

Bruce Jugan—was a fencer and finished ninth in the 1977 NCAA Fencing Championships. He had also been a member of the U.S. international squad in foil fencing. He had been training 20 hours per week for more than three years for the 1980 Olympic Summer Games.

Carlie Geer—was a rower and placed in the top third of the Head of the Charles Race in Boston in 1978 and 1979. She raced in the national championships the previous three years, placing third in the intermediate singles in '78. She had been training 25-to-30 hours per week.

Judy Geer—was a rower and member of the 1976 U.S. Olympic team. She was a national singles champion in amateur women's rowing in '76, and together with Jan Palchikoff was the 1979 national doubles champion.

Peter Schnugg—was a member of the 1980 U.S. Olympic water polo team. He was also a member of the Athletes' Advisory Council to the USOC.

Allan Feuerbach—was a member of the 1972 and 1976 U.S. Olympic teams who took fifth and fourth place in shot put, respectively. He held the sport's world record from 1973 to '76.

Jan Harville—was a rower and had been on the women's national team for the previous two years. In the 1979 World Championship, she finished third, and in 1978, she finished fourth. She practiced an average of 30 hours per week.

Patricia Brink—was a rower and a member of the 1979 Women's National Rowing Team. She trained 30 hours per week.

Patricia Spratlen—was a rower and a member of the U.S. Development Team in 1979. She had been practicing 30 hours per week in preparation for the 1980 Olympic Summer Games.

Arnie Robinson—was a long jumper and member of the 1972 and 1976 U.S. Olympic teams, winning a bronze medal and gold medal, respectively. He also won his event in the 1978 USA-USSR competition.

Jan Palchikoff—was a rower and member of the 1976 U.S. Olympic team and took fifth place in the double sculls event in the Montreal Olympics. She also was a member of the 1975 Women's National Rowing Team. In 1979, she was the national champion in double sculls and trained 20 hours per week in preparation for the 1980 Olympic Summer Games.

Robert Douglas Espeseth—was a rower and an alternate on the 1976 U.S. Olympic rowing team. He was a member of the 1978 Men's World Rowing Team and trained 25 hours per week.

Jeff Taylor—was a pole vaulter and had competed in several international competitions in his event. He was ranked second in the U.S. for the 1979–80 indoor winter season.

Holly Hatton—was a coxswain and a member of the women's national eight-oared crew in 1977, 1978 and 1979. The crew was second in the world championships in '78 and third in '79.

Tom Woodman—was a rower and member of the national team in 1978 (four with coxswain) and 1979 (eight-oar). He also was a member of the U.S. eight-oared crew at the Pan American Games.

Blaise Stanek—was a canoeist and member of the U.S. National Team in 1978, 1979 and 1980. He also competed in the '78 and '79 World Championships.

Cosema Crawford—was a rower and member of the national team in her event in 1978 and 1979. She was a national champion in the coxed-fours in '79.

Jim Curry—was a weightlifter and national champion in his class in 1979. He won a bronze medal in the '79 Pan American Games. At the time of the lawsuit he was ranked first in the U.S.

Arthur Drechsler—was a weightlifter and on the national team in his event in 1973. He was on the Executive Board of the Weightlifting Federation, the sport's national governing body. He also sat on the USOC House of Delegates.

Burton William Shaw—was the chairman of the national governing body for water polo and a member of the Executive Board of the U.S. Olympic Committee.[29]

* * * * *

As stated in the complaint filed in the United States District Court, District of Columbia, Civil Action No. 80-1013, *Anita DeFRANTZ v. UNITED STATES OLYMPIC COMMITTEE,* the suit was described as follows :

DEFENDANT

> The defendant is the United States Olympic Committee. The USOC is a corporation created and chartered by Congressional enactment in 1950 and is registered to do business in the District of Columbia. Its charter was substantially revised by the Amateur Sports Act of 1978. Congress has conferred upon the USOC "exclusive jurisdiction" and authority over all matters pertaining to the participation of United States citizens in the Olympic Games, subject to the restrictions on that authority specified in the Amateur Sports Act.[30]

CLASS ACTION

> The athlete plaintiffs bring this action on their own behalf and as a class action on behalf of all others similarly situated. The class consists of those United States citizen amateur athletes who have been, or seek to be and have a reasonable prospect of being, recommended

by their respective national sports governing bodies to the defendant USOC for selection as members of the United States Olympic Team, and who wish to compete in the XXIInd Olympiad to be staged in Moscow in the Summer of 1980 or at least to be free to make an individual decision whether so to compete or to boycott the Games.

* * * * *

The athletes' suit was predicated on three legal theories: a statutory argument; a constitutional argument; and a corporate governance argument that the USOC had violated its constitution, by-laws and governing statute by injuring the USOC and violating one of its Executive Board member's rights to comply with its constitution, by-laws and governing statute.

* * * * *

The first and principle argument made in the athletes' suit was a statutory argument that centered on the congressionally-enacted Amateur Sports Act of 1978.

The Amateur Sports Act was enacted by Congress and signed into law by President Carter in 1978. The Moscow Games would serve as a landmark because, due to this act, these Games were the first in which U.S. participation was organized, financed and controlled under a new amateur sports regime ordained by Congress.

The Act, which amended the congressional charter first granted to the USOC in 1950, was a response to two related problems. The first was long-standing and constant bickering between national sports federations, in particular the National Collegiate Athletic Association (NCAA) and the

Amateur Athletic Union (AAU), concerning jurisdiction over athletic events and the adverse effect the quarrels had on the athletes. The second problem was the perceived decline in the quality of performance by U.S. athletes in the Olympic Games, particularly in 1972 and 1976.

The Act enlarged the role of the USOC by making it a more central governing body and by giving it powers to select and control the national governing bodies for the various amateur sports. The Act also gave the USOC a new and heavier emphasis on the rights of the athletes to compete in international events and to make the newly-constituted and reinvigorated USOC the guarantor and protector of these rights. And for the first time, federal funds were authorized for the USOC.

* * * * *

The Amateur Sports Act of 1978 grew out of a study by the President's Commission on Olympic Sports, which was appointed in 1975 and issued its final report in 1977. The report identified a host of problems that were viewed as afflicting amateur sports in the U.S., including jurisdictional disputes and power struggles between the NCAA and AAU in which athletes were being denied their right to compete in events because of their affiliations with one group or the other.

Enacted in the aftermath of the African boycott of the 1976 Summer Olympics, and in advance of the Moscow Games, the legislation that was introduced and considered by Congress also reflected a general concern over the politicization of the Games. It conferred on the USOC in broad terms exclusive power to "organize, finance and control" U.S. representation in the Olympic Games. It did not explicitly confer the power to decline to participate in the Olympic Games unless the USOC felt the United States could not competently represent itself with athletes in one-or-more of the events and competitions.

If there was any justification for not participating in the Olympics, the Act made it clear it could be only because of sports-related considerations. The statute provided that unless a federation demonstrated clear and convincing evidence that "holding or sponsoring an international amateur athletic competition would be detrimental to the best interest of the sport," the USOC was obligated to sanction holding an international competition in the U.S. or sponsoring a U.S. team to compete abroad.

The provision of the 1950 charter which stated that the USOC "shall be non-political and, as an organization, shall not promote the candidacy of any person seeking public office," took on a significantly new meaning after 1978. The USOC was now explicitly authorized "to represent the U.S. as its national Olympic committee in relations with the International Olympic Committee." And thus the USOC was bound by Rule 24C of the IOC's Olympic Charter stating that national committees "must be autonomous and must resist all pressures of any kind whatsoever, whether of political, religious or economic nature."

The enactment of the Amateur Sports Act by Congress, and its signing into law by President Carter, was a commitment to an autonomous Olympic committee. President Carter also hoped that the signing of this legislation would help strengthen the United States' participation in international competitions, broaden opportunities for amateur athletics in the U.S., and help contribute to a stronger representation by the U.S. team in the 1980 Games compared to previous Olympics.

However, with the powers granted to the USOC within the Act, there also was a risk that the presence of a U.S. Olympic team in Moscow, or a U.S. team in other international competitions, could be interpreted as an endorsement of the local regimes and their policies.[31]

* * * * *

"We felt at the time, our strongest argument was the statutory one," explains Mackiewicz. "We believed, and argued before the court, that the statute made clear several things, including that the Olympic Committee had exclusive jurisdiction over these issues—namely, whether to accept an invitation from the International Olympic Committee to participate in the Games, and that their exclusive jurisdiction was constricted in a way by making it clear, in our view, that the only allowable basis for turning down such an invitation would have to be sports-related. And, politics could not enter into any decision whether to accept or decline an invitation to an Olympiad."

The legal team pointed to a number of provisions in the Amateur Sports Act that they believed supported their argument that the USOC could not decline the invitation, given that the sole basis for that decision was political.

The athletes argued in the first cause of action that the Amateur Sports Act guaranteed them statutory rights to participate in international competitions. Furthermore, they asserted that those rights were guaranteed in order to ensure the participation of teams from the U.S. in international sports events—including, in particular, the Olympics—which were described in the Act as "protected competition."[32]

The first cause of action also pointed out that the stated purpose of the Amateur Sports Act was "to recognize certain rights for United States amateur athletes," including "the opportunity of any amateur athlete, coach, trainer, manager, administrator, or official to participate in national and international amateur athletic competition." The claim further cited the Act's declaration that the USOC's object and purpose was to protect the athletes' opportunity to compete, and that the USOC was "required to establish and maintain in its Constitution and By-laws provisions for resolving disputes over the opportunity of such persons to participate 'in the Olympic Games' and 'other such protected competition.'"[33]

The suit also cited provisions from the Amateur Sports Act that pertained to the USOC's obligation "to obtain for the United States, either directly or by delegation to the appropriate national governing body, the most competent amateur representation possible in each competition and event of the Olympic Games," and that empowered the USOC to "organize, finance, and control the representation of the United States in the competitions and events of the Olympic Games... and obtain, either directly or by delegation to the appropriate national governing body, amateur representation for such game."[34]

The athletes also cited the USOC's constitution: "No member of the USOC may deny or threaten to deny any amateur athlete the opportunity to compete in the Olympic Games."

The USOC failing or refusing to ensure the representation of the U.S. in the Olympics was clearly not a part of the Amateur Sports Act. The only similar authority granted by Congress could be wielded only if the USOC found "clear and convincing evidence" that participation "would be detrimental to the best interest of the sport."[35]

The final provision in the first cause of action argued that Congress did not authorize the USOC power to abridge the athletes' statutory right to compete in international competitions and events for political, national-interest or national-security reasons, or for any reason that is not directly related to sports. In fact, the Amateur Sports Act had specifically stated the opposite.[36]

Clearly, the athletes argued, with the April 12 vote to boycott the Moscow Games, the House of Delegates of the United States Olympic Committee had violated the athletes' statutory rights, and had exceeded its authority under the Amateur Sports Act of 1978 and ignored congressional limitations on that authority in several respects, including:

[The USOC] exercised a power that it does not have to decide that no United States amateur athletes shall participate in the 1980 Games.

[The USOC] breached a duty to organize, finance and control participation in the events and competitions of the Olympic Games by the United States athletes.

[The USOC] denied to United States amateur athletes the opportunity to compete in these Games on a basis other than their want of athletic merit, or for a sports-related reason.

[The USOC] yielded its exclusive jurisdiction over Olympic matters to the political leaders of the nation.

[The USOC] acted in a political manner.

[The USOC] yielded its autonomy and has succumbed to political and economic pressure.

* * * * *

The athletes felt that their strongest argument was based on statutes in the Amateur Sports Act. But they were also aware that their secondary points were not nearly as strong. If the statutory argument failed, their constitutional arguments alone were unlikely to withstand enough judicial scrutiny to give them a legal victory.

"First we had to argue that in effect the USOC, taking the action that it did, was in fact controlled by, to some extent, the federal government, and this constituted state action," Mackiewicz explains. "And this action violated the athletes' First, Fifth and Ninth Amendment rights—basically, self expression, the ability to freely travel and things of that sort."

Based on the premise that Congress had intended the USOC to exist independent of the government, the claim further asserted that because of the intrusion by the government and its officials, the actions of the USOC must be regarded as governmental actions, or "state actions," and were thus subject to the U.S. Constitution.

The athletes argued that their Constitutional rights and their right to make their own decision about whether to participate in the Olympics had been deprived by the USOC because of that governmental action.

★ ★ ★ ★ ★

In the lawsuit's final claim, Mackiewicz and the legal team argued that the USOC had violated its constitution, by-laws and governing statute, thus injuring the USOC. Because one of the plaintiffs, Burton William Shaw, was a member of the USOC's executive committee, they argued on his behalf that, similar to a shareholder derivative action (in which a shareholder sues on behalf of a corporation for alleged mismanagement or waste), his right to require the organization to comply with its own governing documents had been violated.

Such an argument is usually used in cases against profit-making corporations (alleging that the corporation injured its ability to make a profit), but the athletes' claim targeted a non-profit organization. They argued that the USOC was established for the purpose of coordinating the United States' amateur sports program by ensuring the country was represented in the Olympic Games by the "most competent amateur representation;" consequently, because its decision not to send a U.S. Olympic team to Moscow injured the USOC, the organization was therefore subject to Shaw's claim.

* * * * *

In concluding their arguments, the athletes maintained that the decision by the House of Delegates of the USOC not to send a team to represent the United States in the 1980 Olympic Summer Games was illegal because it violated their federal statutory and constitutional rights.

In so stating, they asked the court to ensure that there would be representation by the U.S. in the events and competitions of the Games by over-ruling the USOC's decision and giving the athletes the right to choose for themselves whether to participate.

It was further noted that if the president of the United States were to advise the USOC on-or-before May 20, 1980, that international events had become compatible with national interest and that national security was no longer threatened, the USOC should enter its athletes in the 1980 Olympic Summer Games.

"If you had to say what was *the* most important principle that we were trying to uphold, and a right that we were trying to enforce, it was the fact that politics was not an appropriate factor," Mackiewicz says. "In fact, it was an inappropriate factor to be used in making determinations with respect to the participation in a particular Olympic Games. The whole idea of the sports movement was to be above the fray of politics. It was to bring together a group of athletes that was beyond geographic, political borders and it was to promote, in effect, world peace by allowing athletes to compete against each other. That was contemplated both by the International Olympic Committee in its constitution by-laws, and there, the USOC was similarly created. That is what we argued—that the Amateur Sports Act made it clear that politics is not supposed to be used. The only way [the administration] could do what they did was for sports-related reasons and not for political reasons."

* * * * *

The following day, April 24—Day 172 of the American hostage crisis in Iran—President Carter launched his plan to free the 52 hostages with an airborne commando raid unit of seven helicopters and a rescue plane. But the mission ended in disaster when the plane and a helicopter collided in the Iranian desert. Amidst the twisted wreckage of the burning aircraft, eight American soldiers were dead, and the mission was aborted due to a now-insufficient number of helicopters.

* * * * *

Despite all that was happening at the time, Vice President Walter F. Mondale was sympathetic to the athletes' cause. "I never thought that we didn't do the right thing, but I can understand why some athletes might have brought a lawsuit," he says. "We [called for the boycott] for strategic reasons, for security reasons. As painful as it was, it was a real body blow to the Soviet Union. And as regrettable as it was, I think it was something we had to do. I can't believe that a court would've interfered with that."

Soviet officials also were sympathetic to the U.S. athletes' cause to compete, because of their own interests and propaganda. But they weren't the least bit sympathetic toward the USOC as they called for the IOC to levy a suspension from the Olympic movement against the American committee for deciding to boycott the Games. Like the athletes in their lawsuit, the Soviets charged that the USOC broke Rule 24C of the Olympic Charter by ceding to political pressure and going along with President Carter's call for the boycott.

Others in the U.S. were not as sympathetic to the athletes' cause. A pre-vote op-ed in *The New York Times* was accompanied by the headline "Olympian Hubris." It warned, "By excluding the will of the public from their stewardship of the Games, the Olympians risk a fate about which the ancient Greeks gave appropriate warning: After hubris comes nemesis, a just retribution."[37]

Legendary columnist Shirley Povich wrote in *The Washington Post* that a proposal from the president's top legal counsel Lloyd Cutler for a special medal to be struck honoring the athletes was "absurd." The headline over which his April 25 column appeared coldly announced, "Olympic 'Heroes' Deserve Nothing." Povich went on to describe the athletes' lawsuit as "petty, whining law games" and called the athletes "self interest[ed]" for voting against the boycott and bringing the lawsuit.[38]

Throughout the athletes' ordeal, DeFrantz and others also had been receiving hate mail and phone calls. In some instances, it was suspected their phones were being tapped.

They also received a call from the Stalin Society, which was prepared to enable any U.S. athlete who so desired to attend the Olympic Games in Moscow as a spectator. If the athletes felt they were being used as political pawns by their own government, they were absolutely sure of it when they received this obvious propagandized invitation.

* * * * *

The defendant, the USOC, contended that Congress, through the enactment of the Amateur Sports Act of 1978, had neither explicitly nor implicitly prohibited the USOC from considering the national interest, and declining on that ground, to participate in an Olympic Games. They further contended that the act recognized no rights of the athletes to participate in the Olympic Games if the USOC decided not to enter a team.

The athletes' lawyers believed the USOC was hiding behind the defense of defining "national interest" and "endangering national security." "To say that it is not in the national interest, you leave it to the president and the politicians to describe and shade, to tell you what the national interests are at any one point," Mackiewicz says. "But to say that it endangered national security? Quite frankly, no one to this day has shown me, or even made an argument to support that. They were hiding behind 'endangering national security' arguments, waving the American flag saying, 'You have to do this [boycott].' That was, in effect, what they were telling the USOC, 'You have to do this, otherwise you'd be endangering national security.'"

* * * * *

When it came time for Judge John H. Pratt, a decorated U.S. Marine Corps veteran who won a Purple Heart and Bronze Star and lost an arm in World War II, to render a decision, he was not sympathetic to the athletes' cause.

On May 16, 23 days after filing the suit, the plaintiffs' lawsuit in *Anita De-FRANTZ, et al v. UNITED STATES OLYMPIC COMMITTEE* was dismissed by the court.

At oral argument, the USOC's counsel conceded the plaintiffs' arguments about the defendant USOC "yielding its autonomy and succumb[ing] to political and economic pressure"; "act[ing] in a political manner"; and "yield[ing] its exclusive jurisdiction over Olympic matters to the political leaders of the nation." The judge agreed:

> The significant statutory questions could be decided without reference as to whether the administration exerted political pressure on the defendant.

With respect to the plaintiffs' claim of a "[breaching] of duty to organize, finance, and control participation in the events and competitions of the Olympic Games by United States athletes," Judge Pratt highlighted the use of a broad interpretation of the powers of the USOC based on the Amateur Sports Act in determining its right not to accept the invitation to participate in the Olympics.

The "objects and purposes" section of the act speaks in broad terms, stating that the USOC shall exercise "exclusive jurisdiction" over "all matters pertaining to participation of the United States in the Olympic Games." We read this broadly-stated purpose in conjunction with the specific power conferred on the USOC by the act to "represent the United States as its national Olympic committee in relations with the International Olympic Committee," and in conjunction with the IOC rules and by-laws, which provide that "representation" includes the decision to participate. In doing so, we find a compatibility and not a conflict between the act and the IOC rules on the issue of the authority of the USOC to decide whether or not to accept an invitation to field an American team at the Olympics. The language in the statute is broad enough to confer this authority.... We accordingly conclude that the USOC has the authority to decide not to send an American team to the Olympics.

Judge Pratt continued his decision by dealing with the athletes' argument regarding sports-related reasons for non-participation. In his decision, he said the original purpose of this clause was to curb the unrestrained and arbitrary power struggle and infighting of various athletic organizations subordinate to the USOC.

This purpose has nothing to do with a decision by the USOC to exercise authority granted by the IOC to decide not to participate in an Olympic competition.... We therefore conclude that the USOC not only had the authority to decide not to send an American team to the Summer Olympics, but also that it could do so for reasons not directly related to sports considerations.

The judge's ruling then dealt with the athletes' argument that they had a "private cause of action under the Amateur Sports Act of 1978 to maintain an action to enforce their rights under that act."

This argument assumes (1) the existence of a right and (2) the capability of enforcing that right by a private cause of action.... We have that the statute does not guarantee plaintiffs a right to compete in the Olympics if the USOC decides not to send an American team to the Olympic Games and we have found that defendant has violated no provision of the Act. Thus, the "right" the plaintiffs seek to enforce under the Act simply does not exist. (Plaintiffs have pointed to no express private right of action in the statute, and none exists.) Under these circumstances, we cannot find that plaintiffs have an implied private right of action under the Amateur Sports Act to enforce a right which does not exist.

The decision continued with the plaintiffs' constitutional claims that the USOC's decision not to enter an American team in the 1980 Olympic Summer Games violated their rights guaranteed under the First, Fifth and Ninth Amendments. This argument presented two main questions: whether the USOC's decision was governmental action ("state action"), and whether the USOC's decision abridged any constitutionally protected rights of the athletes, assuming that "state action" was found. In arguing the first part, the plaintiffs had claimed that the campaign of persuasion personally conducted by the Carter administration crossed the line from "governmental recommendation," which they found acceptable and necessary in certain instances, into an area of "affirmative pressure that effectively place[d] the government's prestige behind the challenged action," thus resulting in state action. The court did not agree.

Plaintiffs can point to no case outside the area of discrimination law which in any way supports their theory, and we can find none.

Despite each party citing numerous cases dealing with varying amounts of governmental involvement with private entities, the court concluded there was no such control in this case.

The USOC is an independent body, and nothing in its chartering statute gives the federal government the right to control that body or its officers. Furthermore, the facts here do not indicate that the federal government was able to exercise any type of "de facto" control over the USOC. The USOC decided by a secret ballot of its House of Delegates. The federal government may have had the power to prevent the athletes from participating in the Olympics even if the USOC had voted to allow them to participate, but it did not have the power to make them vote in a certain way. All it had was the power of persuasion. We cannot equate this with control.... We accordingly find that the decision of the USOC not to send an American team to the Summer Olympics was not state action, and therefore, does not give rise to an actionable claim for the infringements of the constitutional rights alleged.

Because the decision found no state action, the argument of whether the athletes' constitutional rights were abridged was moot. But, the judge in his decision dealt with that claim as well by ruling:

Were we to find state action in this case, we would conclude that defendant USOC has violated no constitutionally protected rights of plaintiffs.

Judge Pratt expanded more on his ruling regarding the athletes' constitutional arguments. And then he concluded his decision with a very passionate and heartfelt final statement:

Plaintiffs have been unable to draw our attention to any court decision which finds that the rights allegedly violated here enjoy constitutional protection, and we can find none. Plaintiffs would expand the constitutionally-protected scope of liberty and self-expression to include the denial of an amateur athlete's right to compete in an Olympic contest when that denial was the result of a decision by a supervisory athletic organization acting well within the limits of its authority. Defendant has not denied plaintiffs the right to engage in every amateur athletic competition. Defendant has not denied plaintiffs the right to engage in their chosen occupation. Defendant has not even denied the plaintiffs the right to travel, only the right to travel for one specific purpose. We can find no justification and no authority for the expansive reading of the Constitution which plaintiffs urge. To find as plaintiffs recommend would be to open the floodgates to a torrent of lawsuits. The courts have correctly recognized that many of life's disappointments, even major ones, do not enjoy constitutional protection. This is one such instance.

At this point, we find it appropriate to note that we have respect and admiration for the discipline, sacrifice, and perseverance which earns young men and women the opportunity to compete in the Olympic Games. Ordinarily, talent alone has determined whether an American would have the privilege of participating in the Olympics. This year, unexpectedly, things are different. We express no view on the merits of the decision made. We do express our understanding of the deep disappointment and frustrations felt by thousands of American athletes. In doing so, we also recognize that the responsibilities of citizenship often fall more heavily on some than on others.

Some are called to military duty. Others never serve. Some return from military service unscathed. Others never return. These are the simple, although harsh, facts of life, and they are immutable.[39]

Judge Pratt's decision was appealed to the U.S. Court of Appeals but was dismissed within a day.

* * * * *

Despite the court's ruling, Anita DeFrantz remains steadfast and true to her beliefs. The issue is as clear to her today as it was then. "It was up to the athletes to make that decision and no one else had the right to make that decision."

For her and several of the 24 others who had already experienced the joy and meaning of participating in the Olympics, the lawsuit was filed probably more for their Olympic rookie teammates than for them.

"The moment is gone," she says 28 years later. "Having taken that away can never be given back. I knew what it meant to be a part of the Olympic movement. It is powerful. If anything, I had become an ambassador for peace. It's a life-changing experience to compete in the Games. And when you're successful, in the eyes of this country, which usually means a gold medal—it changes you. But just being there changes you. The truly tragic part was that athletes from other countries were brought into it and their dreams were taken away for no purpose as well. Fortunately, it was a test of the Olympic movement, and the Olympic movement showed it was much stronger and continued without the other nations."

Luci Collins – 1980 U.S. Olympic Gymnastics Team

Luci Collins
Gymnastics

"It was devastating," U.S. women's gymnast Luci Collins recalls. "It was something that continued to set in afterwards." And the stress from the decision to boycott the 1980 Olympic Summer Games in Moscow had unimaginable repercussions that the 16-year-old had no idea were coming.

"Initially, we heard that we were boycotting the Olympics but still had to perform at the Olympic Trials. [The boycott] wasn't presented to us as really completely set in stone. There was still a hopefulness of us going even at the Olympic Trials in Jacksonville, Fla. I guess me being 16 and naive, I didn't completely understand that it wasn't going to happen. After the Olympic Trials they tried to do things for us. They invited us to the White House and gave us our Olympic stuff. We did an exhibition tour through the United States. That was all fun and everything but when we got home it was like, 'All that work we had done for nothing.' It was devastating and disappointing."

Collins' mother was an astute observer of the sport of gymnastics and had realized the top gymnasts in the world were Russian and European. "My mom, who knew the Russian gymnasts were at the top of the gymnastics world as far as coaching and technique, saw there were Russian coaches coming to Culver City," remembers the Englewood, Calif., native.

Luci Collins had been training in Torrance, just 15 miles from Culver City, so the elder Collins made sure her daughter would be part of the Russian coaches' class. "Right from the start they were very into the quality of the gymnastics," Collins recalls. "Everything had to be balletically-correct moves with gymnastics acrobatics mixed in. Toe points were important no matter what tricks you were doing. Completely straight legs when you were doing tricks was always emphasized and very, very important. And doing the basics exactly correct as far as technique and form. Form was really, really emphasized. That is what the Russians were known for—really clean gymnastics lines. Even within the harder tricks they had perfect form."

She took strict ballet classes in addition to gymnastics classes. Gymnasts coming from her gym in Culver City were looking very different from some of the others they were competing against. Collins had very clean lines and clean form and looked like the Russian gymnasts at the top level.

Going to the Soviet Union and Moscow was supposed to be somewhat of a homecoming for Collins. The California teenager, with no real familial roots to the United States' Cold War nemesis, still felt a kindred connection to the Soviets because of her training. "I remember watching Olga Korbut on the TV from early on and saying that I wanted to do what she was doing," Collins says, excited at the memory. "I wanted to do gymnastics like her. She was a Russian gymnast and, as I continued to progress, that meant Olympic dream."

Once the boycott was confirmed, Collins set her sights on the future, on the Los Angeles Olympics in 1984. But it was hard to imagine anything could be worse than the feeling she had as she watched the XXII Olympiad commence in Moscow without Team USA in attendance. Then soon after, Luci Collins' athletic career took a freefall.

At 16, Collins wasn't thinking her career was over because of the boycott. She was trying to look to the future. And then, she broke her back. "I was training to go to another exhibition in China," Collins says. "I was training in the gym and finishing my beam routine assignment. I was finishing up and getting ready to go home and pack up to go to China the next day. What happened is one of my coaches didn't see any of my routines on the beam and wanted to see one more. I guess my mindset at the time was, 'I'm sick of this, I can't believe I have to do another one.' All in my head I'm thinking this. I went through the motions and I did my last beam routine. I got to the dismount and I had just started doing a round-off, back-step dismount off the beam. I went to do the round-off and my foot slipped off. I was thinking, 'Just go for it so you won't have to do another one.' I wasn't high enough because I was only pushing off one leg and I did one and-a-half landing on my upper back, compressing two vertebrae [C3 and C4] and knocking the wind out of myself. Instead of China, I ended up in the hospital."

Collins miraculously recovered from the injury and started to train again, with thoughts of Los Angeles always in her mind. "I didn't want to miss out on that Olympic experience," she says. "I had wanted that for my whole life. At 16, I still felt like I had a lot of gymnastics in me. I was still improving and got over the injury and was doing better than ever."

Collins' skills were improving daily at the side of Don Peters, who would become the 1984 U.S. Olympic women's gymnastics coach. But while training at his gym in Huntington Beach, Calif., she suffered another freefall, this one permanent.

"I developed an eating disorder," she admits. "I ended up with bulimia and that pretty much ended my career. I just couldn't recover from that."

For Collins—the 5-foot, 94-pound sprite and potential medallist in the beam and floor exercise events—representing the U.S. on foreign soil was what had energized her and gave meaning to her years of hard work and sacrifice. "I felt so proud of myself and my country and my family at those times," she says. "I felt bigger than life. That was another adjustment that was really, really difficult to come out of it. In a sense, to be a nobody and completely not recognized was such an adjustment because I had had a 'bigger than life' feeling in a world where everyone knew you and were proud to pay money and fill a stadium to see you. And then to not have that big dream recognized by the world because there was no Olympic medal or Olympic

Games for you, you have to come out of that and fit back into the real world. That was a huge, huge adjustment."

That adjustment, combined with the disappointment and the stress and the injury and not feeling in control of her own destiny, had a major impact on Collins' state of mind. All of that opened the door for the eating disorder. "Bulimia was one way I felt in control of myself," she says. "Bulimia is all about control—the one way you can control your life when other people have so much control over it."

As 1984 approached and the world again was preparing for the Olympic Summer Games, Collins' bulimia stayed with her. "I struggled with it," she says. "I couldn't even watch the 1984 Olympic Games on TV because I was so disappointed to not be there. It was heartbreaking for me. There were people on that team that I had placed ahead of just four years prior, even a year or two prior because I was still competing. To see them on that team and not me was just... just... I couldn't even watch. As I've grown up I've come around to be able to watch and enjoy gymnastics again. It took a while, though."

What has not come around for the one-time gymnastics prodigy is her sense of what the boycott was all for and why politics had to be brought into the Olympic arena in the first place. The why and what-for of the 1980 boycott ultimately led Collins to years of inner turmoil and despair as she tried to grow up and handle the most disappointing experience of her life.

"In my opinion," Collins says, "the Olympics has always been known to be where all the countries of the world come to unite no matter what differences we have. President Carter used the Olympics to prove his point, and that was wrong."

Eventually, Collins broke the cycle of despair and started an ascent toward a healthier life away from gymnastics and Olympic dreams. "You just realize that life is about a lot of special moments. Again, I have beautiful, wonderful memories of the times when gymnastics was great to me. The boycott was one huge devastating moment of my gymnastics career. It is easy to let that overshadow all of the other beautiful memories I have, but I just can't. I have to go on with my life. As you do other things in life, and get older and mature, there are other things that are disappointing and somewhat devastating. You realize that life is bigger than that and you can't live the rest of your life on that one disappointment. Things may have just [been] meant to be that way."

Collins' current outlook is one of a mature mother of two girls she wants to see grow up in an environment without the pressure she experienced as a budding gymnastics star. She still carries scars from her past and is not bashful about sharing her thoughts on exposing kids to that type of stress. "I would rather they just enjoy being regular people and dabbling in lots of different things—play the piano, try music, drama classes," Collins says, laughing. "Just being happy kids without the restrictions. I wonder if that is because I channeled all of my energy into one direction and gave up so many things along the way and was completely disappointed by it."

To say Collins' Olympic journey was empty would be incorrect, but not entirely far from the truth. In her mind, and the minds of many others who saw her perform, it could have been so much different. "I truly did believe that if I had done my best performance during those Olympic Games, which I was on track to do, there could've been a possible medal for me and some worldwide recognition past the gymnastics world. Missing out on that will always leave me with an empty space, because I never got the chance to fulfill that dream."

David Kimes – 1980 U.S. Olympic Shooting Team

David Kimes
Shooting

David Kimes has a pioneer spirit as unrelenting as that which carried his great-great-grandparents west from Missouri along the Oregon Trail in conestoga wagons in the 1800s.

Kimes' ancestors made their way into the unorganized territory of the United States through such outlets as Courthouse Rock, Fort Laramie, Soda Springs and Whitman Mission before ultimately settling in Summerlake, Ore. The same perseverance that carried them half a continent west inspired Kimes' grandfather to make his way down the coast to Central California's Kings County in the early years of the 20th century.

In what was still very much the wild west, Kimes' grandfather decided to run for office. "He was walking around the county fair—at that point he was running for sheriff," says Kimes, recalling the story told to him by his father. "He always had his .45 strapped to his side and the bootleggers used to taunt him by asking if he ever shot that thing because he wore it all the time. Well, one day, on a post with a safe background, he put a playing card and walked 10 paces. He took three shots and cut the card in half. When he turned around all the bootleggers were seen walking off back into the crowd. My dad told me that was the start of my shooting, because it was ingrained in your grandfather."

The current Kimes started his journey toward the Olympics when he was in sixth grade, after finding an old rifle behind the door of his great-great-grandparents' homestead in Oregon. "I remember saying, 'Hey Dad, can we go shoot that?' We found a dirt bank, set up some tin cans and he taught me some sighting, aiming, breathing and trigger control and we started shooting at tin cans. That piqued my interest and got me started."

Two years later as a freshman in high school, Kimes was talking to a classmate and mentioned his interest in shooting. It happened the classmate's father was the coach at the South Coast Gun Club in Irvine, Calif. "I started shooting more rifle there and getting some coaching. The Southern California Junior Rifle League was really big in those days and shooters would go to different ranges every month and have matches," Kimes says. "One of the top shooters around the nation would come and shoot matches there. I was around and got to rub shoulders with some of those folks—some of whom were world champions. That piqued my thoughts about those guys being so darned good that I didn't think I could ever get to that point. That was all through high school."

Following graduation, Kimes maintained his passion for rifle shooting and continued to shoot in college. He started his collegiate career at Orange Coast College, a two-year school, and then headed to the University of California, Berkeley, for his final two years. At Berkeley, Kimes participated in NCAA rifle on the ROTC team. There, he earned first- and second-team All-America honors and then put his rifle down until November 22, 1963.

"I got my draft notice the same day President Kennedy was assassinated," remembers Kimes. "They let us off early from my first job out of college. I went home and it said 'Greetings from the President.' I had heard about the Army International Rifle Team at Fort Benning, Ga. I applied to have a tryout for that team and that is where I got my higher level start at shooting."

When Kimes arrived at Fort Benning, he was assigned to the United States Marksmanship Unit where he had a 90-day tryout period. Afterward he traveled throughout Europe shooting at various competitions from 1964 to '66, but never set foot in Vietnam. "President Eisenhower had started that marksmanship program after the Melbourne Olympics, where the Russians were at the top and the United States was at the bottom of the shooting events," Kimes explains. "He started that unit wanting the military to look into how we could get our United States teams more competitive. It was more of a PR thing in those days."

Following his three-year stint in the Army, Kimes entered the Army Reserve (where he would eventually serve 23 years) and decided to go back to school to work toward a master's degree. It was during that time when one morning, at 3:00 a.m., the phone rang. "I got a call from the chief of the Army Reserves in Washington, D.C.—Mr. Joe Berry," Kimes says. "What they were doing was starting to pick up people who were going back into civilian life [and] pull them into the Army Reserve so the United States could have an Army Reserve and a National Rifle Team, as well. There was Maj. Bruce Meredith on the team at Fort Benning. He and Joe Berry got this idea to form a team. That's what happened to me, too. They helped us out with ammunition and we would go to the inner-service championships and tryouts for the team every year. We got some training on the side, as well."

Kimes had first gotten a taste of the Olympics in 1964 when he was still at Fort Benning. "I shot in the Olympic tryouts but was nowhere near competitive enough to make the team," he says. "That was for the Summer Olympics in Tokyo. A couple of the people on my Army team made the Olympic team. One of them was Lones Wigger and he won a gold and silver in those Games. I have a picture of him when he got back from the Olympics and he had both medals around his neck. So, being in the tryouts, seeing someone I shot next to win and come home and talk about it was something that started pulling at me to try and make an Olympic team. I was 23 at the time."

That experience started a 28-year quest to try to compete in a sport that dates back to the first of the modern-day Olympics in 1896. "I tried again in '68, '72, '76. Each time getting better, more experience and learning more about the match pressure."

Besides training the mental aspect of his mind, Kimes also spent thousands of hours at the range perfecting his physical skills. "In shooting it's three positions: prone, standing and kneeling," explains Kimes. "I was better at the prone event but the other positions had a slot for the Olympics. My world record and world championship was in three-position shooting at 300 meters in '74 and '78. I would go out and shoot for five hours a day. You would shoot for 1 1/2 hours prone and then standing for an hour or two, take a break and then go back and shoot kneeling. Go back to prone. You organized your schedule on what you thought was most important to polish. You would make notes on anything that needed to be tweaked and the next day you would go out and work on that."

In 1980, realizing computers were doing lots of the work in those days, Kimes took classes to familiarize himself with programming. When the Olympic tryouts took place that year (despite the announced boycott), Kimes was working fulltime at Rockwell International. "The tryouts were in Phoenix, Ariz. They had built ranges for the World Shooting Championships in 1970 and held all the tryouts there for the Olympics."

After four previous attempts at making an Olympic team, Kimes spent most of his time working hard on the mental aspect of the sport. Additionally, he practiced shooting in outdoor conditions in which the wind plays on the bullet. "You need to know how to dope the wind, or change your sights, whatever you had to do. I worked a lot on Kentucky Windage, or 'shading,' as we called it."

When the wind picked up, Kimes would aim his sight a little off-center. "All the shooting we would do was at metallic sites and it takes a lot of practice to perfect that. When I went to the 1980 tryouts we would shoot three days in each event. I made the Olympics after the first day, and it was kind of medium to light wind, but it was switching all over the place," Kimes says, relishing the memory. "Most people were really having problems with that.

Out of a 60-shot match I shot maybe 40 shots from the Kentucky Windage and I had a 599 out of 600."

Kimes and his fellow competitors were shooting at targets with centers the size of a dime from more than half a football field away. The black, which contains the highest-scoring rings, was no bigger than a softball. Kimes made the Olympic team in the event known as Prone English Match. The years of training and steely nerves gave Kimes the confidence to incorporate the Kentucky Windage method. "It takes a pile of experience to get to know that and how far off-sight to hold it. I would practice holding off a wide 10 or maybe a mid-ring nine in my sights but click over to the center 10 ring trying to shoot 10 or 20 shots [in] a tight group. I would hold off six different shades that way, 10 o'clock, 4 o'clock and different places so that I had the confidence to do it in a really important match. That was the big difference."

It was the difference for Kimes in 1980 but it didn't result in his competing in the Olympic Games. He would try again in 1984, 1988 and finally in 1992, to no avail. Being a member of the 1980 Olympic team, having secured a place in history one time in his eight attempts, gives Kimes a unique perspective and added responsibility that he does not regard lightly. "When I'm giving talks or clinics to young shooters, it gives me a chance to put things into perspective and say there is always something good that comes from something bad," he says. "Also, being an Olympian has given me that extra character that keeps me doing everything ethical and moral. When I speak to young kids I try to instill in them the same values for life—hard work, determination, sticking to your guns and staying focused."

That same attitude has served him well throughout his life, especially in between his Olympic bids. Kimes proved to be a pioneer himself in 1968. He joined Rockwell in February of that year as a computer programmer in the burgeoning aerospace industry that was working on the Apollo program.

Eighteen months later, he watched as Apollo 11 and Neil Armstrong took "one small step" on the surface of the moon.

Years later, Kimes would blaze more trails with his work in the space-shuttle program. "That was a neat run. I got a lot of the 1980 Olympic pins and it was fun to give a pin to a special person. I gave a pin to one of the astronauts and signed the back. He ended up taking that pin into orbit, bringing it back and mounting it on a board with pictures of the launch. I've never felt so honored when that happened."

Today, Kimes is retired after 26 years in the aerospace industry. No doubt his adventures were not as rugged and individual as his ancestors'. But his great-great-grandparents would surely be proud to know he continued living the pioneering spirit that once carried them through the unknown terrains of the glorious country that now calls David Kimes an Olympian.

CHAPTER **VII**

The Games Go On

As the May 24 deadline for accepting the invitation to the 1980 Summer Olympic Games approached, other nations' Olympic committees that had held off deciding whether to boycott the Games started to weigh in. In a display of unanimity, many of the European nations, including most of Western Europe, were trying to salvage the Moscow Olympics. A desperate appeal from 18 national committees, including all nine Common Market members, called for all nations to participate and issued a proposal to eliminate politics from the Olympics.

The proposal outlined several steps, including: each national delegation being represented by a flag bearer and a name board, but no athletes, in the Opening Ceremony; each team using the Olympic flag instead of its nation's flag; the singing of the Olympic hymn instead of national anthems at the opening, closing and medal ceremonies; athletes' clothes displaying only their national Olympic committee logo and an identification badge; political speeches being barred from the Opening Ceremony; each delegation confining its activities to sporting events; and no national committee participating in the international youth camp organized by the Russians in conjunction with the Olympics.

Of course, these proposed actions would have required approval from the IOC and the organizing committee in Moscow.

The Carter administration had hoped that such unanimity would be shown by all of the United States' allies, as well as other countries, in supporting the boycott. Their hopes were only partially realized. Canada, Norway, Turkey and Israel officially voted to support the boycott, joining several other nations, such as West Germany, Japan, China and Kenya, which had decided the same weeks before. But several other nations' committees chose otherwise: France, Italy, Spain, Australia, Greece, Austria, Belgium, Ireland, Sweden, Finland, Iceland, the Netherlands, Luxembourg and Puerto Rico voted to accept their invitations to attend the Moscow Games. For many—including the French, Italians, Dutch, Greeks and Irish—the vote to attend was in direct defiance of their government's wishes, much like the situation in Great Britain weeks earlier.

Still, the boycott received support from smaller contingents within the countries that were planning to compete in Moscow. Despite their committees' vote to play, some of the individual sports federations—including yachtsmen from Great Britain and Australia, and equestrians from France and Switzerland—decided to boycott the Games, depriving those events of much of their competitive stature. A quarter of the Australian Olympic-bound athletes withdrew in the face of public outcry over the country's decision not to boycott, as well as the prospect of poor competition in certain events. Some Italian athletes saw their Olympic dreams shattered as their government banned team members who were policemen and soldiers from competing in Moscow. Italy also refused to alter exam schedules for student-athletes wanting to compete, thus forcing them to decide whether competing was worth losing a year's credit at their university.

As the scorecard of countries that were competing or boycotting fluctuated depending on whose propaganda each chose to believe, U.S. and Soviet officials continued to push their causes. A deadline extension to accept invitations by the Moscow Olympic Organizing Committee motivated the hopes of Soviet officials that some boycotting countries would have a change of heart. On the other hand, U.S. officials saw the extension as a chance for countries that had accepted to reconsider.

To help change the minds of some of the countries that had decided to stay away, Soviet officials began offering inducements such as free travel packages that included transportation on the Soviet airline Aeroflot. That was enough for a cash-strapped Costa Rica Olympic Committee to renege on its boycott. For other South American and Latin American teams, Soviet officials also offered free room and board, as well as round-trip Aeroflot charters. Thailand was offered a 50 percent discount on Aeroflot in exchange for canceling its boycott, which it declined. Several African nations were offered the same incentives, plus Soviet athletic gear and coaching assistance in preparation for the Games. Jordan, which was sending a team, was promised a visit by the Bolshoi Ballet.

* * * * *

Soviet officials were acutely aware that like all Olympic Games host cities before, Moscow, the capital of the Soviet empire and Eastern bloc, would be showcased like no other time in its history. They took great strides to make sure the city and its people were seen by the rest of the world as a positive representation of the communist way of life. With an estimated 85,000 Russian troops stationed in Afghanistan and another 15,000 amassed north of the border, this was especially important in light of the brutality the Soviet Red Army was inflicting on their neighbors.

The Olympics were more than just games to the Soviet hierarchy and its citizenry. The Soviet Union, and specifically Moscow, was still a relatively closed society, one few foreigners ever dreamed of setting foot in. "The Iron Curtain was still very much there," explains reputed Russian journalist Vladimir Pozner. "This was something new, and in many respects exhilarating, for a lot of people in Moscow."

Reports by foreign journalists prior to the opening of the Games told of Soviet officials gathering up thousands of known "drunks" and "troublemakers" and removing them from Moscow to the suburbs for the two weeks of the Olympics. Soviet rabble-rousers like dissident physicist Andrei Sakharov were nicely tucked away in isolated exile in the closed city of Gorky 250 miles away, and most of the other prominent Soviet dissidents were conveniently on vacation in order to avoid a similar fate. Reports of teachers warning kids not to mix with foreigners or accept chewing gum because it could be laced with poison raised Soviet xenophobia to new heights. And the Soviet government travel agency, Intourist, saw a major drop in the already scant visits planned by tourists from the United States, as well as other boycotting nations, and were reluctant to refund any advance payments.

For a couple of weeks, the average Muscovite was able to live in a completely different environment than they were accustomed. Gone were the never-ending lines to stand in to buy what little food was available in the stores. Citizens from the suburbs were barred from the city, allowing Muscovites to move freely throughout the streets and stores, able to buy ample amounts of many different foods they had never seen before—such as yogurt. Sidewalk cafes with tables, chairs and umbrellas began popping up on Moscow's main streets. And though the shopkeepers didn't know what pizza was, two pizzerias were set up on Moscow's main ring road, the Sadovoye Koltso.

"For the people of Moscow it was like suddenly being in some kind of wonderland," Pozner remembers. "There was all of this stuff and you didn't have to stand in line for it. You could buy as much of it as you wanted. There were no crowds of people pushing and shoving. People weren't getting into fights. These were things that are very difficult for people in the West, and especially America, to understand."

* * * * *

Throughout the days, weeks and years leading up to the Games, it was widely known that the Soviet Union and its leaders would try to use the Olympics as a propaganda tool to validate its world position, as well as to extend its foreign policy initiatives. Soviet officials did not hide that fact as their Olympic handbook, "Soviet Sport: Questions and Answers," stressed their claim that the willingness of the International Olympic Committee to let the Games be held in Moscow was an endorsement of the foreign policy and the peace-loving nature of the Soviet Union. Its pages also espoused their views on the relationship of sports and politics. "In times of political turmoil, countries tend to use different things to prove the superiority of their system," Pozner explains. "Look back to 1936 and the Olympic Games in Berlin. The majority of gold medals, overall, were won by the German team. That gave Hitler reason to proclaim that his system, the National Socialist System, was indeed the best in the world. It was used as a political instrument."

During the Cold War, competition between the U.S. and the Soviet Union—including athletic competition—was used by both sides to prove their system was superior. Americans had a notion of Soviet people, especially Soviet athletes, as robots and machines with no individualism or personality. The Soviets saw Americans as representing freedom, and believed that was the source of their successes on the playing fields and beyond. "When Russian athletes won gold medals at Olympic Games, when Soviet musicians or scientists were honored internationally, or when the world-famous Bolshoi Ballet performed throughout the world to adoring adulation, the Politburo did not hesitate to use those successes as a propaganda tool," explains Pozner. "There was no doubt about that."

* * * * *

As the Opening Ceremony drew closer, the world, including people of the Soviet Union, were aware the U.S. was leading a boycott of the Olympic Games as a protest to Soviet involvement in Afghanistan. The Soviet media did not hesitate to report the story as they wanted it told. "The Soviet people were absolutely aware of the boycott," Pozner says. "They were told the United States and certain Western countries were boycotting the Games because the Soviet Union was being true to its duty of solidarity with the people of Afghanistan, who asked the Soviet Union for military support. This was a reaction of the West not supporting the Afghan people, while here in the Soviet Union it was our duty to do so. Clearly, Afghanistan was the reason. But if you went deeper into explaining—the explanations on both sides were very different."

* * * * *

No matter what explanations were offered for why more than 60 countries were deciding not to compete in the Moscow Games, one thing was very clear: The absence of some of the world's greatest athletes certainly would have an impact on the quality of competition.

The 21 Olympic sports would still be contested with spirit and emotion, but some of the bigger events that would have normally included all-star fields of the world's best certainly stood to lose much of their glamour. Also missing would be the undercurrent of East-West rivalry palpable at any Olympic competition.

Some sports, such as team handball, weightlifting, and canoeing and kayaking, would be virtually unaffected, as they were dominated by Eastern bloc nations before the Olympics, and continued to be so with their teams at full strength in Moscow. Other events—such as yachting, in which the Scandinavians, Americans and Australians were the powers; and equestrian, for which the Americans, British, French, Irish and West Germans were the gold, silver and bronze-standard—would be reduced to folly.

Men's and women's field hockey, another sport dominated by the West, would be reduced practically to scrimmages; nine of the top 12 men's qualifiers would be missing and the boycott would deprive the inaugural women's tournament of all its entrants except the Soviet Union. A team of women from Zimbabwe accepted an invitation to compete five weeks before the Games, put together a team in less than a week, and stunned their hosts by winning the gold.

The glamour sports of basketball, swimming, track and field, gymnastics, boxing and volleyball would most certainly see their medals devalued because of the competition that was not present.

The U.S. men had won gold in nine of 10 Olympic basketball tournaments, with the only exception being the controversial victory by the Soviet Union over the Americans at Munich in 1972. The U.S., U.S.S.R. and Yugoslavia were clearly the "big three." In the women's tournament, the Russians were the defending Olympic champions and looking every bit the favorite whether the U.S. team competed or not.

The U.S. swim team would have been the strongest in both the men's and women's events, though the Soviets were formidable for the men, and the East German women were more than formidable against the U.S. women. Sweden, Canada and Australia were also expected to provide depth in the pool for the swimming competition. The U.S. men were boasting an impressive team that would have included many of the 1976 Olympic gold medallists, such as freestyler Rowdy Gaines, distance freestyler and butterflyer Mike Bruner, backstrokers Peter Rocca and Bob Jackson, freestyler Brian Goodell, and 1978 World Championships Outstanding Swimmer Jesse Vassallo. Seventeen-year-old Tracy Caulkins and 16-year-old Cynthia Woodhead were expected to lead the American women against strong competition from the East Germans and Russians.

The U.S., Soviet Union and East Germany were clearly the superpowers in track and field, with West Germany as a probable fourth. The U.S. had potential gold medallists in hurdlers Renaldo Nehemiah and Edwin Moses, long jumper Larry Myricks, decathlete Bob Coffman, distance runner Mary Decker, and all the relay teams. Kenya's Henry Rono, who set four world records in 1978, was also expected to challenge. Many nations had outstanding individual athletes that would compete, and Great Britain, which had decided to let their athletes compete if they chose, had two of the best long-distance runners in the world in Sebastian Coe and Steve Ovett.

Though there was no real chance of any U.S. men's gymnast knocking off the Soviet's Alexander Dityatin for the individual all-around title, there was hope for individual apparatus events with Bart Conner and Ron Galimore. There was also the possibility the U.S. could win a team medal, given the fact that they had edged East Germany for the bronze—behind the Soviet Union and Japan—at the World Championships. But without the Americans and the perennially strong Japanese team, the Soviets and East Germans were sure to dominate the Olympics.

The boycott was sure to have no impact on the women's side of the vaults, beams, bars and floormats—the Romanians, led by 1976 darling Nadia Comaneci, and the Soviet Union were set to monopolize what promised to be one of the highlighted events of the Games.

In boxing, the U.S. team was not as impressive as its 1976 Olympic brethren that featured gold medallists Sugar Ray Leonard, Howard Davis and Leon and Michael Spinks, but they were the major powers in amateur boxing, along with the Soviet Union and Cuba. The U.S. team would have been punching for gold in several weight divisions, including Richard Sandoval (light flyweight), Jackie Beard (bantamweight) and Bernard Taylor (featherweight). Without the U.S. and Western Europeans in the competition, it was sure to be a pugilistic party of socialists contending for the medals.

In volleyball, the Japanese men weren't what they had been in previous years, but without them competing, any medal won would be somewhat tarnished. The women's side saw the Cubans as defending world champions, but a newfound U.S. training program made the latter more than optimistic that they could win their first Olympic medal.

The Soviet Union and East Germany, as well as other Eastern European countries, were dominant in wrestling, water polo and diving. But the Americans and athletes from other boycotting nations had been expected to impact these competitions as well. The U.S. wrestling team was experienced and successful in the previous two Olympics, having won six medals in each, and seemed poised for a very strong showing in Moscow. U.S. wrestler Gene Mills was on a mission to pin his way to the gold, and there was no indication from previous international events that he wouldn't accomplish that feat.

Eastern European teams like Hungary, the U.S.S.R., Yugoslavia and Romania were expected to be very strong in the water polo competition. But optimism had abounded for the U.S. team here as well, after a strong showing in the previous year's World Championship where they lost to Yugoslavia in the closing seconds of the final.

The diving events were sure to see the Soviets and East Germans have their share of success, but the U.S. team, led by 1976 Olympic silver medallist Greg Louganis, was very strong. Louganis had been expected to compete for gold in the platform and springboard events, while divers from China, Australia and Canada would also have provided legitimate competition.

Archery, historically a very successful event for Americans (they won all four men's and women's gold medals since it became an official Olympic sport in 1972), and shooting, another traditionally strong event for the Americans, would provide somewhat hollow victories with the absences of U.S. athletes.

The 16-team soccer tournament lost perennial world power Argentina, as well as Norway, Egypt and the U.S., who were not expected to compete for a medal.

But despite the competition suffering, and despite the value of medals being undermined in some of the events, the Games went on.

* * * * *

On July 19, with trumpets blaring and elaborately costumed dancers celebrating their Russian heritage and culture while creating a joyous and festive atmosphere of celebration, the Games of the XXII Olympiad in Moscow began.

More than 100,000 spectators held up designated cards on cue to create visual mosaics of art, including the Olympic mascot, Misha, and the symbol of the Soviet Union, a hammer and sickle. Men and women dressed in togas portraying Greek gods and goddesses ushered in the Olympic rings on chariots, and the trumpets soon gave way to classical music that filled the stadium during the parade of athletes.

The procession began as any other Opening Ceremony of the modern age of the Olympics, with the congregation from Greece leading the parade. As the athletes entered Central Lenin Stadium, the spectators displayed the usual signs of national pride as thousands of Russian flags were waved, Australian flags were waved and supporters of Mexico waved sombreros.

From the joyous celebration and production of the event, spectators were at first hard-pressed to realize anything vastly different from the previous cultural celebrations that Olympic Opening Ceremonies had embodied. But after Greece entered the stadium, any semblance of prior openings ceased to exist. In a sign of what was missing, two men unfurled an American flag and waved it. Athletes from only 81 nations, the lowest number of countries to participate in the Olympics since Melbourne in 1956, started to file in. Sixteen countries entered the stadium marching under the flag of the Olympic rings as a sign of disapproval of the Soviet invasion of Afghanistan. Normally, approximately 140 nations would have been participating.

All the athletes made their way into the stadium and were positioned on the infield grass. It was at that point those in attendance saw the reality of the U.S.-led boycott. Full attendance would have covered the stadium's entire infield with athletes from across the world; instead, only half was covered, leaving big, empty patches of green grass where athletes should have been.

Despite it all, Soviet President Leonid I. Brezhnev, Soviet dignitaries, members of the Politburo and others responsible for helping bring the Olympic Games to a socialist country for the first time in Olympic history stood on their feet accepting their guests.

Following the parade of athletes, President Brezhnev greeted and welcomed the spectators and more than 5,000 athletes to Moscow as he officially declared the Games of the XXII Olympiad open.

* * * * *

The following list represents the nations that participated in Moscow. The number in parentheses indicates the number of athletes from each nation that competed. Nations in italics competed under the Olympic flag and New Zealand competed under their National Olympic Committee flag.

- Afghanistan (11)
- Algeria (59)
- *Andorra* (2)
- Angola (13)
- *Australia* (126)
- Austria (89)
- *Belgium* (61)
- Benin (17)
- Botswana (7)
- Brazil (109)
- Bulgaria (295)
- Burma (2)
- Cameroon (26)
- Colombia (23)
- Congo (23)
- Costa Rica (30)
- Cuba (216)
- Cyprus (14)
- Czechoslovakia (216)
- *Denmark*(63)
- Dominican Repuplic (6)
- East Germany (362)
- Ecuador (11)
- Ethiopia (41)
- Finland (124)
- *France* (125)
- *Great Britain* (231)
- Greece (42)
- Guatemala (10)
- Guinea (9)
- Guyana (8)
- Hungary (279)
- Iceland (9)
- India (74)
- Iraq (44)
- *Ireland* (48)
- *Italy* (163)
- Jamaica (18)
- Jordan (4)
- North Korea (50)
- Kuwait (58)
- Laos (19)
- Lebanon (17)
- Lesotho (5)
- Liberia (0)
- Libya (32)
- *Luxembourg* (3)
- Madagascar (11)
- Mali (7)
- Malta(8)
- Mexico (45)
- Mongolia (43)
- Mozambique(14)
- Nepal (11)
- *Netherlands* (86)
- New Zealand (5)
- Nicaragua (5)
- Nigeria (44)
- Peru(30)
- Poland (320)
- *Portugal* (11)
- *Puerto Rico* (3)
- Romania (243)
- *San Marino* (17)
- Sierra Leone (14)
- Senegal (32)
- Seychelles (11)
- *Spain* (159)
- Sri Lanka (4)
- Sweden (148)
- *Switzerland* (84)
- Syria (69)
- Tanzania (41)
- Trinidand and Tobaggo (9)
- Uganda (13)
- USSR (506)
- Venezuela (38)
- Vietnam (30)
- Yugoslavia (162)
- Zambia (40)
- Zimbabwe (46)

* * * * *

Ultimately, the Games did go on. Not surprisingly in the Western Hemisphere, the Moscow Games were summarized as disappointing due to the low level of competition. The 506-member Soviet team dominated the medal count like no other nation since the U.S. in 1904, winning a lopsided 197 medals—80 gold, 70 silver and 47 bronze. In all, 4,064 men and 1,115 women competed in 203 events in 21 sports.

* * * * *

Sixteen days of competition resulted in athletes realizing the dreams of their lifetime. When they concluded on August 3, the Games of the XXII Olympiad in Moscow were relegated to history. As the athletic dreams of thousands of athletes became a footnote in a saga that still reverberates today, one of the most lasting images of the Moscow Games was Misha, who shed a single tear at the Closing Ceremony.

It was an image that not only came to symbolize the closing of the Moscow Games, but that also expressed the feelings of hundreds of American athletes, as well as the thousands of other athletes, who had their Olympic dreams stolen in the summer of 1980.

Brian Gust – 1980 U.S. Olympic Greco-Roman Wrestling Team

Brian Gust
Greco-Roman Wrestling

"There but for the grace of God go I" is a phrase not trivialized or uttered tritely by 1980 U.S. Olympian and Greco-Roman wrestler Brian Gust.

Gust, who has seen his share of trials and tribulation before, during and after 1980, is keenly aware of the fragility of life. He also has experienced and remembers the many twists and turns life presents when pursuing an Olympic dream and living beyond it. But Gust may have learned even greater lessons from his Olympic experience than he could have imagined.

In 1978, unable to afford both training and supporting his growing family, Gust figured he was approaching the end of his Greco-Roman wrestling career. "As amateur athletes, we were pretty much broke," Gust recalls. "I had a wife and two kids. By 1978, I was flat broke and had no concept of how I was even going to continue my career. I got to a point where I cried out to God and said, 'I can't go on because I can't afford to go and compete and leave my wife and two little babies to fend for themselves.' I was on my knees at work and crying. I remember telling God that this was it, because the money wasn't there. But I felt like he was telling me what to do and I was trusting him for my direction."

Several years earlier, Gust had taken a job at the Sports & Health Club of Minneapolis, in part so he could have access to a facility to train in for the 1976 Montreal Olympics while also supporting his family. "I was on a starvation salary [that was] based on commissions to sell memberships," Gust says. "But, when you're not there, it's pretty hard to sell memberships." Though Gust was able to train at the club, he didn't get paid to travel to important

U.S. and international tournaments that would help solidify his credentials for an Olympic berth.

Having reached the top of the U.S. rankings in his 125-pound weight class in 1976, Gust seemed poised to fulfill his Olympic destiny as an experienced 27-year-old competitor. But one week before the U.S. National Championship, the unthinkable occurred. Gust tore the cartilage in his right knee and could not compete for the championship that would have brought him one step closer to the Olympics. "Because of my credentials up to that point, I got a waiver from having to compete in the Nationals and subsequent Olympic tournament wrestle-offs," Gust remembers. "As the top American wrestler, I was invited to the final Olympic wrestle-offs in Brockport, N.Y. As a waived, or 'invited,' wrestler, you have to start at the bottom and beat everyone two-out-of-three up to the finals. I made it to the finals and lost and became the U.S. Olympic alternate in 1976."

Consequently, Gust set his sights on Moscow and 1980. He would be 31, effectively a generation older than the 23-year-old average age of his competitors.

But Gust was exceptionally well trained, even for an elite athlete. He was a U.S. Army Special Forces veteran who served three years as a Green Beret during the Vietnam era and worked covertly overseas helping to train insurgent groups. So he didn't think his age would be an issue. The real obstacle turned out to be a matter not of health, but of economics. He couldn't even afford a plane ticket from his home in Camby, Minn., to attend the World Championships in California.

Back at the Sports & Health Club in Minneapolis, Gust, who turned to religion prior to his 1976 Olympic experience, told no one of his prayer when it seemed his career would finally end in 1978. "One week later the owner of the company called me into his office," Gust recalls. "He said, 'Brian, we've been looking at your career. We know your goals are for the Olympics and we're excited about them. What we've decided to do as a corporation is take you off the payroll and put you on our advertising budget.'" The club would pay Gust $1,000 per month until the end of the 1980 Olympic Games so that he could continue to train and pursue his Olympic dream. Gust felt his prayers were answered. Little did he know that the sacrifices he was making as an Olympic athlete would pay even bigger dividends years later.

"I would travel around the world competing, carrying organic baked potatoes, organic raisins, organic dates, dried pineapple, and had learned that would be very instrumental in a performance context," Gust says. "Interestingly enough, the results of my nutrition plan were successful. As we got pooh-poohed originally traveling around the world—'What are you eating now, Gust? Baked potatoes?'—it wasn't long before six out of the 10 Olympians in '80 were doing the same thing. I realized it was better to sit down and eat organic foods after weigh-ins because they were going to be effective for you on the mat in three hours versus going down to the cafeteria with the rest of the world in attendance and having bacon and eggs. We were drinking liquid vitamin E and eating high, high carbohydrate foods that were easily digested. No protein foods. We were really concentrated on this high organic diet for the purpose of being able to compete at 120 percent when you weren't able to eat. I would go from 140 pounds to 125 pounds, so you really had to put this thing together. The results were great."

Though Gust's Olympic dream was extinguished in 1980, he again toyed with the idea of representing his country and competing in the Games. This time Gust aimed for Los Angeles and 1984. Fitness was still of little concern, and he'd solved the financial problem.

"I took a head coaching job in 1982 at Lakeville [Minn.] High School and coached there [until] '86," Gust says. "As 1983 came around, all my kids were going, 'Mr. Gust, you gotta go for the Olympic Games again.' So I started training and ended up wrestling with a broken disk in my neck. I didn't know how serious it was but ended up having surgery between Christmas and New Year's. The surgery was very successful. I ended up coming back in March, which was the start of the Olympic Trials. I won two pre-qualifying tournaments building up to the final Olympic Trials in Minneapolis and ended up getting beat."

Brian Gust's Olympic dream was finally over.

Unfortunately, his health problems were not. And they would prove to be a bigger fight than any he could have imagined in Montreal, Moscow or Los Angeles.

On December 20, 2004, Gust was diagnosed with squamous cell carcinoma. The primary tumor filled the right side of his throat, and the cancer had metastasized into the lymph nodes in his neck. "I went through a series of interviews to determine the best series of action to take, starting with the University of Minnesota," Gust says two years to the date of his first visit. "Originally, they had said I was in huge trouble and they gave me as little as four months to live."

At that point, Gust knew his body was breaking down, so he relied on his nutrition regimen from 25 years before. "I instantly went back to my organic diet that helped me become an Olympic athlete," Gust says. "Just with diet alone, over the next 45 days, we retested and the tumor was reduced 25 percent."

Gust's battle with cancer continues today, but he sees the parallel journey of his cancer fight and his Olympic odyssey as a blessing. "I had determined pretty early on in my career—because I had studied nutrition in college—that if you put the right fuel into your body, your body is going to be able to perform more adeptly. So I had a quest to do that." That quest may very well have saved his life in 2004.

Looking back at 1980 and his one chance at Olympic glory, Gust does not stop to ponder the what-ifs. "Financially, I think it really wouldn't have made that much of a significant difference even if I went to Moscow and won the gold medal," he says. "For me, as a wrestler, which is a blue-collar sport, it really didn't have that impact."

Gust was happy to be a member of the 1980 team and has stood by President Carter's decision for nearly three decades. "I love America," exclaims the emotional wrestler. "And as I traveled around the world competing as an amateur athlete, I would come home and realize this is the greatest country in the world—bar none. I respected what the president of the United States had to say and whatever his command was. That is what I was going to accept willingly. I felt that was the right thing to do. Unfortunately, a lot of the athletes, once the boycott occurred, were very bitter and in a lot of cases had so much to lose."

Today, Brian Gust is a volunteer wrestling coach at Minnesota's Eagan High School and the owner of his own painting business—Olympic Colors—that generates more than $1 million in revenue. His hardships, heartaches, disappointments and trials have rivaled the patience of Job, but the scrappy Greco-Roman Olympian carries on and is honored to be a member of such a distinguished Olympic alumni.

"It's interesting because in 1972, having come out of the military, I watched the Olympics on TV," Gust says. "And I recall to the day, like it was yesterday, that I was watching wrestling, and I set a goal in 1972 that I could do that. I can remember putting on my running shoes, and running that night, having set the goal of becoming an Olympian.

"Unfortunately, it took eight years and thousands and thousands and thousands of dollars out of my pocket. And even though I didn't get the chance to compete, America is the greatest country in the world and it was an honor to represent the United States on that Olympic team. It was an honor for my parents, my family, and something [no one will] ever take away from me."

Lisa Buese – 1980 U.S. Olympic Swim Team

Lisa Buese
Women's Swimming

Eleven years after Lisa Buese was denied the opportunity to swim in the 1980 Olympic Summer Games in Moscow, her resilience and determination were to be tested in a way the 28-year-old former world-class swimmer would never have imagined.

Her life perspective had been profoundly tested by the unimaginable disappointment of 1980. Still, that paled in comparison to what happened while running along the scenic Boston paths near the Charles River. "I was living in Boston, my second year out of business school," Buese explains. "I had done several marathons and triathlons. One day I was running outside along the Charles River and basically, what happened, to make a long story short, I ended up at Massachusetts General Hospital with an episode of sudden cardiac death." Buese's heart, the heart of an Olympian who, based on her times, would have undoubtedly won an Olympic medal in Moscow, had stopped. Twenty-eight-years-old and clinically dead.

"It was a an eye-opener," says Buese matter-of-factly 17 years later. "I had never been in the hospital before. Being a very physically fit person, I had taken to running and other things to keep myself healthy and fit. Lo and behold, I had this episode of sudden cardiac death at 28 years old. I remember lying in the hospital and them asking me if I had done any drugs and I said, 'No. No. No.' I was extremely lucky to be living so close to the hospital and have some of the world's leading cardiologists at the hospital I was in.

"I had a congenital condition. It was an electrical problem that caused my heart to beat incredibly fast. They said had I not been so incredibly fit I may not have survived it. I had my swimming days to thank for that, as far as taking care of my body and paying attention to it."

Buese was born in Chicago and grew up in Louisville, Ky., two cities more known for big-shouldered athletes and thoroughbreds, not for producing world-class swimmers. At an early age, Buese's parents got all five of their children involved in swimming. Lisa, number four in line with three older brothers and a younger sister, immediately excelled in the water. "At some point in time they realized I had a little bit of talent, and I was enjoying doing it, so they had me swimming in summer club leagues," Buese says. "I had won a few races here and there. The next thing I knew I was swimming all year round and competing for an Amateur Athletic Union team."

Buese's progress stalled at age 10, so her father suggested switching back to the coach who had originally taught her to swim—Dennis Pursley. From then on, Buese's improvement was dramatic. Like anything, Buese knew her success did not come without help and support. "My father, who was an executive and worked extremely hard, made time to get me up at 4:30 in the morning to take me to practice. My mother would do the afternoon shift while raising five kids without any help. They were committed to my success, as were my siblings."

As Buese advanced into the 12 to 13-year-old age group, she was part of a core group of swimmers that started doing well and performing on a national level. One in particular, a girl from the Plantation Swim Team in Louisville, was also beginning to turn heads with her talent as a but-terflyer—Mary T. Meagher. "We grew up across the street from each other," remembers Buese of one of USA Swimming's all-time greats. "We were both butterflyers. I was also a freestyler. Our coach did something unique for girls that age. We would swim morning workouts at the age of 13. I had school so I would get up at 4:30 and my father would make a bagel and take me and the rest of my carpool, including Mary T., over to the pool. We would swim morning practice. Mary T. and I would come a little bit later than everybody else and stay a little later so that we would have more room in the pool to swim one-on-one and train against each other. I think we were both complementary to each other, having that other person there to push each other to do their best."

Around that time, Buese's Olympic dream began to take focus. At 13 years old, she made the National Junior Olympic team and placed second. From there, she competed in the 1976 nationals and was becoming a top-caliber swimmer. If she was looking for inspiration for her next step, she didn't have to look far. "In my hometown there was a woman by the name of Camille Wright who swam in the Olympics," Buese recalls. "There was a lot of local talent with national caliber. Then there was a group a few years older than me that were all national-caliber swimmers—a woman by the name of Robin Wright, no relation [to the actress], Rosemary Boone and a couple other swimmers."

Buese knew the Olympics was not a pie-in-the-sky dream anymore. "A lot of it probably came from my coach," she admits. "I think he knew I had the talent to get there, and dedication and determination. It wasn't something I thought about every day. It was more like day-to-day and taking each season as it came. I happened to peak at the right time in 1980."

Buese's Olympic odyssey hit a crossroad when she was 16—one year before the 1980 Olympic trials. Pursley had taken a job in nearby Ohio coaching the Cincinnati Marlins swimming club. Buese, and the rest of her teammates, contemplated what Pursley's departure meant. At the time, Lakeside Swim Club, Buese's training facility in Louisville, didn't have an indoor Olympic-size pool. With Pursley headed to Cincinnati, Buese discussed the situation with her parents. "We all decided that I shouldn't change my coach one year before the Olympic Trials," Buese says. "One: He taught me how to swim. Two: He came back and helped turn me into an elite national swimmer. I made the conscious decision to move to Cincinnati for my junior year in high school and boarded with a family."

The Caseys of Cincinnati became Buese's surrogate family. They had three daughters and only one was still at home. They had nothing to do with swimming and created an ideal environment for Buese to continue training for the Olympics and to continue her junior year in high school. Eventually, other individuals Buese had trained with and gotten to know migrated to Cincinnati to train with Pursley as well. It paid off for everyone—six swimmers trained by Pursley would make the 1980 team.

At the Olympic Trials, Buese needed to finish in the top three of an event to earn a spot on the Olympic team. It came down to her best event, the 100 butterfly. After spending thousands of hours swimming, working out and focusing on the moment at hand, the 17-year-old was poised and ready for the final race. Unfortunately, domestic politics forced her to wait a little longer. "At the time, Ronald Reagan was the governor of California and they always had someone like that to present the awards after each event," Buese remembers. "This was my last opportunity and I just remember we had to wait for Ronald Reagan to land because he was coming in his helicopter to hand out the awards at the end of the race. We had to wait for an extra half hour to begin."

When Buese finally got to race she touched the wall and immediately turned to the scoreboard. "It was a funky scoreboard so every time someone touched, it reorganized itself," Buese recalls. "When I touched, it actually looked like I had finished fourth, but I finished third. It was a bittersweet moment.

"Even though we knew we weren't going to go [to Moscow], it was a goal that I wanted to make the team. I think back to my coach, Dennis Pursley, and when I had accomplished the goal of making the Olympic team. He said, 'You're in the top one percent of Americans in terms of accomplishments.'"

Buese didn't let the boycott stop her from continuing her life and swimming career. She attended Stanford University on a scholarship and decided to shun thoughts of 1984 and Los Angeles. "After 1980, it was always very important to me to have balance in my life. My parents stressed that if you put too much focus into one thing you're going to get out of whack. So, I pursued different opportunities while at Stanford. I went over to Florence, Italy, in 1984. I was over there on an academic program in the spring of 1984 before the Olympic Trials. I had consciously decided—I had spent so much of my childhood focused on swimming, not necessarily at the expense of other things, but there was a cost for everything—given the boycott and things you couldn't control, that I had attained my goal of making the Olympic team and felt like there were other things in life to move on to."

The bittersweet remnants of that time, though faded, still resonate when an event triggers a memory of the 17-year-old butterflyer from Louisville by way of Chicago. The first time Buese appreciated the reality of missing the 1980 Olympics was during the 1996 Summer Games in Atlanta. Buese had travelled to Georgia to visit her brother. "My niece and I went [to the Games]. I remember, my coach Dennis Pursley was the U.S. swim team director and he was on deck there. That to me brought it full circle, because here was someone who taught me how to swim and helped me attain my goals and was still involved in the sport and excelling quite well as a coach and manager. Here I was, a spectator. That was the first time I ever really thought back on it."

If that day in Atlanta brought Buese back to one of the darker times of her athletic career, surely her fateful run along the Charles River brought perspective to her life of today. In the middle of her run, Buese started to feel faint. "Like Dorothy in the *Wizard of Oz* in the poppy fields," she recalls with a chuckle. Buese managed to get herself to an office building with no identification and no money. With her heart racing away inside her chest,

Buese explained to the security guard that she needed to get to a hospital and asked if he could lend her the cash to get there.

With $5 of the guard's money, Buese got into a cab. "When I got in … there was a quarter on the floor of the cab. I don't know what I was thinking but I picked it up," Buese remembers with exasperation. "I was on the other side of the Charles River, the Cambridge side of the river, and I remember sitting at a red light thinking, 'I'm going to die. I'm going to die.' Luckily, he got me there and the fare was exactly $5.25."

For Lisa Buese, a gold, silver or bronze medal from Moscow would have served as the symbol of the sacrifice and hard work of her youth. But the 25 cents she found on the floor of a Boston cab may well be the unknowing symbol of her life's perspective and ultimate achievement.

"It didn't dawn on me at the time, maybe because of the insular world I was in, what a huge achievement that I would hold onto my whole life," says the 45-year-old mother about making the 1980 U.S. Olympic team. "It really was. It is something I'll always have and no one can ever take away from me. When I'm faced with difficult situations, I know I have it in me to rise up to the challenge no matter what the challenge is."

CHAPTER VIII

Results

Results compiled from WWW.OLYMPIC.ORG—Official website of the Olympic Movement

Archery Individual Fita Round: Men
Gold	Finland	POIKOLAINEN, Tomi
Silver	USSR	ISACHENKO, Boris
Bronze	Italy	FERRARI, Giancarlo

Archery Individual Fita Round: Women
Gold	USSR	LOSABERIDZE, Keto
Silver	USSR	BUTUZOVA, Natalia
Bronze	Finland	MERILUOTO-AALTONEN, Paivi

Artistic Gymnastics Balance Beam: Women
Gold	Romania	COMANECI, Nadia
Silver	USSR	DAVYDOVA, Elena
Bronze	USSR	SHAPOSHNIKOVA, Natalia

Artistic Gymnastics Floor Exercises: Men
Gold	East Germany	BRÜCKNER, Roland
Silver	USSR	ANDRIANOV, Nikolay
Bronze	USSR	DITYATIN, Aleksandr

Artistic Gymnastics Floor Exercises: Women
Gold	USSR	KIM, Nelli
Gold	Romania	COMANECI, Nadia
Bronze	USSR	SHAPOSHNIKOVA, Natalia
Bronze	East Germany	GNAUCK, Maxi

Artistic Gymnastics Horizontal Bar: Men
Gold	Bulgaria	DELTCHEV, Stoyan
Silver	USSR	DITYATIN, Aleksandr
Bronze	USSR	ANDRIANOV, Nikolay

Artistic Gymnastics Individual All-round: Men
Gold	USSR	DITYATIN, Aleksandr
Silver	USSR	ANDRIANOV, Nikolay
Bronze	Bulgaria	DELTCHEV, Stoyan

Artistic Gymnastics Individual All-round: Women
Gold	USSR	DAVYDOVA, Elena
Silver	East Germany	GNAUCK, Maxi
Silver	Romania	COMANECI, Nadia

Artistic Gymnastics Parallel Bars: Men
Gold	USSR	TKACHEV, Aleksandr
Silver	USSR	DITYATIN, Aleksandr
Bronze	East Germany	BRÜCKNER, Roland

Artistic Gymnastics Pommel Horse: Men
Gold	Hungary	MAGYAR, Zoltan
Silver	USSR	DITYATIN, Aleksandr
Bronze	East Germany	NIKOLAY, Michael

Artistic Gymnastics Rings: Men
Gold	USSR	DITYATIN, Aleksandr
Silver	USSR	TKACHEV, Aleksandr
Bronze	Czechoslovakia	TABAK, Jiri

Artistic Gymnastics Team Competition: Men
Gold	USSR
Silver	East Germany
Bronze	Hungary

Artistic Gymnastics Team Competition: Women
Gold	USSR
Silver	Romania
Bronze	East Germany

Artistic Gymnastics Uneven Bars: Women
Gold	East Germany	GNAUCK, Maxi
Silver	Romania	EBERLE, Emilia
Bronze	East Germany	KRÄKER, Steffi
Bronze	Romania	RÜHN, Melita
Bronze	USSR	FILATOVA, Maria

Artistic Gymnastics Vault: Men
Gold	USSR	ANDRIANOV, Nikolay
Silver	USSR	DITYATIN, Aleksandr
Bronze	East Germany	RÜCKNER, Roland

Artistic Gymnastics Vault: Women
Gold	USSR	SHAPOSHNIKOVA, Natalia
Silver	East Germany	KRÄKER, Steffi
Bronze	Romania	RÜHN, Melita

Athletics 10000m: Men
Gold	Ethiopia	YIFTER, Miruts
Silver	Finland	MAANINKA, Kaarlo
Bronze	Ethiopia	KEDIR, Mohammed

Athletics 100m Hurdles: Women
Gold	USSR	KOMISOVA, Vera
Silver	East Germany	SCHALLER-KLIER, Johanna
Bronze	Poland	LANGER, Lucyna

Athletics 100m: Men
Gold	Great Britain	WELLS, Allan
Silver	Cuba	LEONARD SARRIA, Silvio
Bronze	Bolivia	PETRomania, Peter

Athletics 100m: Women
Gold	USSR	KONDRATIEVA, Liudmila
Silver	East Germany	OELSNER-GÖHR, Marlies
Bronze	East Germany	AUERSWALD-LANGE, Ingrid

Athletics 110m Hurdles: Men
Gold	East Germany	MUNKELT, Thomas
Silver	Cuba	CASANAS RAMIREZ, Alejandro
Bronze	USSR	PUCHKOV, Aleksandr

Athletics 1500m: Men
Gold	Great Britain	COE, Sebastian
Silver	East Germany	STRAUB, Jürgen
Bronze	Great Britain	OVETT, Steve

Athletics 1500m: Women
Gold	USSR	KAZANKINA, Tatiana
Silver	East Germany	STOLL-WARTENBERG, Christiane
Bronze	USSR	OLIZARENKO, Nadezhda

Athletics 200m: Men
Gold	Italy	MENNEA, Pietro
Silver	Great Britain	WELLS, Allan
Bronze	Jamaica	QUARRIE, Donald

Athletics 200m: Women
Gold	East Germany	ECKERT-WÖCKEL, Bärbel
Silver	USSR	BOCHINA, Natalia
Bronze	Jamaica	OTTEY-PAGE, Merlene

Athletics 20km Walk: Men
Gold	Italy	DAMILANO, Maurizio
Silver	USSR	POCHINCHUK, Piotr
Bronze	East Germany	WIESER, Roland

Athletics 3000m Steeplechase: Men
Gold	Poland	MALINOWSKI, Bronislaw
Silver	Tanzania	BAYI, Filbert
Bronze	Ethiopia	TURA, Eshetu

Athletics 400m Hurdles: Men
Gold	East Germany	BECK, Volker
Silver	USSR	ARKHIPENKO, Vasili
Bronze	Great Britain	OAKES, Gary

Athletics 400m: Men
Gold	USSR	MARKIN, Viktor
Silver	Australia	MITCHELL, Richard
Bronze	East Germany	SCHAFFER, Frank

Athletics 400m: Women
Gold	East Germany	KOCH, Marita
Silver	Czechoslovakia	KRATOHVILOVA, Jarmila
Bronze	East Germany	BREHMER-LATHAN, Christina

Athletics 4x100m Relay: Men
Gold   USSR
Silver   Poland
Bronze   France

Athletics 4x100m Relay: Women
Gold   East Germany
Silver   USSR
Bronze   Great Britain

Athletics 4x400m Relay : Men
Gold   USSR
Silver   East Germany
Bronze   Italy

Athletics 4x400m Relay : Women
Gold   USSR   PROROCHENKO, Tatiana
Silver   East Germany   LÖWE, Gabriele
Bronze   Great Britain   MACDONALD, Linsey

Athletics 5000m: Men
Gold   Ethiopia   YIFTER, Miruts
Silver   Tanzania   NYAMBUI, Suleiman
Bronze   Finland   MAANINKA, Kaarlo

Athletics 50km Walk: Men
Gold   East Germany   GAUDER, Hartwig
Silver   Spain   LLOPART RIBAS, Jorge
Bronze   USSR   IVCHENKO, Evgeni

Athletics 800m: Men
Gold   Great Britain   OVETT, Steve
Silver   Great Britain   COE, Sebastian
Bronze   USSR   KIROV, Nikolai

Athletics 800m: Women
Gold   USSR   OLIZARENKO, Nadezhda
Silver   USSR   MINEEVA, Olga
Bronze   USSR   PROVIDOKHINA, Tatiana

Athletics Decathlon: Men
Gold   Great Britain   THOMPSON, Daley
Silver   USSR   KUTSENKO, Yuri
Bronze   USSR   ZHELANOV, Sergei

Athletics Discus Throw: Men
Gold   USSR   RASHCHUPKIN, Viktor
Silver   Czechoslovakia   BUGAR, Imrich
Bronze   Cuba   DELIS, Luis

Athletics Discus Throw: Women
Gold   East Germany   SCHLAAK-JAHL, Evelin
Silver   Bulgaria   VERGOVA-PETKOVA, Maria
Bronze   USSR   LESOVAIA, Tatiana

Athletics Hammer Throw: Men
Gold   USSR   SEDYKH, Yuri
Silver   USSR   LITVINOV, Sergei
Bronze   USSR   TAMM, Yuri

Athletics High Jump: Men
Gold   East Germany   WESSIG, Gerd
Silver   Poland   WSZOLA, Jacek
Bronze   East Germany   FREIMUTH, Jörg

Athletics High Jump: Women
Gold   Italy   SIMEONI, Sara
Silver   Poland   KIELAN, Urszula
Bronze   East Germany   KIRST, Jutta

Athletics Javelin Throw: Men
Gold   USSR   KULA, Dainis
Silver   USSR   MAKAROV, Aleksandr
Bronze   East Germany   HANISCH, Wolfgang

Athletics Javelin Throw: Women
Gold   Cuba   COLON, Maria
Silver   USSR   GUNBA, Saida
Bronze   East Germany   HOMMOLA, Ute

Athletics Long Jump: Men
Gold   East Germany   DOMBROWSKI, Lutz
Silver   East Germany   PASCHEK, Frank
Bronze   USSR   PODLUZHNYI, Valeri

Athletics Long Jump: Women
Gold   USSR   KOLPAKOVA, Tatiana
Silver   East Germany   WUJAK, Brigitte
Bronze   USSR   SKACHKO, Tatiana

Athletics Marathon: Men
Gold   East Germany   CIERPINSKI, Waldemar
Silver   Netherlands   NIJBOER, Gerard
Bronze   USSR   DZHUMANAZAROV, Setymkul

Athletics Pentathlon: Women
Gold   USSR   TKACHENKO, Nadezhda
Silver   USSR   RUKAVISHNIKOVA, Olga
Bronze   USSR   KURAGINA, Olga

Athletics Pole Vault: Men
Gold   Poland   KOZAKIEWICZ, Wladyslaw
Silver   Poland   SLUSARSKI, Tadeusz
Silver   USSR   VOLKOV, Konstantin

Athletics Shot Put: Men
Gold   USSR   KISELEV, Vladimir
Silver   USSR   BARYSHNIKOV, Aleksandr
Bronze   East Germany   BEYER, Udo

Athletics Shot Put: Women

Gold	East Germany	SCHOKNECHT-SLUPIANEK, Ilona
Silver	USSR	KRACHEVSKAIA, Svetlana
Bronze	East Germany	DROESE-PUFE, Margitta

Athletics Triple Jump: Men

Gold	USSR	UUDMAE, Yaak
Silver	USSR	SANEEV, Viktor
Bronze	Brazil	DE OLIVEIRA, Joao Carlos

Basketball: Men

Gold	Yugoslavia
Silver	Italy
Bronze	USSR

Basketball: Women

Gold	USSR
Silver	Bulgaria
Bronze	Yugoslavia

Boxing + 81kg (Heavyweight): Men

Gold	Cuba	STEVENSON, Teofilo
Silver	USSR	ZAEV, Piotr
Bronze	Hungary	LEVAI, Istvan
Bronze	East Germany	FANGHÄNEL, Jürgen

Boxing 48kg (Light-flyweight): Men

Gold	USSR	SABIROV, Shamil
Silver	Cuba	RAMOS, Hipolito
Bronze	North Korea	LI, Byong Uk
Bronze	Bulgaria	MUSTAFOV, Ismail

Boxing 48–51kg (Flyweight): Men

Gold	Bulgaria	LESOV, Petr
Silver	USSR	MIROSHNICHENKO, Viktor
Bronze	Ireland	RUSSELL, Hugh
Bronze	Hungary	VARADI, Janos

Boxing 51–54kg (Bantamweight): Men

Gold	Cuba	HERNANDEZ, Juan
Silver	Venezuela	PINANGO, Bernardo Jose
Bronze	Romania	CIPERE, Dumitru
Bronze	Guyana	ANTHONY, Michael

Boxing 54–57kg (Featherweight): Men

Gold	East Germany	FINK, Rudi
Silver	Cuba	HORTA, Adolfo
Bronze	USSR	RYBAKOV, Viktor
Bronze	Poland	KOSEDOWSKI, Krzysztof

Boxing 57–60kg (Lightweight): Men

Gold	Cuba	HERRERA VERA, Angel
Silver	USSR	IANENKO, Viktor
Bronze	Poland	ADACH, Kazimierz
Bronze	East Germany	NOWAKOWSKI, Richard

Boxing 60–63.5kg (Light-welterweight): Men

Gold	Italy	OLIVA, Patrizio
Silver	USSR	KONAKBAEV, Serik
Bronze	Great Britain	WILLIS, Anthony
Bronze	Cuba	AGUILAR, Jose

Boxing 63.5–67kg (Welterweight): Men

Gold	Cuba	ALDAMA CABRERA, Andres
Silver	Uganda	MUGABI, John
Bronze	Poland	SZCZERBA, Kazimierz
Bronze	East Germany	KRÜGER, Karl-Heinz

Boxing 67–71kg (Light-middleweight) : Men

Gold	Cuba	MARTINEZ, Armando
Silver	USSR	KOSHKIN, Aleksandr
Bronze	Czechoslovakia	FRANEK, Jan
Bronze	East Germany	KÄSTNER, Detlef

Boxing 71–75kg: Men

Gold	Cuba	GOMEZ, Jose
Silver	USSR	SAVCHENKO, Viktor
Bronze	Romania	SILAGHI, Valentin
Bronze	Poland	RYBICKI, Jerzy

Boxing 75–81kg (Light-heavyweight): Men

Gold	Yugoslavia	KACAR, Slobodan
Silver	Poland	KRZECZ, Pawel
Bronze	East Germany	BAUCH, Herbert
Bronze	Cuba	ROJAS, Ricardo

Canoe / Kayak Flatwater C-1 1000m (Canoe Single): Men

Gold	Bulgaria	LIUBENOV, Liubomir
Silver	USSR	POSTREKHIN, Sergei
Bronze	East Germany	LEUE, Eckhard

Canoe / Kayak Flatwater C-1 500m (Canoe Single): Men

Gold	USSR	POSTREKHIN, Sergei
Silver	Bulgaria	LIUBENOV, Liubomir
Bronze	East Germany	HEUKRODT, Olaf

Canoe / Kayak Flatwater C-2 1000m (Canoe Double): Men

Gold	Romania	PATZAICHIN, Ivan
Gold	Romania	SIMIONOV, Toma
Silver	East Germany	HEUKRODT, Olaf
Silver	East Germany	MADEJA, Uwe
Bronze	USSR	YURCHENKO, Vasili
Bronze	USSR	LOBANOV, Yuri

Canoe / Kayak Flatwater C-2 500m (Canoe Double): Men

Gold	Hungary	FOLTAN, Laszlo
Gold	Hungary	VASKUTI, Istvan
Silver	Romania	PATZAICHIN, Ivan
Silver	Romania	CAPUSTA, Petre
Bronze	Bulgaria	ANANIEV, Borislav
Bronze	Bularia	LKOV, Nikolai

Canoe / Kayak Flatwater K-1 1000m (Kayak Single): Men
Gold	East Germany	HELM, Rüdiger
Silver	France	LEBAS, Alain
Bronze	Romania	BIRLADEANU, Ion

Canoe / Kayak Flatwater K-1 500m (Kayak Single): Men
Gold	USSR	PARFENOVICH, Vladimir
Silver	Australia	SUMEGI, John
Bronze	Romania	DIBA, Vasile

Canoe / Kayak Flatwater K-1 500m (Kayak Single): Women
Gold	East Germany	FISCHER, Birgit
Silver	Bulgaria	GESHEVA, Vania
Bronze	USSR	MELNIKOVA, Antonina

Canoe / Kayak Flatwater K-2 1000m (Kayak Double): Men
Gold	USSR	PARFENOVICH, Vladimir
Gold	USSR	CHUKHRAI, Sergei
Silver	Hungary	SZABO, Istvan
Silver	Hungary	JOOS, Istvan
Bronze	Spain	RAMOS MISIONE, Luis Gregorio
Bronze	Spain	MENENDEZ RODRIGUEZ, Herminio

Canoe / Kayak Flatwater K-2 500m (Kayak Double): Men
Gold	USSR	PARFENOVICH, Vladimir
Gold	USSR	CHUKHRAI, Sergei
Silver	Spain	MENENDEZ RODRIGUEZ, Herminio
Silver	Spain	DEL RIEGO GORDON, Guillermo
Bronze	East Germany	HELM, Rüdiger
Bronze	East Germany	OLBRICHT, Bernd

Canoe / Kayak Flatwater K-2 500m (Kayak Double): Women
Gold	East Germany	GENÄUSS, Carsta
Gold	East Germany	BISCHOF, Martina
Silver	USSR	KREFT-ALEKSEEVA, Galina
Silver	USSR	GOPOVA-TROFIMOVA, Nina
Bronze	Hungary	RAKUSZ, Eva
Bronze	Hungary	ZAKARIAS, Maria

Canoe / Kayak Flatwater K-4 1000m (Kayak Four): Men
Gold	East Germany	HELM, Rüdiger
Gold	East Germany	OLBRICHT, Bernd
Gold	East Germany	MARG, Harald
Gold	East Germany	DUVIGNEAU, Bernd
Silver	Romania	ZAFIU, Mihai
Silver	Romania	DIBA, Vasile
Silver	Romania	GEANTA, Ion
Silver	Romania	ESEANU, Nicusor
Bronze	Bulgaria	BORISOV, Borislav
Bronze	Bulgaria	MILENKOV, Bojiar
Bronze	Bulgaria	KHRISTOV, Lazar
Bronze	Bulgaria	MANEV, Ivan

Cycling Road Individual Road Race: Men
Gold	USSR	SUKHORUCHENKOV, Sergei
Silver	Poland	LANG, Stanislaw
Bronze	USSR	BARINOV, Yuri

Cycling Road Team Time Trial: Men
Gold	USSR	KASHIRIN, Yuri
Gold	USSR	LOGVIN, Oleg
Gold	USSR	SHELPAKOV, Sergei
Gold	USSR	YARKIN, Anatoli
Silver	East Germany	BODEN, Falk
Silver	East Germany	DROGAN, Bernd
Silver	East Germany	LUDWIG, Olaf
Silver	East Germany	HARTNICK, Hans-Joachim
Bronze	Czechoslovakia	KLASA, Michal
Bronze	Czechoslovakia	KONECNY, Vlastibor
Bronze	Czechoslovakia	KOSTADINOV, Alipi
Bronze	Czechoslovakia	SKODA, Jiri

Cycling Track 1km Time Trial: Men
Gold	East Germany	THOMS, Lothar
Silver	USSR	PANFILOV, Aleksandr
Bronze	Jamaica	WELLER, David

Cycling Track Individual PUSSRuit: Men
Gold	Switzerland	DILL-BUNDI, Robert
Silver	France	BONDUE, Alain
Bronze	Denmark	ÖRSTED, Hans-Henrik

Cycling Track Sprint Individual: Men
Gold	East Germany	HESSLICH, Lutz
Silver	France	CAHARD, Yave
Bronze	USSR	KOPYLOV, Sergei

Cycling Track Team PUSSRuit (4000m): Men
Gold	USSR
Silver	East Germany
Bronze	Czechoslovakia

Diving 10m Platform: Men
Gold	East Germany	HOFFMANN, Falk
Silver	USSR	ALEINIK, Vladimir
Bronze	USSR	AMBARTSUMYAN, David

Diving 10m Platform: Women
Gold	East Germany	JÄSCHKE, Martina
Silver	USSR	EMIRZIAN, Servard
Bronze	USSR	TSOTADZE, Liana

Diving 3m Springboard: Men
Gold	USSR	PORTNOV, Aleksandr
Silver	Mexico	GIRON, Carlos
Bronze	Italy	CAGNOTTO, Giorgio Franco

Diving 3m Springboard: Women

Gold	USSR	KALININA, Irina
Silver	East Germany	PROEBER, Martina
Bronze	East Germany	GUTHKE, Karin

Equestrian / Dressage Individual: Mixed

Gold	Austria	THEURER-MAX, Elisabeth
Gold	Austria	MON CHERIE
Silver	USSR	KOVSHOV, Yuri
Silver	USSR	IGROK
Bronze	USSR	UGRYUMOV, Viktor
Bronze	USSR	SHKVAL

Equestrian / Dressage Team: Mixed

Gold	USSR
Silver	Bulgaria
Bronze	Romania

Equestrian / Eventing Individual: Mixed

Gold	Italy	ROSSINAN
Gold	Italy	ROMAN, Federico Euro
Silver	USSR	BLINOV, Aleksandr
Silver	USSR	GALZUN
Bronze	USSR	SALNIKOV, Yuri
Bronze	USSR	PINTSET

Equestrian / Eventing Team: Mixed

Gold	USSR
Silver	Italy
Bronze	Mexico

Equestrian / Jumping Individual: Mixed

Gold	Poland	KOWALCZYK, Jan
Gold	Poland	ARTEMOR
Silver	USSR	KOROLKOV, Nikolai
Silver	USSR	ESPADRON
Bronze	Mexico	ALYMONY
Bronze	Mexico	PEREZ DE LA HERAS, Joaquin

Equestrian / Jumping Team: Mixed

Gold	USSR
Silver	Poland
Bronze	Mexico

Fencing Épée Individual: Men

Gold	Sweden	HARMENBERG, Johan
Silver	Hungary	KOLSZONAY, Ernö
bronze	France	RIBOUD, Philippe

Fencing Épée Team: Men

Gold	France
Silver	Poland
Bronze	USSR

Fencing Foil Individual: Men

Gold	USSR	SMIRNOV, Vladimir
Silver	France	JOLYOT, Pascal
Bronze	USSR	ROMANKOV, Aleksander

Fencing Foil Individual: Women

Gold	France	TRINQUET-HACHIN, Pascale
Silver	Hungary	MAROS, Magda
Bronze	Poland	WYSOCZANSKA, Barbara

Fencing Foil Team: Men

Gold	France
Silver	USSR
Bronze	Poland

Fencing Foil Team: Women

Gold	France
Silver	USSR
Bronze	Hungary

Fencing Sabre Individual: Men

Gold	USSR	KROVOPUSKOV, Viktor
Silver	USSR	BURTSEV, Mikhail
Bronze	Hungary	GEDOVARI, Imre

Fencing Sabre Team: Men

Gold	USSR
Silver	Italy
Bronze	Hungary

Football: Men

Gold	Czechoslovakia
Silver	East Germany
Bronze	USSR

Handball: Men

Gold	East Germany
Silver	USSR
Bronze	Romania

Handball: Women

Gold	USSR
Silver	Yugoslavia
Bronze	East Germany

Hockey: Men

Gold	India
Silver	Spain
Bronze	USSR

Hockey: Women

Gold	Zimbabwe
Silver	Czechoslovakia
Bronze	USSR

Judo + 95kg (Heavyweight): Men
Gold   France   PARISI, Angelo
Silver   Bulgaria   ZAPRIANOV, Dimitar
Bronze   Yugoslavia   KOVACEVIC, Radomir
Bronze   Yugoslavia   KOCMAN, Vladimir

Judo–60 kg: Men
Gold   France   REY, Thierry
Silver   Bulgaria   RODRIGUEZ, Jose
Bronze   Hungary   KINCSES, Tibor
Bronze   USSR   EMIZH, Arambi

Judo 60–65kg (Half-lightweight): Men
Gold   USSR   SOLODUKHIN, Nikolai
Silver   Mongolia   DAMDIN, Tsendying
Bronze   Bulgaria   NEDKOV, Ilian
Bronze   Poland   PAWLOWSKI, Janusz

Judo 65–71kg (Lightweight): Men
Gold   Italy   GAMBA, Ezio
Silver   Great Britain   ADAMS, Neil
Bronze   East Germany   LEHMANN, Karl-Heinz
Bronze   Mongolia   DAVAADALAI, Ravdan

Judo 71–78kg (Half-middleweight): Men
Gold   USSR   KHABARELI, Shota
Silver   Cuba   FERRER, Juan
Bronze   France   TCHOULLOUYAN, Bernard
Bronze   East Germany   HEINKE, Harald

Judo 78–86kg (Middleweight): Men
Gold   Switzerland   RÖTHLISBERGER, Jürg
Silver   Cuba   AZCUY OLIVA, Isaac
Bronze   East Germany   ULTSCH, Detlef
Bronze   USSR   YATSKEVICH, Aleksandr

Judo 86–95kg (Half-heavyweight): Men
Gold   Belgium   VAN DE WALLE, Robert
Silver   USSR   KHUBULURI, Tengiz
Bronze   Netherlands   NUMAN, Henk
Bronze   East Germany   LORENZ, Dietmar

Judo Open Category: Men
Gold   East Germany   LORENZ, Dietmar
Silver   France   PARISI, Angelo
Bronze   Great Britain   MAPP, Arthur
Bronze   Hungary   OZSVAR, Andras

Modern Pentathlon Individual Competition: Men
Gold   USSR   STAROSTIN, Anatoli
Silver   Hungary   SZOMBATHELYI, Tamas
Bronze   USSR   LEDNEV, Pavel

Modern Pentathlon Team Competition: Men
Gold   USSR
Silver   Hungary
Bronze   Sweden

Rowing Coxless Pair: Men
Gold   East Germany   LANDVOIGT, Bernd
Gold   East Germany   LANDVOIGT, Jörg
Silver   USSR   PIMENOV, Yuri
Silver   USSR   PIMENOV, Nikolai
Bronze   Great Britain   WIGGIN, Charles
Bronze   Great Britain   CARMICHAEL, Malcolm

Rowing Double Sculls (2x): Men
Gold   East Germany   DREIFKE, Joachim
Gold   East Germany   KRÖPPELIEN, Klaus
Silver   Yugoslavia   PANCIC, Zoran
Silver   Yugoslavia   STANULOV, Milorad
Bronze   Czechoslovakia   PECKA, Zdenek
Bronze   Czechoslovakia   VOCHOSKA, Vaclav

Rowing Double Sculls (2x): Women
Gold   USSR   KHLOPTSEVA, Elena
Gold   USSR   ALEXANDROVA-POPOVA, Larissa
Silver   East Germany   LINSE, Cornelia
Silver   East Germany   WESTPHAL, Heidi
Bronze   Romania   HOMEGHI-BULARDA, Olga
Bronze   Romania   ROSCA-RASILA, Valeria

Rowing Eight With Coxswain (8+): Men
Gold   East Germany
Silver   Great Britain
Bronze   USSR

Rowing Eight With Coxswain (8+): Women
Gold   East Germany
Silver   USSR
Bronze   Romania

Rowing Four Without Coxswain (4-): Men
Gold   East Germany
Silver   USSR
Bronze   Great Britain

Rowing Four-oared Shell With Coxswain: Men
Gold   East Germany
Silver   USSR
Bronze   Poland

Rowing Four-oared Shell With Coxswain: Women
Gold   East Germany
Silver   Bulgaria
Bronze   USSR

Rowing Pair Without Coxswain (2-): Women
Gold   East Germany   STEINDORF, Ute
Gold   East Germany   KLIER, Cornelia
Silver   Poland   DLUZEWSKA, Malgorzata
Silver   Poland   KOSCIANSKA, Czeslawa
Bronze   Bulgaria   KELBETCHEVA-BARBULOVA, Siika
Bronze   Bulgaria   GRUITCHEVA-KUBATOVA, Stoyanka

Rowing Pair-oared Shell With Coxswain: Men

Gold	East Germany	JÄHRLING, Harald
Gold	East Germany	ULRICH, Friedrich-Wilhelm
Gold	East Germany	SPOHR, Georg
Silver	USSR	PEREVERZEV, Viktor
Silver	USSR	KRIUCHKIN, Gennadi
Silver	USSR	LUKYANOV, Aleksandr
Bronze	Yugoslavia	MRDULJAS, Dusko
Bronze	Yugoslavia	CELENT, Zlatko
Bronze	Yugoslavia	REIC, Josip

Rowing Quadruple Sculls With Coxswain: Women

Gold	East Germany	
Silver	USSR	
Bronze	Bulgaria	

Rowing Quadruple Sculls With Coxswain: Men

Gold	East Germany	
Silver	USSR	
Bronze	Bulgaria	

Rowing Single Sculls (1x): Men

Gold	Finland	KARPPINEN, Pertti
Silver	USSR	YAKUSHA, Vasili
Bronze	East Germany	KERSTEN, Peter

Rowing Single Sculls (1x): Women

Gold	Romania	TOMA, Sanda
Silver	USSR	DUMCHEVA, Antonina
Bronze	East Germany	SCHRÖTER, Martina

Sailing 470–two Person Dinghy: Men

Gold	Brazil	SOARES, Marcos Pinto Rizzo
Gold	Brazil	PENIDO, Eduardo Henrique
Silver	East Germany	BOROWSKI, Jörn
Silver	East Germany	SWENSSON, Egbert
Bronze	Finland	LINDGREN, Jouko
Bronze	Finland	TALLBERG, Georg

Sailing Fleet/match Race Keelboat Open (Soling): Mixed

Gold	Denmark	JENSEN, Poul Richard Hoj
Gold	Denmark	BANDOLOWSKI, Valdemar
Gold	Denmark	HANSEN, Erik Hermann
Silver	USSR	BUDNIKOV, Boris
Silver	USSR	BUDNIKOV, Aleksandr
Silver	USSR	POLYAKOV, Nikolai
Bronze	Greece	BOUDOURIS, Anastassios
Bronze	Greece	GAVRILIS, Anastassios
Bronze	Greece	RAPANAKIS, Aristidis

Sailing Flying Dutchman: Mixed

Gold	Spain	ABASCAL GARCIA, Alejandro
Gold	Spain	NOGUER CASTELLVI, Miguel
Silver	Ireland	WILKINS, David
Silver	Ireland	WILKINSON, James
Bronze	Hungary	DETRE, Szabolcs
Bronze	Hungary	DETRE, Zsolt

Sailing Single-handed Dinghy (Finn): Men

Gold	Finland	RECHARDT, Esko
Silver	Austria	MAYRHOFER, Wolfgang
Bronze	USSR	BALASHOV, Andrei

Sailing Tornado–Multihull: Mixed

Gold	Brazil	WELTER, Alexandre
Gold	Brazil	BJORKSTROM, Lars Sigurd
Silver	Denmark	DUE, Peter
Silver	Denmark	KJERGARD, Per
Bronze	Sweden	MARSTRÖM, Göran
Bronze	Sweden	RAGNARSSON, Jörgen

Sailing Two-person Keelboat Open (Star): Mixed

Gold	USSR	MANKIN, Valentyn
Gold	USSR	MUZYCHENKO, Aleksandr
Silver	Austria	RAUDASCHL, Hubert
Silver	Austria	FERSTL, Karl
Bronze	Italy	GORLA, Giorgio
Bronze	Italy	PERABONI, Alfio

Shooting 25m Rapid Fire Pistol (60 Shots): Mixed

Gold	Romania	ION, Corneliu
Silver	East Germany	WIEFEL, Jürgen
Bronze	Austria	PETRITSCH, Gerhard

Shooting 50m Pistol (60 Shots): Mixed

Gold	USSR	MELENTIEV, Aleksandr
Silver	East Germany	VOLLMAR, Harald
Bronze	Bulgaria	DIAKOV, Lubtcho

Shooting 50m Rifle 3 Positions (3x40 Shots): Mixed

Gold	USSR	VLASOV, Viktor
Silver	East Germany	HARTSTEIN, Bernd
Bronze	Sweden	JOHANSSON, Sven

Shooting 50m Rifle Prone (60 Shots): Mixed

Gold	Hungary	VARGA, Karoly
Silver	East Germany	HEILFORT, Hellfried
Bronze	Bulgaria	ZAPRIANOV, Petar

Shooting 50m Running Target (30+30 Shots): Mixed

Gold	USSR	SOKOLOV, Igor
Silver	East Germany	PFEFFER, Thomas
Bronze	USSR	GAZOV, Aleksandr

Shooting Skeet (125 Targets): Mixed

Gold	Denmark	RASMUSSEN, Hans Kjeld
Silver	Swededn	CARLSSON, Lars-Göran
Bronze	Cuba	CASTRILLO GARCIA, Roberto

Shooting Trap (125 Targets): Mixed

Gold	Italy	GIOVANNETTI, Luciano
Silver	USSR	YAMBULATOV, Rustam
Bronze	East Germany	DAMME, Jörg

Swimming 100m Backstroke: Men
Gold	Sweden	BARON, Bengt
Silver	USSR	KUZNETSOV, Viktor
Bronze	USSR	DOLGOV, Vladimir

Swimming 100m Backstroke: Women
Gold	East Germany	REINISCH, Rica
Silver	East Germany	KLEBER, Ina
Bronze	East Germany	RIEDEL, Petra

Swimming 100m Breaststroke: Men
Gold	Great Britain	GOODHEW, Dunkan
Silver	USSR	MISKAROV, Arsen
Bronze	Australia	EVANS, Peter

Swimming 100m Breaststroke: Women
Gold	East Germany	GEWENIGER, Ute
Silver	USSR	VASILKOVA, Elvira
Bronze	Denmark	NIELSSON, Susanne Schultz

Swimming 100m Butterfly: Men
Gold	Sweden	ARVIDSSON, Pär
Silver	East Germany	PYTTEL, Roger
Bronze	Spain	LOPEZ-ZUBERO PURCELL, David

Swimming 100m Butterfly: Women
Gold	East Germany	METSCHUCK, Caren
Silver	East Germany	POLLACK, Andrea
Bronze	East Germany	KNACKE, Christiane

Swimming 100m Freestyle: Men
Gold	East Germany	WOITHE, Jörg
Silver	Sweden	HOLMERTZ, Per
Bronze	Sweden	JOHANSSON, Per

Swimming 100m Freestyle: Women
Gold	East Germany	KRAUSE, Barbara
Silver	East Germany	METSCHUCK, Caren
Bronze	East Germany	DIERS, Ines

Swimming 1500m Freestyle: Men
Gold	USSR	SALNIKOV, Vladimir
Silver	USSR	CHAEV, Aleksandr
Bronze	Australia	METZKER, Maxwell

Swimming 200m Backstroke: Men
Gold	Hungary	WLADAR, Sandor
Silver	Hungary	VERRASZTO, Zoltan
Bronze	Australia	KERRY, Mark

Swimming 200m Backstroke: Women
Gold	East Germany	REINISCH, Rica
Silver	East Germany	POLIT, Cornelia
Bronze	East Germany	TREIBER, Birgit

Swimming 200m Breaststroke: Men
Gold	USSR	ZHULPA, Robertas
Silver	Hungary	VERMES, Alban
Bronze	USSR	MISKAROV, Arsen

Swimming 200m Breaststroke: Women
Gold	USSR	KACHUSHITE, Lina
Silver	USSR	VARGANOVA, Svetlana
Bronze	USSR	BOGDANOVA, Yulia

Swimming 200m Butterfly: Men
Gold	USSR	FESENKO, Sergei
Silver	Great Britain	HUBBLE, Philip
Bronze	East Germany	PYTTEL, Roger

Swimming 200m Butterfly: Women
Gold	East Germany	GEISSLER, Ines
Silver	East Germany	SCHÖNROCK, Sybille
Bronze	Australia	FORD, Michelle

Swimming 200m Freestyle: Men
Gold	USSR	KOPLYAKOV, Sergei
Silver	USSR	KRYLOV, Andrei
Bronze	Australia	BREWER, Graeme

Swimming 200m Freestyle: Women
Gold	East Germany	KRAUSE, Barbara
Silver	East Germany	DIERS, Ines
Bronze	East Germany	SCHMIDT, Carmela

Swimming 400m Freestyle: Men
Gold	USSR	SALNIKOV, Vladimir
Silver	USSR	KRYLOV, Andrei
Bronze	USSR	STUKOLKIN, Ivar

Swimming 400m Freestyle: Women
Gold	East Germany	DIERS, Ines
Silver	East Germany	SCHNEIDER, Petra
Bronze	East Germany	SCHMIDT, Carmela

Swimming 400m Individual Medley: Men
Gold	USSR	SIDORENKO, Aleksandr
Silver	USSR	FESENKO, Sergei
Bronze	Hungary	VERRASZTO, Zoltan

Swimming 400m Individual Medley: Women
Gold	East Germany	SCHNEIDER, Petra
Silver	Great Britain	DAVIES, Sharron Elizabeth
Bronze	Poland	CZOPEK, Agnieszka

Swimming 4x100m Freestyle Relay: Women
Gold	East Germany
Silver	Sweden
Bronze	Netherlands

Swimming 4x100m Medley Relay: Men
Gold   Australia
Silver USSR
Bronze Great Britain

Swimming 4x100m Medley Relay: Women
Gold   East Germany
Silver Great Britain
Bronze USSR

Swimming 4x200m Freestyle Relay: Men
Gold   USSR
Silver East Germany
Bronze Brazil

Swimming 800m Freestyle: Women
Gold   Australia   FORD, Michelle
Silver East Germany   DIERS, Ines
Bronze East Germany   ÄHNE, Heike

Volleyball: Men
Gold   USSR
Silver Bulgaria
Bronze Romania

Volleyball: Women
Gold   USSR
Silver East Germany
Bronze Bulgaria

Water Polo: Men
Gold   USSR
Silver Yugoslavia
Bronze Hungary

Weightlifting + 110kg, Total (Super Heavyweight): Men
Gold   USSR   RAKHMANOV, Sultan
Silver East Germany   HEUSER, Jürgen
Bronze Poland   RUTKOWSKI, Tadeusz

Weightlifting–52kg, Total (Flyweight): Men
Gold   USSR   OSMONALIEV, Kanybek
Silver North Korea   HO, Bong Chol
Bronze North Korea   HAN, Gyong Si

Weightlifting–56kg, Total (Bantamweight): Men
Gold   Cuba   NUNEZ AGUIAR, Daniel
Silver USSR   SARKISIAN, Yurik
Bronze Poland   DEMBONCZYK, Tadeus

Weightlifting 100–110kg, Total (Heavyweight): Men
Gold   USSR   TARANENKO, Leonid
Silver Bulgaria   CHRISTOV, Valentin
Bronze Hungary   SZALAI, György

Weightlifting 56–60kg, Total (Featherweight): Men
Gold   USSR   MAZIN, Viktor
Silver Bulgaria   DIMITROV, Stefan
Bronze Poland   SEWERYN, Marek

Weightlifting 60–67.5kg, Total (Lightweight): Men
Gold   Bulgaria   RUSEV, Yanko
Silver East Germany   KUNZ, Joachim
Bronze Bulgaria   PASHEV, Mincho

Weightlifting 67.5–75kg, Total (Middleweight): Men
Gold   Bulgaria   ZLATEV, Asen
Silver USSR   PERVI, Aleksandr
Bronze Bulgaria   KOLEV, Nedelcho

Weightlifting 75–82.5kg, Total (Light-heavyweight): Men
Gold   USSR   VARDANIAN, Yurik
Silver Bulgaria   BLAGOEV, Blagoi
Bronze Czechoslovakia POLIACIK, Dusan

Weightlifting 82.5–90kg, Total (Middle-heavyweight): Men
Gold   Hungary   BACZAKO, Peter
Silver Hungary   LEKSANDROV, Rumen
Bronze East Germany   MANTEK, Frank

Weightlifting 90–100kg, Total (First-heavyweight): Men
Gold   Czechoslovakia ZAREMBA, Ota
Silver USSR   NIKITIN, Igor
Bronze Cuba   BLANCO FERNANDEZ, Alberto

Wrestling Freestyle + 100kg (Super Heavyweight): Men
Gold   USSR   ANDIEV, Soslan
Silver Hungary   BALLA, Jozsef
Bronze Poland   SANDUSSRKI, Adam

Wrestling Freestyle–48kg (Light-flyweight): Men
Gold   Italy   POLLIO, Claudio
Silver North Korea   JANG, Se Hong
Bronze USSR   KORNILAEV, Sergei

Wrestling Freestyle 48–52kg (Flyweight): Men
Gold   USSR   BELOGLAZOV, Anatoli
Silver Poland   STECYK, Wladyslaw
Bronze Bulgaria   SELIMOV, Nermedin

Wrestling Freestyle 52–57kg (Bantamweight): Men
Gold   USSR   BELOGLAZOV, Sergei
Silver North Korea   LI, Ho Pyong
Bronze Mongolia   OUINBOLD, Dugarsuren

Wrestling Freestyle 57–62kg (featherweight): Men
Gold   USSR   ABUSHEV, Magomedgasan
Silver Bulgaria   DOUKOV, Mikho
Bronze Greece   HADJIIOANNIDIS, Georgios

Wrestling Freestyle 62–68kg (Lightweight): Men

Gold	USSR	ABSAIDOV, Saipulla
Silver	Bulgaria	YANKOV, Ivan
Bronze	Yugoslavia	SEJDI, Saban

Wrestling Freestyle 68–74kg (Welterweight): Men

Gold	Bulgaria	RAICHEV, Valentin
Silver	Mongolia	DAVAAJAV, Jamtsying
Bronze	Czechoslovakia	KARABIN, Dan

Wrestling Freestyle 74–82kg (Middleweight): Men

Gold	Bulgaria	ABILOV, Ismail
Silver	USSR	ARATSILOV, Magomedkhan
Bronze	Hungary	KOVACS, Istvan

Wrestling Freestyle 82–90kg (Light-heavyweight): Men

Gold	USSR	OGANISIAN, Sanasar
Silver	East Germany	NEUPERT, Uwe
Bronze	Poland	CICHON, Aleksander

Wrestling Freestyle 90–100kg (Heavyweight): Men

Gold	USSR	MATE, Ilia
Silver	Bulgaria	CHERVENKOV, Slavcho
Bronze	Czechoslovakia	STRNISKO, Julius

Wrestling Greco-roman + 100kg (Super Heavyweight): Men

Gold	USSR	KOLCHINSKY, Aleksandr
Silver	Bulgaria	TOMOV, Aleksandr
Bronze	Lebanon	BCHARA, Hassan

Wrestling Greco-roman 48kg (Light-flyweight): Men

Gold	USSR	USHKEMPIROV, Zhaksylyk
Silver	Romania	ALEXANDRU, Constantin
Broze	Hungary	SERES, Ferenc

Wrestling Greco-roman 48–52kg (Flyweight): Men

Gold	USSR	BLAGIDZE, Vakhtang
Silver	Hungary	RACZ, Lajos
Bronze	Hungary	MLADENOV, Mladen

Wrestling Greco-roman 52–57kg (Bantamweight): Men

Gold	USSR	SERIKOV, Shamil Moscow 1980
Silver	Poland	LIPIEN, Josef
Bronze	Sweden	LJUNGBECK, Benni

Wrestling Greco-roman 57–62kg (Featherweight): Men

Gold	Greece	MIGIAKIS, Stilianos
Silver	Hungary	TOTH, Istvan
Bronze	USSR	KRAMORENKO, Boris

Wrestling Greco-roman 62–68kg (Lightweight): Men

Gold	Romania	RUSU, Stefan
Silver	Poland	SUPRON, Andrzej
Bronze	Sweden	SKIOLD, Lars-Erik

Wrestling Greco-roman 68–74kg (Welterweight): Men

Gold	Hungary	KOCSIS, Ferenc
Silver	USSR	BYKOV, Anatoli
Bronze	Finland	HUHTALA, Mikko

Wrestling Greco-roman 74–82kg (Middleweight): Men

Gold	USSR	KORBAN, Gennadi
Silver	Poland	DOLGOWICZ, Jan
Bronze	Bulgaria	PAVLOV, Pavel

Wrestling Greco-roman 82–90kg (Light-heavyweight): Men

Gold	Hungary	NOTTNY, Norbert
Silver	USSR	KANYGIN, Igor
Bronze	Romania	DICU, Petre

Wrestling Greco-roman 90–100kg (Heavyweight): Men

Gold	Bulgaria	RAIKOV, Georgi
Silver	Poland	BIERLA, Roman
Bronze	Romania	ANDREI, Vasile

Linda Cornelius Waltman – 1980 U.S. Olympic Pentathlon Team

Linda Cornelius Waltman
Pentathlon

The first thing Linda Cornelius Waltman wanted to do was call her parents. "They were not able to be at the trials," she emotionally recalls. "I'll always remember calling my parents—who were, basically, uneducated, poor people—and saying, 'Your daughter made an Olympic team.'"

Linda Cornelius Waltman enjoyed her greatest Olympic triumph in the trials, on the track at the University of Oregon in Eugene, and not in Central Lenin Stadium in Moscow. "They gave us a dozen roses and then we took our victory lap," Waltman recalls. "It is probably the closest feeling that I would've ever had to being in the Olympics, because everybody in that stadium stood up and they never stopped clapping from the time they announced you and the three of us took our victory lap. They cheered and stayed on their feet the entire time."

The fans in Eugene lustily cheered that day because they knew, as the athletes did, that the U.S. Olympic team would not be traveling to Moscow later in the summer for the XXII Olympiad. "For me, it was a once-in-a-lifetime shot," Waltman says.

The journey toward earning that once-in-a-lifetime started in Fort Worth, Texas. "I remember my dad coached me in high school," she says. "He would get off of work at General Motors and we would go up to this four-lane cinder track. He grew up in a one-room schoolhouse in the Ozark Mountains. This was a man who just loved his daughter. He didn't have a knowledge of track or a fancy camera or anything to train with. He just did what he thought was right. He went out there and put in hour after hour after hour with me. It's amazing that I made the team."

Waltman was from a generation of female athletes that did not enjoy today's benefits of Title IX. Her R.L. Pascal High School didn't even field a girl's track team until she was an upperclassman. "Prior to that I ran on summer teams, clubs, and participated in AAU Track and Field and other club track," Waltman remembers. "Through the efforts of several people, my father being one of them, they continued to push the Fort Worth athletic director to implement track for girls in high school. So, when I was a junior, they implemented a pilot program in five high schools to see if the girls really could run and like it."

In 1975, Waltman's senior year, all the high schools in the Fort Worth area offered track and field for girls. "You could do three running and two field, or two running and three field, and that was the maximum," she recalls. "Every single meet I went to I did the maximum amount of events I could do. My specialties were the quarter-mile and long jump. My senior year, I set a national high school record in the long jump at the state meet."

Not having money to further her education following high school, a full scholarship was the only way the burgeoning pentathlete could afford to go to college. Ideally, Waltman wanted to stay close to home and compete in the Southwest Conference. "My dream was to go to the University of Texas, but no Southwest Conference school offered full scholarships for women," Waltman explains. "So, I ended up going to the University of Nevada, Las Vegas on a full athletic scholarship."

With the burden of having to pay tuition off her shoulders, the UNLV track coach asked Waltman about her goals. She said she wanted to make the Olympic team. Since she had competed in five events in high school, her coach reasoned she would become a pentathlete. Waltman enthusiastically accepted that challenge in 1976, the first step of which was learning to hurdle and throw shot put. So she embarked on learning two new disciplines to accompany three others—high jump, long jump and running the 800-meter.

Still wanting to return to her native Texas, Waltman decided to leave the Nevada desert. "Texas A&M said they had never offered a female athlete a full athletic scholarship, [but] they told me they wanted me," she says. "So I applied to transfer and remain on eligibility. It was approved and I transferred to A&M my sophomore year."

At Texas A&M, Waltman not only became the first woman in school history to receive an athletic scholarship, but she was also the first female student-athlete on scholarship in the entire Southwest Conference. "A lot of it back then was you had to be real self-motivated," Waltman says. "There was a lot of pressure, I guess, to perform well. My vision was still the Olympic team, and I got a lot of support there."

With her style of training established from her early days working with her father, Waltman never really needed the push of a coach's words. When she arrived on the Aggie campus, the Athletic Department had just allotted a paid position for a full-time track and field coach. The year before, the coach had been a volunteer and member of the school's cross country team. The new coach didn't know much, so Waltman was told to just continue her previous training regime. "A lot of what I did was on natural talent," Waltman says. "My fiancé actually ended up coaching me. I was never filmed—there was not a lot available to us back then. You had to use a lot of common sense. Basically, he coached me the year I made the Olympic team and we squeezed in workouts between school and work."

Having graduated in 1979, Waltman needed financial help to continue her pursuit of Olympic glory. "In 1980, my husband was still in his senior year at A&M and we had to squeeze in workouts," Waltman recalls. "Many times during the day, between classes, we were out there by ourselves. A&M supported me. The athletic director for women at the time, Kay Don, went around to the Aggie clubs all over the state and told them, 'We have a girl who wants to make the Olympic team and we have to support her.' She actually got donations from Aggie clubs that went into a fund, and she created a checking account that funded my training and travel for the year so that I could commit most of my time to working out."

But then came the boycott. Waltman's "happily-ever-after" ending to her Olympic story concluded in Eugene, Ore., as she circled the track in the victory of realizing her dream. The 1980 Olympic Summer Games in Moscow would have been her only chance to test herself at the highest level of competition. Her husband had been accepted to law school in Lubbock, Texas, and they were moving on with their lives. "For me," Waltman says, "that was the one chance I had. One of us had to go to work, so I started teaching and coaching."

After moving to Lubbock, she tried to regain the spirit that carried her to work toward Moscow. Unfortunately, the 23-year-old couldn't muster the energy to train and sacrifice four more years. "I remember that Fall thinking I would start training again. I was running and trying to do some things, but I could never get it back. There was a sadness, and I just couldn't get that high again that soon. For me it was the end of my athletic career, and I moved on with my life."

Waltman has since been inducted into the Texas A&M Hall of Fame, and now works as the superintendent for Public Parks and Recreation in Boerne, Texas, and has served as commissioner of the Texas Amateur Athletic Federation for the past 23 years.

Despite the loss of a dream, Waltman contends that losing the chance to compete in the Olympics has not been the biggest disappointment of her life. "As you become a mature person and lose friends to illness, those are things that are big disappointments," she says. "Has it been a big disappointment? It's up there. I had never made an Olympic team. Several of the others had made several Olympic teams prior to '80, and they knew what it was all about. I don't know that I had that understanding at the time. I have since gotten that understanding of all the things that I've missed, and it angers me. I'm very angry because it shouldn't have happened."

Waltman, a mother of four, ponders her missed opportunity each time the world gathers to celebrate youth and sport every four winters and summers. "I don't think I've ever watched a Winter or Summer Olympic Games, and seen the American team march in, that I don't think about missing out on that. Every time," she says. "It never feels any better. It's really not about what you do at the Olympics. It's being a part of the Olympics. You've heard that statement before and it really is true. That is something you shouldn't take away from an athlete who's given so much and worked really hard."

Though she doesn't dwell on it, the ultimate sadness that resides in the recesses of her soul reappears when she's reminded about her experience in 1980. "I don't feel like one of the lucky ones, that's for sure. It's just sad. It's being unique without really wanting that uniqueness."

In the end, though, she is proud. Proud to have accomplished a goal that, by today's standards, is probably unachievable in the way Waltman pursued it. "My parents were both working-class folks. They did not have high school degrees, and they worked in factories. I just really wanted to do well to bring honor to them. Along the way, that became very important to me. I wanted to do something with my life, and I knew my route was going to be through athletics. That's why I pursued that vision of a scholarship with the next thing on the list being the Olympics. That is the ultimate—to make the Olympic team."

Thomas Schuler – 1980 U.S. Olympic Cycling Team

Thomas Schuler
Cycling

"I just tell people, if they ask, that I was in the Olympics once." 1980 Olympic cyclist Thomas Schuler inadvertently misspeaks a sentiment which he doesn't have to follow with an explanation. "Or, I 'was an Olympian.' And they ask me, 'What year?' And I tell them '80. If they don't ask anymore I leave it at that. If they say 'Where was it?' I tell them Moscow. If they are the right age they remember."

Schuler knew what a big deal the Olympics were to Americans, even though he wasn't overly upset about the boycott. Most people would think an athlete would be crushed to fall so closely short of competing in the Olympics and realizing a lifelong dream—especially since, as a 19-year-old would-be college freshman, Schuler was named as the first alternate on the 1976 U.S. Olympic cycling team and would later suffer the same fate in 1984. "There are people like me that only had that one chance," Schuler explains with little emotion. "I was not as adamant then about being denied that opportunity. More so now as I realize the Olympics *are* a special thing no matter how long a professional career you have. The Olympics are special."

For Schuler, cycling was just one of many sports he enjoyed while growing up in the Detroit suburb of Birmingham, Mich. "Generally, I did sports all through school. I got into cycling by just enjoying riding bikes with my friends, the neighborhood gang."

Schuler, like lots of kids living in suburbia in the 1960s and '70s, occupied his time playing sports and dreaming about athletic heroes such as Olympian Jim Ryun, baseball Hall of Famer Al Kaline and hockey legend Gordie Howe.

"I did all the sports I could—football, baseball, wrestling, track and field, then soccer in high school. And hockey—I played a lot of hockey growing up," Schuler says. Along the way, when he got more serious about cycling, the names John Howard and John Allis, two American cyclists finding some fame on the roads, also became important to him.

It wasn't until Schuler was a young teenager that cycling and the thought of the Olympics and beyond caught on with him. "I was always competitive in whatever sport or activity I was doing, so I got hooked up with the Wolverine Sports Club," Schuler remembers. "It's one of the older, more established clubs in the United States that has produced many national [and] world champions and Olympic medallists."

Schuler participated and competed with the club casually until his junior year in high school. At that point, cycling became more than a pastime for the future Cycling Hall of Fame inductee. A bout with mononucleosis during the track season left Schuler, who was a miler, on the sidelines for the season. "Not being able to run track, I focused a little more on cycling that year," Schuler recalls. "I got a little more serious, and by the time my senior year rolled around I was very serious because I had had some success around the Midwest. I went to the National Championships in 1973."

After graduating from high school in 1974, Schuler decided he would forego the start of his college education at the University of Michigan and stay closer to home, where he could focus on training and eventually trying out for the 1976 U.S. Olympic Cycling team. "The '76 trials were in Saranac Lake [N.Y.] and I got ready and had a good series of races," Schuler says. "I won one race. I was third in two and crashed out of another one. I probably should've made the '76 team, but I was one of the younger ones. The coach had discretion in the selection so he made me an alternate."

The 19-year-old Schuler had his first sniff of what his life might someday become. "Leading up to '80 I was sure that I wanted to make that team, since

I was so close to making the team in '76," Schuler says. "My expectations were not so much that I was going to make that '76 team. I was on the cusp. Leading up to '80, I was finishing up my college and participating in all of the nationalteam stuff.

"All of my other national team peers had been living in Colorado Springs at the training center for two or three years. I wasn't interested in doing that. I was interested in finishing my college. A lot of my peers weren't going to college—they were just full-time cycling. I was determined to finish my undergraduate degree and still try out for the Olympic team."

So it wasn't until after graduating from Michigan in the spring of 1980 that Schuler moved to Colorado Springs, lived in the dorms and began training in full sight of the Olympic coaches. By June, when the Olympic Trials took place, it had been pronounced to the world the U.S. would not send a team to Moscow. For Schuler, who had committed himself since 1976 to return to the Olympics, his attitude was ambivalent at best. "During that time, my disappointment of the boycott sort of evaporated," Schuler says. "In cycling, like a lot of other sports in the Olympics, the professional side of the sport is what athletes are striving for. I'm probably more disappointed now than at the time because I was so focused on being professional. After '80, I raced for another 10 years, and those were probably my best years."

Schuler and his U.S. cycling teammates so quickly moved on from the disappointment of not competing in the Olympics that they even bypassed the gala thrown for the U.S. team by President Carter in Washington, D.C. "There was a group of us who had better things to do than go to that ceremony. We were pursuing our sport." For them, professional cycling was the goal of their game. The Olympics was mostly a nice road to making a living.

Still, Schuler and his peers kept their amateur status through 1984 to finally get to compete in the Olympics, to be held in Los Angeles. For Schuler, it didn't work out. His life in Chicago now included his future wife, as well as a steady job—moving back to Colorado Springs to train was not part of his plan, and it probably cost him a spot on the '84 team.

Though he went to the trials that year, Schuler was pretty well convinced he would not be racing in the Olympics. He reasoned that the race points he accumulated should have been enough to put him on the team, but he did not have a good relationship with the coach, who had the final say as to who would represent the U.S. in Los Angeles.

Again, Schuler's mild disappointment was quelled in 1985 as he and his teammates all turned professional, comprising the 7-Eleven cycling team which they had originally organized in 1981. His ultimate goal was realized.

Today, Schuler is still unsure about whether the boycott of 1980 was necessary or useful. "I didn't disagree with Carter because I don't know if I would've done it differently," Schuler says. "It was the Cold War and almost appropriate at the time. Though, I didn't agree with it either. I wasn't adamant or infuriated about it. I felt bad for some of the athletes that weren't going to be able to continue with their sport for another four years.

"Now it is more of a disappointment that I never got to do it, but at the time I was really focusing on being professional. We all knew that even if we got to compete in the Olympics, that really wasn't the pinnacle of the sport. I knew what the Olympics were and what it meant to Americans. It was a big deal to me personally but among my peer group it was, 'That's great but what's next?' "

"What's next" for Schuler turned out to be a professional career racing bicycles and founding Team Sports Inc., a sports management company that focuses on cycling, mountain biking, triathlon and inline skating. But after sending nearly 30 clients of his to the Olympic Games over the years and having several of them become medal winners, Schuler knows what he missed in 1980. "Opening Ceremonies are probably the one thing I regret about not having an Olympic experience. I would've liked to have experienced that maybe even more than the competition."

Message to President Carter

In certain respects, the group of 25 U.S. athletes that sued the United States Olympic Committee on behalf of their teammates for their right to participate in the 1980 Summer Olympic Games made their statement against President Jimmy Carter's and the USOC's decision to boycott. Of course, not all of the 1980 team agreed with the lawsuit, just as not all of the team agreed with the boycott. Though their sentiments were expressed in the courtroom, many of the rank and file never truly got the opportunity—or, out of respect, took the opportunity—to ask President Carter about the decision that had such a profound impact on their lives.

Nearly three decades and seven Summer Olympic Games later, some members of the 1980 team were asked what they would say to President Carter if they had the chance to speak with him today:

"Athletes are humanitarians. We are the voice of the people and don't have political motives. We don't have other hidden agendas. We just want to do the best at what we can do. I think other very, very good people sacrificed a lot for this. Again, I want to footnote this by saying it is nothing compared to people who have given up their lives or risked their lives. It is a small price to pay. [But] it was the wrong direction to take. Politics and sports. If anything, you need more sports in the world and people to cross those boundaries and share what we have in common."
—**Craig Beardsley**

"I read a lot of stuff about the world and see all the things Jimmy Carter has done as a humanitarian in that vein, and his intentions are noble and pure. He won a Nobel Peace Prize and he's a good man. That's how I feel about him. I read his book *Palestine: Peace Not Apartheid*, which I enjoyed tremendously. And I'm respectful of him certainly as a president and human being."
—**Carol Blazejowski**

"I had an opportunity to say something to him when I met him in the White House. You know, I think looking at it and taking a mature approach to it, I would say 'Doggone, why didn't you think through the decision a little bit more and realize who you were ultimately impacting?' It's the same thing with the war [in Iraq]. All of these families are losing loved ones. We really need to think through these decisions and the impact and whether we can ultimately achieve the political agenda that will be positive for the country. I don't have any bitterness towards [Carter] personally. It's more the decision and the decision-making process that led him to the boycott. I think Jimmy Carter has been a much stronger politician now and someone who has been able to make an impact in the country in a positive way much more than when he was in office. His heart was in the right place, but the decision-making process wasn't."
—**Lisa Buese**

"I believe he was doing what he thought was best for the country. Now, the fact is I don't believe it ended up *being* the best solution for the country, because what he was trying to accomplish didn't even happen. It didn't affect [the Soviets] because we didn't go to the Olympics. I don't know. I don't know what I would say to him, honestly. I think he was doing what he thought was best for the country, but he destroyed so many dreams by using the Olympics. It's supposed to be a non-political part of the world."

—Luci Collins

"I would say it was a mistake. It does not mean that we're not Americans and we don't understand the big decisions that are made and why they are made. It is not anti-American. I can go back and look at it historically, retrospectively, and say it would've been better to let the athletes go and ask to leave every medal back in Moscow. You trained your whole life to prove and show everyone you were the best in the world. I was up for one or two medals and I would've left them there, easily, in exchange for the ability to go and compete. I know those were big, hard decisions but…."

—Ron Galimore

"I just think he made a mistake and deprived us athletes the opportunity to participate."   **—Gwen Gardner**

"What I would say to President Carter today is that I respected his decision as the president of the United States. However, my research has documented that nothing changed relative to the flow of money. The measly little athletes were the pawns, and the grain embargo on the farmers, who had no voice, were the pawns [in his attempt] to make a political statement that meant nothing in the end. In the end, all of the computer technology, the trade, all of that, never missed a blink."   **—Brian Gust**

"I don't know all the political things that were involved but I probably would ask him, 'Do you think you made the right decision? Do you think it was a mistake? And how would that have changed if we had gone? What would've happened differently?'"

—Bill Hanzlik

"I'd tell him it was a big mistake and they should've let us go and get our medals and then boycott by not being in the Opening and Closing ceremonies. The Russians were known to cheat anyhow. In Moscow, during the track and field, they had these big doors they used to open up when the Russians were throwing the javelin and then close them when others were throwing. So, you know, that was not good. It was a big mistake and it could've been done so much better."

—David Kimes

"I don't know what I could say. He had a very difficult job at the time. I don't know why he thought that was the answer. Or why he thought it would get the response he wanted. Once you say it, you can't take it back."

—Amy Koopman

"I respect his decision. I think he was doing what he thought was the right thing to do. I don't think he truly understood the scope of that problem from the athletes' perspective. I can't begrudge him for trying to lead the country and do what he thought was in the best interest of our country. I would guess that he would look back on it and realize it wasn't such a great decision, but I don't really know that for sure. It's one of those things. In his position, he thought he was doing the best he could for the country. I wouldn't say anything that would be bitter. It is something in the past. I know it wasn't an individual decision on his part. He was counseled by several people and he made this decision thinking it was going to be an important part of the whole package of the things they were doing at the time."

—**Debbie Landreth**

"I honestly don't know. Inside I'm still so mad that I don't want to think about what I would say or do because it wouldn't be appropriate. I'm a teacher and I try to preach making the right decisions. So, I really shouldn't say."

—**Gene Mills**

"Butt out. The U.S. government has nothing to do with the sport. They don't support us financially. Never have and never will. He obviously wasn't an athlete, because anyone who has ever been involved in international athletics will realize the way we're going to bring this world together is by kids coming together to compete. As soon as the race is over, you're making new friends. You're meeting people from all over the world and this was supposed to be a coming together of nations, not a divide-and-separate. The Olympics are for the youth of the world to come together to play these games. If you want to beat me, you have to follow these rules and go for it. If you do, then great, congratulations, because I know you had to work really hard to do it. The thing that has always amazed me the most—we had an administration, or a guy, politician—that was supposed to see what things do to society. And follow what societal trends are doing. Didn't he just see the hockey team win? Didn't he just see people stopping their cars on the side of the road to cheer? The unification that that did to our country? I mean, what was he watching? How could he have missed that? And then to turn around and say, 'Things are going really well now.' The hostage crisis was in full swing. Our farmers couldn't trade their corn overseas. There was all kinds of political unrest. We don't want to feel good about anything again, so let's not go to the Olympics.

It was the most asinine thing I had ever heard of. He had no understanding of athletics and should've just stayed out of it."   —**Glenn Mills**

"There is no ill will. He took all the information he had at the time. I'm not a big fan of being a Monday-morning quarterback. Hindsight is a wonderful thing in this world, and he had to make a tough decision which I'm sure crushed him when he had to make a stand worldwide. And those people who want to say politics should never be mixed in with sports don't live in the real world. Politics has always been in sports. You don't think there were politics involved when Jesse Owens had to run in 1936 in front of Adolf Hitler? There sure was. There will always be politics in sports, and I believe Jimmy Carter made the best decision he could at the time. I'm not going to sit here and say he made a bad decision. I still say maybe because Don Paige did not go to the Olympics, maybe I spared one life in Afghanistan. And, if I did, I sleep really well at night because of that. It makes me feel good and proud."   —**Don Paige**

"There are so many things that go on behind the scenes and so many conversations that we as citizens are not aware of. The trust we place in our president, we have to honor and follow his judgment. Whatever decision he made I still support to this day."   —**Isiah Thomas**

"Could you rethink that one? It's really hard because I am a firm believer in whoever is the president, regardless of whether I think every decision they make is the decision I'd make, I'm pretty supportive. I didn't agree with it. I wish it could've been different. Ultimately, it didn't accomplish what he had hoped, but I feel like he made the best decision he felt at the time. You know, it was people's lives versus my dreams. How do you ever weigh that against one another? My response would be: Was there no other way? If not, then

I take it on the chin. Ultimately, what would his other choices have been? Would we have had to send troops there? My brother and sister were in the Marine Corps. Watching the war we're in now, I hate the thought of that. People having to risk their lives to defend us and what we believe in. So, if this was another way, to accomplish something without people losing their lives, then so be it."

—Sue Walsh

"Anything I said to him, it wouldn't make a difference. He'd probably still think he made the right decision. I don't think I would have harsh words for him. I don't think I would say anything harsh. No one has ever asked me that question before. Earlier, I would have said he made a mistake. I would probably still say, "You made a mistake.' I don't know. I don't hold grudges. I'm not one of those kinds of people."

—Linda Cornelius Waltman

Ron Galimore — 1980 U.S. Olympic Gymnastics Team

Ron Galimore
Gymnastics

Following the United States men's gymnastics Olympic Trials, NBC Sports commentator Bryant Gumbel approached 22-year-old Ron Galimore, who had just earned the right to represent the U.S. at the 1980 Summer Games in Moscow. Gumbel informed Galimore he was the first African-American to make a U.S. Olympic gymnastics team.

"I was shocked," admits Galimore more than 25 years later. "I was surprised because I didn't even think of it in those terms. I had such tunnel vision at that point, not even realizing I was a minority at most of the meets I went to, if not all of them. I was just having a great time. I just had fun with it. I was very focused."

At his Tallahassee, Fla., home in 1969, 11-year-old Ron Galimore mastered a running front flip, and then turned it around and started trying to flip backwards. That's when the rambunctious youngster's mother knew it was time to get him to an organized and safe environment to learn the tricks he had been teaching himself. "I think my mother decided to sign me up for a program so someone could teach me how to do it so I didn't kill myself," Galimore remembers. "She actually went to a city-run program at that time called the Tallahassee Tumbling Tots and asked if they accepted blacks. They said, 'By all means.' And I started my first gymnastics class on September 23, 1969, at 3:30 p.m."

From there, Galimore's tunnel vision did not include any thoughts of becoming the Jackie Robinson of men's gymnastics. "When I started out there weren't a lot of black gymnasts," Galimore says. "There were a couple.

Gymnasts like Mike Carter, who was originally from Philly and was a big reason I went to [Louisiana State University]. He made a couple of international teams, but I think he just missed making the Olympic team in 1976. He competed internationally on the national team. There were other collegiate gymnasts that inspired me. Mel Carr from the Temple [University] team. Michael Foster from LSU. There were a few, but the number was small without a doubt."

Despite the lack of same-race role models in gymnastics, Galimore's athletic prowess and desire to excel were never in question. "My father was an all-pro running back for the Chicago Bears who passed away when I was very young—five or six years old," Galimore says. "Sports were always in our family. Going to gymnastics was not something anyone in my family thought I would do. I loved sports, period. I loved watching anybody who was good at what they did. I can't say there was any one particular athlete in any sport that I said, 'I want to be just like him.' I was just enjoying myself and having a good time, trying to be the absolute best I could be. My goal was to make the Olympic team. I made that a goal at a young age."

Galimore was a sponge as he learned to maneuver his way around the disciplines that comprised the six Olympic events in men's gymnastics. Before long, the Galimores were looking for more in-depth training for Ron. "My mother, sister and I moved to Fort Lauderdale, Fla., for a while and left my brother in Tallahassee so that I could train under a gentleman by the name of Jack Miles," Galimore says. "I was in ninth grade, 10th grade. It was a little bit too much of a strain on my family to be apart, so I moved back during my junior year and trained under a gentleman by the name of Dan Gatsinos, a junior college gymnast and judge in Tallahassee."

Galimore blossomed under Gatsinos' tutelage and in 1976 was offered a scholarship to attend LSU. "I went to LSU for two years," Galimore says. "I won an NCAA title during my freshman year on floor exercises and during my sophomore year I won an NCAA championship in vaulting." Following those two successful seasons, he transferred to Iowa State, all while keeping his sights fixed on making the 1980 U.S. Olympic gymnastics team.

"Once I set my goal to make the Olympic team I had to focus on all six men's events, because in order to make the Olympic team you had to compete and be good on all of them," he explains. "I was among the best in the world in one or two events—floor exercise and vaulting—but I had other events I was weaker on and I had to concentrate on those as well. I had a lot of good supportive friends who were telling me the right things and encouraging me. From family, to friends, coaches and schoolmates, they were the ones who helped me believe that I could accomplish what I wanted."

Galimore's focus remained steadfast throughout the months leading to the Olympic Trials. As the trials moved closer, the U.S. media focused not only on the boycott, but also on some of the special athletes and their stories—stories the rest of the world would not get to hear. One of those athletes was Ron Galimore. "Those are things that I had no control over," he says. "I wanted to focus on the things I had control over. So, I didn't think about it very much at all."

When he finally made the team, Galimore knew it was a special accomplishment. "I was so excited and elated that I accomplished something that only six people every four years have the chance to achieve, let alone be the first African American to accomplish that. I was basking in patting myself on my back once I actually made the team."

Not fully comprehending the political situation, Galimore and his Olympic teammates took their consolation trip to Washington, D.C., as honored guests at the Kennedy Center. "I really didn't understand what it meant to march in the Opening Ceremony, what it meant to wear all the red, white and blue and how it really brings the country together," Galimore says. "You don't know what's been taken away from you. Then, they pull you all together and you see how much they put into trying to make you feel good about not going, and it all hits.

"It wasn't until they flew all of the Olympians to Washington, D.C., and gave a star-studded ceremony in the Kennedy Center that it really hit me what I had achieved. I started pouring down crying in the middle of that celebration. And it hit me like a brick that I had actually made it but I wasn't going to get to go. I started the sport at 11, and 11 years later I made the Olympic team and was told we can't go. It's like going to school for 11 years to become a doctor and then waking up one morning and being told you can't."

Galimore, like so many other members of this unheralded fraternity of athletes, suffered emotionally after the boycott. The hardship was compounded by not knowing if he had it in him to train for four more years and try to make the team again, and then compete at the highest level of the sport at 26 years old. "I don't think there was a morning, once I decided making the Olympic team was my goal, that I didn't wake up with that goal guiding me that day—what I did and didn't do, my diet, my training, what I put into my body. And the depression hit really hard at that point."

Not only had Galimore spent 11 years dreaming and working toward his Olympic ambition, he also had thought about what post-Olympic glory may have been in store for him. "My goal was to make an Olympic team, win a medal at the Olympic Games, and then maybe do some color commentary afterwards, perhaps make all kinds of money because it was so new and unique," Galimore says. "And all of sudden, I hit a brick wall. I didn't know what to do. I woke up and did not know what I wanted to do with my life. I obviously had to finish school, but it really took me five years before I was re-motivated into something."

Galimore headed to Los Angeles where he had some luck acting in commercials and doing stunt work, but his lost dream always managed to rear its head when talk turned to his credentials. "A lot of the comments I got back were, 'You're an Olympian, but you really didn't compete in the Olympics.' And that depressed me even more."

As his healing finally started to take hold in 1984, Galimore found himself in the production trucks of ABC Sports, which was televising the Olympic Summer Games from Los Angeles. Galimore was hired as a spotter identifying athletes on television during the broadcast. His colleagues in the truck didn't recognize who was sitting next to them. "I have red, white and blue in my blood, and I think that is part of what hit me as a truck spotter in 1984," remembers Galimore. "It hit me and I really realized a little of what had been taken away because I could've been a part of getting the nation that excited too. And I would've enjoyed that, not for the spotlight of being in front, but for being a part of pulling the country together. All races, creeds, backgrounds, cheering for USA. That's what the Olympics is all about."

It wasn't until Galimore and his future wife returned to Tallahassee that his five-year fog completely lifted. At that point he re-focused on helping others achieve their dreams by starting a gymnastics program. "I guess I finally woke up and realized if I was able to achieve making the Olympic team, I would be able to achieve something else that is big and great, and that is what I was put on Earth to achieve," Galimore says. "Either you can stay depressed or you can shift your gears and your energy. I decided to do the latter, and was excited about the gymnastics program we started. It was a good thing to go back home and give something back to the community, and that's what I did."

Today, Galimore continues to give back to his sport, serving as vice president of the men's program for USA Gymnastics. He admits to having thought about "what might have been" in the years immediately following 1980, but he does not begrudge his Olympic fate. Quite the contrary. "What it could've meant for me financially to be the first African-American gymnast to win a gold medal could've been huge if I had any personality to go along with it," he says. "And so, I thought about those things selfishly. I thought it was bad to think those things, but I felt it. I think I ran the gamut on all of that. Today it is different. I don't feel that way."

Almost 30 years removed from his days as a world-class gymnast, Galimore feels blessed with the perspective and wisdom that comes with age and experience. He feels no bitterness toward the politicians who rendered his aspirations moot. "It's still good to know that I was able to accomplish something like that. It makes me feel good and keeps me motivated. If I had it to do all over again, knowing the result would be the same, I would do the same thing. I would not hesitate. It has been said, a cliché that has been overused many times, 'It's not about the end result, it's about the journey.' And, you know, the journey that I experienced has given me the tools that I use every day, and I feel blessed and honored. There is no sadness in me today."

Debbie Landreth – 1980 U.S. Olympic Volleyball Team

Debbie Landreth
Volleyball

"It was huge. Absolutely huge," remembers women's volleyball player Debbie Landreth, at the realization that the United States Olympic Committee had decided to vote against sending an Olympic team to the Summer Games in Moscow in 1980.

"It was one of those things where—leading up to the final decision—there was this hope that somehow the decision was going to be reversed and the boycott really wasn't going to happen. It was crushing. It was devastating. We were on tour with the East Germans at the time. We had just finished playing a match and we found out about the decision and it was just so disappointing. Even though we knew there was a good likelihood of [boycotting], it's one of those things where we couldn't really prepare ourselves."

Landreth was dumbfounded, as were the other 10 members of the first American women's volleyball team to ever qualify for the Olympic Games. These volleyball pioneers had achieved a goal of qualifying for the Olympics by putting their lives on hold and moving to Colorado Springs as the first team to live and train full-time at the United States Olympic Training Center, a former military training base which would become the USOC administrative headquarters in July 1978.

Landreth and her teammates had moved to the facility in the spring of '78 and trained for half-a-year before embarking on a fall trip to the World Championships in the Soviet Union. "We had been together for only about six months and we ended up taking fifth at the World Championships," recalls Landreth, now the women's volleyball head coach at the University of

Notre Dame. "It was a pretty big jump, and we realized if we were fifth at the World Championships, we could certainly be one of the top eight teams to qualify for the Olympics. The World Championships were bigger; it was 24 teams and we took fifth, [and] we knew the best teams in the world were playing there. We could see the tangible results with just six months of training and we knew we could do it."

For Debbie Landreth, volleyball was not her first love. The thought of competing in an Olympic Games as a volleyball player was the furthest thing from her mind while growing up in El Segundo, Calif. The youngster was taken with softball and didn't become interested in volleyball until high school. "I played volleyball, basketball and softball in high school," Landreth recalls. "Between my sophomore and junior years, my high school volleyball coach, Barbara Bernlohr, asked me if I wanted to go to a volleyball camp in the summer. I thought that sounded fun so I went. That camp is what really ignited the fire within me to learn the sport of volleyball. I came back from that camp really excited and wanted to learn and get a lot better."

Landreth's natural athleticism combined with her new-found talent prompted her to ponder the possibility of someday making an Olympic team. "I think it was [during] the '72 Olympics, but we didn't have a team," she says. "USA didn't qualify. I thought it would be really cool to be on a USA team. In high school, I had this little spark of thinking, 'Wow, wouldn't that be cool?' But I never really knew how I would ever…It was a hope or dream that was never going to happen, but it was a nice thought."

The reality of making an Olympic team really took shape during Landreth's senior year in high school, when she made the junior national team. "It was when I started training with them that I realized this might be a good way to develop my skills and really make it to the Olympics. It became something that I knew could happen, as opposed to before when it was just a dream.

"I don't think my high school coach had any idea that I would take volleyball to the next level, but she was a good coach who wanted to give her players the best opportunity to learn more about the game. I think she knew I was an athlete who had some God-given talent and she wanted to help refine that. And, while my high school coach introduced me to the game and got me interested, it was Chuck Erbe, coach of the junior national team, who *really* taught me good, solid fundamental skills and gave me a solid foundation."

Landreth's path to the Olympics took a circuitous route after high school as she tried to balance the dream of competing at the highest level of her sport with securing an education for her life beyond the volleyball court.

Following high school, Landreth decided to attend El Camino Junior College. "I continued to train with the junior national team, and in the first semester, my first year out of high school, I had the opportunity to try out for the national team," she says. "So, I tried out for the national team and made the roster for the 1974 World Championships. The national team was pretty lacking at the time. No full-time training. You tried out, they brought people in and you practiced for a couple weeks together and then played teams that were in year-round training programs. I made the team and went to the World Championships and had my 18th birthday in Mexico. We ended up taking 12th out of 24 teams."

Only several years removed from her initial interest in the sport, Landreth was securely on the radar of USA Volleyball coaches. Knowing her Olympic dream was taking shape, she returned from the '74 World Championships and re-enrolled at El Camino. "I knew the Olympics was something I wanted to do and I'd do whatever needed to be done training-wise to make it happen," she says.

Landreth spent 1975 at El Camino before transferring to the University of Southern California, where she played two seasons with the Trojans. After helping lead USC to back-to-back national championships in 1976 and '77, the two-time All-American opted to commit herself full-time to achieving her Olympic dream. "I left school to make it happen," she says. "I didn't graduate until after I finished playing for the national team. I graduated in '82."

Her Olympic vision came into clearer view during the 1979 Zonal Championships to qualify for the 1980 Summer Games. The American team knew they were on the right course after the 1978 World Championships and remained true to their "Aim For '80" motto. "We knew going to the Zonal Championships that we could qualify by winning the whole thing—which is what we wanted to do—but also by finishing second," Landreth explains. "We took second to Cuba. It was huge."

The U.S. women's volleyball team had qualified to participate in the Olympic Summer Games for the first time in their history. Debbie Landreth and her teammates had done it. Then after watching the U.S. hockey team's inspirational win in Lake Placid, their motto became "Go For Gold."

"Seeing the hockey team win, we thought, 'That's us! We're winning a gold medal.' All the notoriety they got was an awesome thing and that is what we were working towards," Landreth recalls.

But America's excitement about the Olympics was about to end.

"I do remember, specifically, that when we learned of [the possibility of a boycott] we thought it was an idle threat," she says. "We were really confused and wondered why this would be something important for us to do as a country or as athletes. Really, what was it going to show? At first we thought, This isn't really going to happen. [But] as the weeks and months went by, it became clearer and clearer that there was a really good likelihood the boycott *would* happen."

As the reality of the political decision settled in, Landreth was faced with the uneasy decision whether to continue pursuing the next Olympiad in 1984, or to move on. "Yes, there was consideration," she admits.

"In the end I thought, I had the chance and now I'm moving in another direction."

That direction involved heading to Arizona. After years of training, Landreth had to find a way to pay for her tuition. "I knew the coach at Arizona State University and talked to him about the possibility of receiving a grad-assistant position with him as an assistant coach and have my tuition paid for." Head Coach Dale Flickinger enthusiastically welcomed Landreth, and thus began her coaching career with the Sun Devils and her farewell to her life as an Olympic hopeful.

"I think about the whole Olympic movement," she reflects. "There are times when I think we were on the right track. We had prepared ourselves to go and compete at the highest level and give ourselves a chance to win a gold medal. I look back and think about what we could've done for the sport of volleyball at the time. What we could've done as a group collectively. It was a great story of people putting their lives on hold and saying, 'Come on, let's do this. We can do this.' There was only one woman on the team who had finished college. All of us had dropped out, left families, all that stuff, on a very, very meager stipend—$80 a month. It never dawned on me that I was sacrificing so much. I was preparing for the Olympics."

Asked what it means to be a member of the 1980 U.S. Olympic Summer Games team, Landreth pauses for a long time, and then confesses, "I don't know." She laughs uneasily and pauses again as she tries to further explain. "You know," she finally says, "it's something that I'm proud of and I feel blessed to have had the opportunity to play at the highest level and represent our country. While I know I was on the Olympic team according to the Olympic Committee and everyone else… it's with an asterisk.

"It's a different thing. Whenever somebody finds out I was on the Olympic team, they always ask, 'Oh my gosh, what was it like?' And nobody remembers that we didn't even go. It's like one of those things where they say, 'You were on the Olympic team but you didn't compete?' It's not really an Olympian, yet I know I am. It always has to be explained. That's a bummer. It's a bummer that I can't just say, 'Oh my gosh, it was awesome.' And again, whether we had gone and won a medal or gone and fallen on our faces, the fact that we went and competed in the Games and represented our country, people want to hear about that stuff. I don't really…" Landreth concludes—like so many of her 1980 Olympic teammates—with a loss for words that still confounds and confuses her as she tries to understand why her Olympic dream was stolen.

Epilogue

It started by not knowing what they had. Ron Neugent read a notice in his local newspaper—*The Wichita Eagle*—that they were looking for readers who'd had their pictures taken with a world leader. The newspaper was seeking photos in anticipation of a June 15 visit to Wichita by President George W. Bush. So, Neugent sent in the photo of him shaking Jimmy Carter's hand after accepting a medal during a trip to the White House as a member of the 1980 United States Summer Olympic Team.

"I didn't know what to properly call the medal when I was writing the caption for the photo," Neugent says. "I didn't know what type of Congressional Medal it was and I wanted to be accurate when I sent in the picture and caption." The newspaper promptly called Neugent back to ask him about the photo. Neugent explained it was a medal given to him by Congress. The reporter then asked him if it was a Congressional Medal of Honor. Neugent wasn't sure but told the reporter he would check.

Neugent went home and immediately googled "Congressional Medal of Honor." Initially his research revealed that the medal in question is awarded only to military personnel. However, he came across a *New York Times* article from 1985 about the Congressional Gold Medal being presented to Elie Weisel. In that article it also mentioned the 1980 U.S. Olympic team.

Surprised at this revelation, Neugent then called his Olympic buddy Dave Sims and asked, "Did I miss something during the ceremony? Do you know our medal is the Congressional Gold Medal?" Neugent had uncovered a 27-year-old mystery that no one even knew was a mystery. The two former 1980 Olympians, who have been friends for almost three decades, went to work trying to officially understand what each of the 461 athletes, as well as numerous other personnel from the 1980 U.S. Olympic Summer Games team, had in their possession.

In 1980, Public Law 96-306 was enacted by Congress. The decree authorized President Carter to present the specially struck gold-plated medals to members of the team on behalf of Congress.

They found an obscure list on the site of the U.S. Mint website that listed the 1980 medal along with all the other Congressional Gold Medals. However, it also was listed as an "FYI." Usually, all the medals are numbered, so Sims and Neugent started to call around asking why their medal was not listed. Staffers in Washington continually answered that their medal was bronze with gold plating and was, therefore, not really a gold medal.

Digging deeper, Neugent and Sims reviewed transcripts of the discussions that took place in the House of Representatives and Senate pertaining to Public Law 96-306. It became clear to the pair that what was awarded to them and to their Olympic teammates was, indeed, intended to be a Congressional Gold Medal. But there was a problem. "The funding for this was not in anyone's budget and the whole ceremony was thrown together at the last minute," Sims explains. Congress had $50,000 to work with, which is a typical budget for a Congressional Gold Medal. In usual circumstances, Congress had to create only one. But in the case of the 1980 Summer Olympians, they had to make 650. Congress couldn't have them cast from solid gold because, at that time, the precious metal cost $600 to $700 per ounce, and each would have weighed 4 to 5 ounces. Therefore, the government instead minted the medals with bronze and gold plating.

Neugent and Sims continued their plight for formal recognition for what most of their 1980 Olympic teammates believed were "souvenir" baubles from their trip to Washington, D.C., to meet with President Carter and attend an Olympic gala.

Neugent sent Representative Todd Tiahrt, (R-Kan.), a letter and included copies of the Congressional record from June and July 1980. He then asked the 13-year Congressman for his help to properly designate the medal as a Congressional Gold Medal. "Representative Tiahrt did a tremendous job," Sims says. "They started to work on this before realizing Ron was a member of the 1980 team. They were great and that speaks very highly of Tiahrt and his staff."

In September 2007, Representative Tiahrt and Jim Scherr, chief executive officer of the United States Olympic Committee, submitted a letter to Lorraine Miller, clerk of the House of Representatives, requesting formal recognition of the medal authorized by the 96th Congress and presented by President Jimmy Carter to the 1980 U.S. Olympic Summer Team. The process was nearly complete.

On October 30, 2007, the Clerk's office designated the medal a Congressional Gold Medal. Additionally, it officially added the 1980 U.S. Olympic Summer Games team to the list of recipients that dates back to 1776 and contains less than 200 names—including George Washington, Thomas Edison, Orville and Wilbur Wright, Douglas MacArthur, Jesse Owens, Jackie Robinson, Ronald and Nancy Reagan, Winston Churchill, Pope John Paul II and the Dalai Lama.

Each member of the Olympic team had been presented a medal. And each, hardly impressed because of the immense disappointment of not going to Moscow, thought the medal was just a trinket that Congress commissioned just for the ceremony. "As an athlete you want to compete in the Olympic Games," Neugent explains. "That is the dream as a child. Naturally, we all wished we could've gone to the Olympic Games. We didn't know the medal was the highest honor Congress bestows to civilians. If we had, it would've made the whole experience much different."

Without the medal being on the Congressional list, the importance of the gesture very easily could have been forgotten forever. "It will always be a part of Olympic history," Sims says. "I never want to see a boycott of an Olympic Games ever again. It's important to me to make sure this stays a part of U.S. history because it was an important part of the Cold War. There was a sacrifice that was made. Having it in the official record is gratifying—to know this is a significant part of American history that will not, cannot, be forgotten."

Appendix

The Official Roster of the 1980 United States Olympic Team as compiled by the United States Olympians Association and the USOC.

Archery

Adams, Judi C. Also member of 1996 U.S. Olympic Archery team

Johnson, Lynette Rae

Kertson, Scott Michael

Pace, Darrell Owen Also member of 1976, 1984, 1988 U.S. Olympic Archery team

Coach: Nyquist, Dwight

Manager: Kremer, Harold

Athletics

Anderson, Colin C. Discus Throw

Anderson, Jodi Also member of 1984 U.S. Olympic team; Heptathlon

Anderson, Lynne

Atwood, Duncan Fuller M. Also member of 1984 U.S. Olympic team; Javelin Throw

Banks, Wm. Augustus Also member of 1984 U.S. Olympic team; Triple Jump

Belle, Roberta J. Also member of 1984 U.S. Olympic team; 4x400 Relay

Bessette, Andy Francis Hammer Throw

Bolden, Jeanette Also member of 1984 U.S. Olympic team; 100-Meter Individual, 4x100 Relay

Brown, Alice Regina Also member of 1984, 1988 U.S. Olympic team; 100-Meter Individual, 4x100 Relay

Brown, Douglas Charles Also member of 1972, 1976 U.S. Olympic team; Steeplechase

Brown, Julie Ann Also member of 1984 U.S. Olympic team; Marathon

Buerkle, Richard Thomas Also member of 1976 U.S. Olympic team; 5000-Meter Individual

Butler, James 200-Meter Individual

Caldwell, Gregory Donnell Triple Jump

Campbell, Anthony Eug. Also member of 1984, 1988 U.S. Olympic team; 110 Hurdles

Campbell, Robin Theresa Also member of 1984 U.S. Olympic team; 800-Meter Individual

Centrowitz, Matthew Also member of 1976 U.S. Olympic team; 1500-Meter Individual

Cheeseborough, Chandra D. Also member of 1976, 1984 U.S. Olympic team; Relays team

Coffman, Robert Edward Decathlon

Cooper, Dedy 110-Meter Hurdles

Dabney, Sharon Ann Relays team

Decker-Slaney, Mary T. Also member of 1984, 1988, 1996 U.S. Olympic team; 1500-, 3000-, 5000-Meter Individual

Dixon, Fred Also member of 1976 U.S. Olympic team; Decathlon

Djerassi, Boris Dov Hammer Throw

Durden, Benji Ray Marathon

Durkin, Michael Kevin Also member of 1976 U.S. Olympic team; 1500-Meter Individual

Evoniuk, Marco Ray Also member of 1984, 1988, 1992 U.S. Olympic team; 50-Kilometer, 20-Kilometer Walk

Ewaliko, Rod J. Javelin Throw

Feuerbach, Allan Dean Also member of 1972, 1976 U.S. Olympic team; Shot Put

Fields III, Benjamin F. High Jump

Fitzgerald, Benita P. Also member of 1984 U.S. Olympic team; 100-Meter Hurdles

Floyd, Stanley 100-Meter Individual

Frazier, Herman R. Also member of 1976 U.S. Olympic team; 400-Meter Individual, 4x400 Relay

Fredericks, Gregory L. 5000-Meter Individual

Gardner, Gwen 400-Meter Individual

Gault, Willie Relays team

Girven, Paula Darcel Also member of 1976 U.S. Olympic team; High Jump

Glance, Harvey Edward Also member of 1976, 1984 U.S. Olympic team; 100-Meter, 4x100 Relay

Green, William Earnest 400-Meter Individual

Greene, Pamela D. Also member of 1972 U.S. Olympic team; 200-Meter Individual

Gregorek, John Stanley Also member of 1984 U.S. Olympic team; 3000-Meter Steeplechase

Griffin, Lorna Joann Also member of 1984 U.S. Olympic team; Discus Throw

Harmon, Marlene Pentathlon

Hawkins, Karen

Heffner, Kyle Daniels Marathon

Heiring, James Anthony Also member of 1984, 1988 U.S. Olympic team; 20-Kilometer Walk

Hightower, Stephanie 100-Meter Hurdles

Hill-Howard, Denean E. Also member of 1984, 1988, 1992 U.S. Olympic team; 4x400 Relay

Hintnaus, Tomas Pole Vault

Howard Jr., James Allen Also member of 1988 U.S. Olympic team; High Jump

Howard, Sherri Francis Also member of 1984, 1988 U.S. Olympic team; 4x400 Relay

Jordan, Paul Triple Jump

Kennedy, Bruce Graham Javelin Throw

Lacy, Steven M. Also member of 1984 U.S. Olympic team; 5000-Meter

Larrieu-Smith, Francis Ann Also member of 1972, 1976, 1988, 1992 U.S. Olympic team; 1500-Meter, 10,000-Meter, Marathon

Lattany, Melvin 100-Meter

Lee, David Kenneth 400-Meter Hurdles

Lewis, Carol Legrant Also member of 1984, 1988 U.S. Olympic team; Long Jump

Lewis, Fred Carlton (Carl) Also member of 1984, 1988, 1992, 1996 U.S. Olympic team; Long Jump, 100-Meter, 200-Meter, 4x100 Relay

Marsh, Henry Dinwoodey Also member of 1976, 1984, 1988 U.S. Olympic team; 3000-Meter Steeplechase

McArdle, John E. Hammer Throw

McChesney, William E. 5000-Meter Individual

McCoy, Walter Lee Also member of 1984 U.S. Olympic team; 4x400 Relay

McMillan, Kathy Laverne Also member of 1976 U.S. Olympic team; Long Jump

Mims, Madeline Manning J. Also member of 1968, 1972, 1976 U.S. Olympic team; 800-Meter Individual, 4x400 Relay

Morehead, Brenda Louise Also member of 1976 U.S. Olympic team; 100-Meter Individual

Moses, Edwin Corley Also member of 1976, 1984, 1988 U.S. Olympic team; 400-Meter Individual Hurdles

Myricks, Larry Ellwyne Also member of 1976, 1984, 1988 U.S. Olympic team; Long Jump

Nehemiah, Renaldo 110-Meter Hurdles

O'Connor, Daniel Also member of 1984 U.S. Olympic team; 20-Kilometer Walk

Osborne, Mary Therese Javelin Throw

Page, Nathaniel High Jump

Paige, Donald James 800-Meter Individual

Palles, Lee Nicholas Decathlon

Plucknett, Ben (Walter) Discus Throw

Powell, John Gates Also member of 1972, 1976, 1984 U.S. Olympic team; Discus Throw

Ripley, Dan Pole Vault

Ritter, Louise Dorothy Also member of 1984, 1988 U.S. Olympic team; High Jump

Robinson Jr., James J. Also member of 1976 U.S. Olympic team; 800-Meter

Rodgers, William Also member of 1976 U.S. Olympic team; Marathon

Salazar, Alberto Bauduy Also member of 1984 U.S. Olympic team; 10,000-Meter, Marathon

Sandoval, Anthony Marathon

Schmidt, Kathryn Joan Also member of 1972, 1976 U.S. Olympic team; Javelin Throw

Schueler, Carl Francis Also member of 1984, 1988, 1992 U.S. Olympic team; 50-Kilometer Walk

Scott, Steven Michael Also member of 1984, 1988 U.S. Olympic team; 1500-Meter

Scully Jr., Clark Todd Also member of 1976 U.S. Olympic team; 20-Kilometer Walk

Seidler, Maren Elizabeth Also member of 1968, 1972, 1976 U.S. Olympic team; Shot Put

Shmock, Peter Carlton Also member of 1976, 1984 U.S. Olympic team; Shot Put

Smith, Karin Kiefer Also member of 1976, 1984, 1988, 1992 U.S. Olympic team; Javelin Throw

Smith, Willie Also member of 1976, 1984 U.S. Olympic team; 400-Meter Individual

Sokolitz, Karen 200-Meter Individual

Spencer, Pamela Ann Also member of 1976, 1984 U.S. Olympic team; High Jump

Taylor, Frederick G. 200-Meter Individual

Thomas, Kim Sandy Relays team

Tully, Michael Scott Also member of 1984 U.S. Olympic team; Pole Vault

Turbyne, Ann Mary Shot Put

Virgin, Craig Steven Also member of 1976, 1984 U.S. Olympic team; 10,000-Meter

Walker, James Andre 400-Meter Hurdles

Walker, Larry A. Also member of 1976 U.S. Olympic team; 20-Kilometer Walk

Waltman, Linda C. Pentathlon

Wiley, Clifford A. 200-Meter Individual

Wilkins, Mac Maurice Also member of 1976, 1984, 1988 U.S. Olympic team; Discus Throw

Williams, Barton 400-Meter Hurdles

Williams, Diane Also member of 1984 U.S. Olympic team; 4x100 Relay, 100-Meter Individual

Williams, Randy Lavelle Also member of 1972, 1976 U.S. Olympic team; Long Jump

Wilson, Randy Byron 800-Meter Individual

Winbigler, M. Lynne Also member of 1976 U.S. Olympic team; Discus Throw

Young, Canzetta (Candy) 100-Meter Hurdles

Head Coach: Carnes, Jimmy

Assistants: Huntsman, Stan
Santos, Jim
Tellez, Tom
Williams, Willie

Head Manager: Newland, Robert

Assistant Managers: Cunliffe, Ernie
Griak, Roy
Simmons, Steve

Basketball

Aguirre, Mark Anthony

Blackman, Rolando

Blazejowski, Carol

Bowie, Sam

Brooks, Michael Anthony

Curry, Denise Marie Also member of 1984 U.S. Olympic team

Donovan, Anne Theresa Also member of 1984 U.S. Olympic team

Hanzlik, William Henry

Heiss, Tara Grey

Kirchner, Kristin Joye (Kris)

Lister, Alton

McCray, Rodney

Miller, Debra

Noble, Cindy Jo Also member of 1984 U.S. Olympic team

Pollard, Lataunya

Rankin, Jill Anne

Thomas III, Isiah Lord

Valentine, Darnell Terrell

Vranes, Daniel Ladrew

Walker, Rosie Marie

Warlick, Frances H.

Williams, Charles Linwood

Wood, Martin Alphonzo

Woodard, Lynette Also member of 1984 U.S. Olympic team

Men's Head Coach: Gavitt, David

Men's Assistant Coaches: Brown, Larry Also Head Coach of 2004 U.S. Olympic Men's Basketball team
Rowe, Dee

Men's Manager: Vancisin, Joe

Women's Head Coach: Gunter, Sue

Women's Assistant Coaches: Head, Pat
Plarski, Lea

Boxing

Beard, Jackie Bantamweight

Broad, Willie James Super Heavyweight

Bumphus, Johnny Light Welterweight

Carter, Charles (Willie) Middleweight

Curry, Don Welterweight

Manley, Joseph Lightweight

Murphy, Lee Roy Light Heavyweight

Sandoval, Richard Flyweight

Shannon, Robert Edward Also member of 1984 U.S.
Olympic team; Light Flyweight, Bantamweight

Shuler, James Light Middleweight

Taylor, Bernard Featherweight

Head Coach: Nappi, Pat

Assistant Coach: Pelligrew, Dick

Manager: Silverglade, Ed

Canoe & Kayak

Barton, Bruce Michael Also member of 1976 U.S.
Olympic team

Barton, Gregory Mark Also member of 1984, 1988, 1992
U.S. Olympic team

Di Martino-Haught, Theresa Also member of 1988 U.S.
Olympic team

Dragan, Linda James Murray Also member of 1972, 1976
U.S. Olympic team

Gillman, David Robert Also member of 1976, 1984, 1988
U.S. Olympic team

Kearney, Jay T.

Kelly, Stephen Paul Also member of 1972, 1976 U.S.
Olympic team

Klein, Leslie Gail Also member of 1984 U.S. Olympic team

Lyda, Charles Clinton Also member of 1976 U.S.
Olympic team

Morrison, Angus Gault Also member of 1972, 1976 U.S.
Olympic team

Muhlen, Roland

Plankenhorn, John (Robert) Also member of 1984 U.S.
Olympic team

Streib, Terry Mathew

Turner, Ann Clare Also member of 1976, 1984 U.S.
Olympic team

Van Cleave, Jonathan E.

Weigand, Andreas John Also member of 1968, 1972, 1976
U.S. Olympic team

White, Carl H. (Terry) Also member of 1984, 1988 U.S.
Olympic team

Coach: Toro, Andy

Assistant Coach: Rademaker, Sperry

Manager: Turner, Howard

Cycling

Barczewski, Les

Cook, Robert

Donaghy, Bruce

Doughty, Thomas

Emery, Brent Also member of 1984 U.S. Olympic team

Gorski, Mark Also member of 1984 U.S. Olympic team

Grylls, David Also member of 1984 U.S. Olympic team

LeMond, Greg

Nitz, Leonard Also member of 1976, 1984, 1988 U.S.
Olympic team

Schuler, Thomas

Shapiro, Douglas Also member of 1984 U.S. Olympic team

Stetina, Dale Also member of 1976 U.S. Olympic team

Stetina, Wayne Also member of 1972, 1976 U.S.
Olympic team

Van Haute, Danny Also member of 1984 U.S. Olympic team

Weaver, Andrew Also member of 1984 U.S. Olympic team

Track Coach: Borysewicz, Edward

Road Coach: Kelly, Timothy

Assistant Coach: Leusenkamp, Carl

Manager: Burke, Ed

Diving

Ableman, Randolph

Phillip W.

Bungum, Brian

Burgering, David Earl

Louganis, Gregory E. Also member of 1976, 1984, 1988
    U.S. Olympic team

Machemer, Kevin Scott

McGrath, Amy

Neyer, Megan

Potter, Cynthia Ann Also member of 1972, 1976 U.S.
    Olympic team

Seufert, Christina Anne

Weinstein, Barbara

Coaches: Kimball, Dick
    O'Brien, Ron

Manager: Robbins, Bryan

Equestrian

Bishop II, Washington D.

Dello Joio, Norman Adrian Also member of 1992 U.S.
    Olympic team

Gray, Lendon Fentress

Homfeld, Conrad E. Also member of 1984 U.S.
    Olympic team

Monahan, Katherine M.

Plumb, John Michael Also member of 1960, 1964, 1968,
    1972, 1976, 1984, 1992 U.S. Olympic team

Rudd, Teresa Lee

Smith, Melanie Ainsworth Also member of 1984 U.S.
    Olympic team

Stives, Karen Elizabeth Also member of 1984 U.S.
    Olympic team

Stockebrand, Gwen Elaine

Watkins, Torrance

Winnett, John Winfield Also member of 1972, 1976 U.S.
    Olympic team

Wofford, James Cunningham Also member of 1968, 1972,
    1984 U.S. Olympic team

Zang, Linda Louise

Manager: Burton, Gen. Jack

Jumping Coach: de Nemethy, Bert

Dressage Coach: van Bruggen, Melle

3-Day Coach: LeGoff, Jack

Fencing

Angelakis, Jana Marie Also member of 1984 U.S.
    Olympic team

Cheris, Elaine Gayle Also member of 1988, 1996 U.S.
    Olympic team

D'Asaro, Gay K. Also member of 1976 U.S. Olympic team

Franke, Nikki Valerie Also member of 1976 U.S.
    Olympic team

Glass, Timothy Carrigan

Ingram, Elaine

Johnson, Stacey Rita

Johnson, Wayne

Lekach, Stanley V.

Losonczy, Thomas John Also member of 1976 U.S.
    Olympic team

Marx, Michael Anthony Also member of 1984, 1988, 1992,
    1996 U.S. Olympic team

Massialas, Gregory David D. Also member of 1984, 1988
    U.S. Olympic team

Nieman, Robert

Nonna, John Michael Also member of 1972 U.S.
    Olympic team

Orban, Alex Also member of 1968, 1972, 1976 U.S.
    Olympic team

Pesthy, Paul Karoly Also member of 1964, 1968, 1976 U.S.
    Olympic team

Reilly, Philip Vincent Also member of 1984 U.S.
    Olympic team

Smith, Mark Jeffrey Troy Also member of 1984 U.S.
    Olympic team

Westbrook, Peter Jonathan Also member of 1976, 1984,
    1988, 1992, 1996 U.S. Olympic team

Captain: Keane, Jack

Coaches: Auriol, Yves
    Elthes, Csaba

Manager: Vaisimis, Marius

Armorer: Byrnes, Joseph

Field Hockey

Anders, Elizabeth Rambo Also member of 1984 U.S. Olympic team

Beglin, Elizabeth Anne Also member of 1984 U.S. Olympic team

Cheeseman, Gwen Wentz Also member of 1984 U.S. Olympic team

Desautels, Denise

Grant, Jill Evans

Johnson, Sheryl Ann Also member of 1984, 1988 U.S. Olympic team

Larson-Mason, Christine Also member of 1984 U.S. Olympic team

Marcellus, Susan

Miller, Anita Corl Also member of 1984 U.S. Olympic team

Milne, Leslie Woods Also member of 1984 U.S. Olympic team

Morett, Charlene Frances Also member of 1984 U.S. Olympic team

Moyer, Diane Marie Also member of 1984 U.S. Olympic team

Shelton, Karen Christina Also member of 1984 U.S. Olympic team

Staver, Julia Ann Also member of 1984 U.S. Olympic team

Strong, Judith Ann Also member of 1984 U.S. Olympic team

White, Nancy Pitkin

Head Coach: Gros, Vonnie

Assistant Coach: van Beaumont, Will

Manager: Watson, Margery

Gymnastics

Cahoy, Philip Michael

Collins, Luci Andrea

Conner, Bart Also member of 1976, 1984 U.S. Olympic team

Frederick, Marcia Jean

Galimore, Ron

Gerard, Larry D.

Hartung, James N. Also member of 1984 U.S. Olympic team

Johnson, Kathy Ann Also member of 1984 U.S. Olympic team

Kline, Beth

Koopman, Amy Richelle

McNamara, Julianne Lyn Also member of 1984 U.S. Olympic team

Talavera, Tracee Ann Also member of 1984 U.S. Olympic team

Vidmar, Peter Also member of 1984 U.S. Olympic team

Wilson, Michael Gower

Men's Head Coach: Allen, Francis

Men's Assistant Coach: Meade, William

Women's Head Coach: Weaver, Ernestine

Women's Assistant Coach: Ziert, Paul

Pianist: Stabisevski, Carol

Judo

Goldstein, Jesse H.

Martin, Tommy Gerard Also member of 1976 U.S. Olympic team

Nakasone, Keith

Santa Maria, Mitch James

Seck, Steven E.

Swain, Michael Lee Also member of 1984, 1988, 1992 U.S. Olympic team

Tudela, Miguel Angel

Yonezuka, Nicholas K.

Head Coach: Maruyama, Maj. Paul

Manager: Fullerton, Frank

Modern Pentathlon

Burley, Michael Edward Also member of 1976 U.S. Olympic team

Fitzgerald, John David Also member of 1972, 1976 U.S. Olympic team

Glenesk, Dean William Also member of 1984 U.S. Olympic team

Nieman, Robert Leef Also member of 1976, 1988 U.S. Olympic team

Rowing

Allsopp, Christopher P. Also member of 1976 U.S. Olympic team

Altekruse, Charles E. B. Also member of 1988 U.S. Olympic team

Barber, Valerie Ann

Barnes, Hope Also member of 1984 U.S. Olympic team

Belden, William Thomas Also member of 1976 U.S. Olympic team

Borchelt, Earl Frederick Also member of 1976 U.S. Olympic team

Borchelt, Mark Raymond Also member of 1976 U.S. Olympic team

Bower, Carol Ann Also member of 1984 U.S. Olympic team

Brown, Carol Page Also member of 1976, 1984 U.S. Olympic team

Carababas, John P.

Cashin Jr., Richard M. Also member of 1976 U.S. Olympic team

Chatzky Jr., John

Christensen, Steven Erik Also member of 1976 U.S. Olympic team

Colgan, Sean Padraic

Cruz, Christina Ann

Darling, Thomas Ward Also member of 1984, 1988 U.S. Olympic team

DeFrantz, Anita L. Also member of 1976 U.S. Olympic team

Dietz, James William Also member of 1972, 1976 U.S. Olympic team

Drewsen, Karla Hull

Epke, Bruce Edward

Espeseth Jr., Robert D. Also member of 1976, 1984, 1988 U.S. Olympic team

Everett, John Gardner Also member of 1976 U.S. Olympic team

Flanagan, Jeanne Ann Also member of 1984 U.S. Olympic team

Geer, Charlotte Mosher Also member of 1984 U.S. Olympic team

Geer, Julia Hand Also member of 1976, 1984 U.S. Olympic team

Gilder, Virginia Anne Also member of 1984 U.S. Olympic team

Graves, Carie Brand Also member of 1976, 1984 U.S. Olympic team

Harville, Janet Christine Also member of 1984 U.S. Olympic team

Hatton, Hollis Straley

Hazeltine, Thomas

Hills, Elizabeth D. Also member of 1976 U.S. Olympic team

Howes, Thomas Andrew

Hull, Thomas W.

Ibbetson, Bruce Bernard Also member of 1984 U.S. Olympic team

Jaugstetter, Robert C. Also member of 1984 U.S. Olympic team

Keeler, Kathryn Elliott Also member of 1984 U.S. Olympic team

Kehoe, David Michael

Kent, Elizabeth Cryer

Kiesling, Stephen H.

Lewis, Bradley Alan Also member of 1984 U.S. Olympic team

Lind, Joan Louise Also member of 1976, 1984 U.S. Olympic team

Lubsen Jr., Walter H. (Chip) Also member of 1976, 1984 U.S. Olympic team

Marden, Anne R. Also member of 1984, 1988, 1992 U.S. Olympic team

McCarthy, Peggy Ann Also member of 1976 U.S. Olympic team

McClain, Valerie Also member of 1984 U.S. Olympic team

Norelius, Kristine Lee Also member of 1984 U.S. Olympic team

O'Brien, Mark Edwin

O'Connor, Mary Irene

Palchikoff, Jan Louise Also member of 1976 U.S. Olympic team

Prioleau, Paul Edward

Purdy, William David

Rickon, Kelly Anne Also member of 1984 U.S. Olympic team

Sayner, Daniel Kevin

Somerville, Kurt

Spratlen, Patricia Maria Also member of 1984 U.S. Olympic team

Stekl, Philip William Also member of 1984 U.S. Olympic team

Storrs, Nancy Hitchcock Also member of 1976 U.S. Olympic team

Terwilliger, John Richard Also member of 1984, 1988 U.S. Olympic team

Tippett-Thaxton, Cathleen Also member of 1976, 1984, 1988 U.S. Olympic team

Tuttle, Susan E.

Van Blom, John Also member of 1968, 1972, 1976 U.S. Olympic team

Vespoli, Nancy P.

Warner, Anne Elizabeth T. Also member of 1976 U.S. Olympic team

Wells, Christopher

Wood, Christopher R. (Tiff) Also member of 1976, 1984 U.S. Olympic team

Woodman, Thomas H.

Men's Head Coach: Parker, Harry

Men's Coach: Gardner, Peter

Men's Sculling Coach: Vespoli, Mike

Men's Manager: Zandbergen, Peter

Boatman: Drelselgacker, Richard

Men's Assistant Coach: Melslahn, Findley

Women's Head Manager: Lippett, Peter

Women's Coaches: Case, Nathaniel
Ernst, Robert
Korzenioswky, Kris
McKibbon, Thomas

Shooting

Anderson, Terence M. Also member of 1996 U.S. Olympic team

Clark, Dean Owen Also member of 1992 U.S. Olympic team

Collins, Steven Keith

Dryke, Matthew A. Also member of 1984, 1988, 1992 U.S. Olympic team

Edmondson, Martin D. Also member of 1976 U.S. Olympic team

Fitz-Randolph Jr., Roderick Also member of 1988 U.S. Olympic team

Goldsby, Boyd D.

Hamilton, Donald Leslie Also member of 1968 U.S. Olympic team

Howard, Terry M.

Kimes, David M.

Neel, Ernest W.

Reiter, Steve Frank

Stewart, Randolph W. Also member of 1984 U.S. Olympic team

Wigger Jr., Lones W. Also member of 1964, 1968, 1972 U.S. Olympic team

Team Manager: Pullum, Bill

Assistant Manager: Berry, Joseph

Gunsmith: Sizemore, James

Soccer

Arnautoff, Peter

Bellinger, Tony

Clark, Timothy

Coffee, Paul

Di Bernardo, Angel Also member of 1984 U.S. Olympic team

Ebert, Donald

Gee, Darryl Lester

Hayes, John Patrick

Keough, William Tyrone

Lawson, Adolphus

McKeon, William

Morrone, Joseph

Nanchoff, Louis

Pesa, Njego

Salvemini, Daniel Michael

Van Der Beck, Perry J.

Villa, Greg

Head Coach: Chyzowych, Walt

Assistant Coach: Gansler, Robert

Manager: Lemm, Kurt

Swimming

Barnicoat, Stephen D.

Barrett, William M.

Baxter, Terri Lynn

Beardsley, Craig R.

Bottom, Michael L.

Bruner, Michael L. Also member of 1976 U.S. Olympic team

Buese, Elisabeth Anne

Carey, Richard J. Also member of 1984 U.S. Olympic team

Carlisle, Kimberly J.

Caulkins, Tracy A. Also member of 1984 U.S. Olympic team

Cavanaugh, Chris

Elkins, Stephanie W.

Float, Jeff

Forrester Jr., William R. Also member of 1976 U.S. Olympic team

Gaines IV, Ambrose (Rowdy) Also member of 1984 U.S. Olympic team

Goodell, Brian S. Also member of 1976 U.S. Olympic team

Gribble, Matthew O. Also member of 1984 U.S. Olympic team

Hencken, John F. Also member of 1972, 1976 U.S. Olympic team

Hogshead, Nancy L. Also member of 1984 U.S. Olympic team

Jackson, Robert S. Also member of 1976 U.S. Olympic team

Jezek, Linda L. Also member of 1976 U.S. Olympic team

Kinkhead, Elizabeth

Kirchner, Kris

LaBerg, Karin Anne

Larson, David E. Also member of 1984 U.S. Olympic team

Linehan, Kimberly A. Also member of 1984 U.S. Olympic team

Linzmeier, Marybeth

Lundquist, Stephen K. Also member of 1984 U.S. Olympic team

Meagher, Mary T. Also member of 1984, 1988 U.S. Olympic team

Mills, Glenn D.

Moffet, John C. Also member of 1984 U.S. Olympic team

Neugent, Ronald K.

Paulus, William G.

Pennington, Mary (Joan)

Rapp, Susan

Rocca, Peter D. Also member of 1976 U.S. Olympic team

Roney, Brian K.

Simons Jr., John N.

Sims, David E.

Sterkel, Jill Ann Also member of 1976, 1984, 1988 U.S. Olympic team

Thayer, Susie S.

Thornton, Richard W.

Vassallo, Jesus D. (Jesse) Also member of 1984 U.S. Olympic team

Walsh, Susan E.

Woodhead, Cynthia L. Also member of 1984 U.S. Olympic team

Head Coach: Haines, George

Assistant Coaches: Bergen, Paul
Gambril, Don
Pursley, Dennis
Reese, Randy
Schubert, Mark

Managers: Breen, George
Burton, Linda
Richardson, Pokey

Volleyball

Baier, Janet Mary

Becker, Carolyn Marie Also member of 1984 U.S. Olympic team

Brassey, Laurel K. Also member of 1988 U.S. Olympic team

Crockett, Rita Louise Also member of 1984 U.S. Olympic team

Dowdell, Patricia T.

Flachmeier, Laurie Jean Also member of 1984 U.S. Olympic team

Green, Debbie Bebe Also member of 1984 U.S. Olympic team

Hyman, Flo

Landreth, Debra Lynn

McCormick, Diane E.

Place, Terry Ann

Woodstra, Susan Jean Also member of 1984 U.S. Olympic team

Head Coach: Sellinger, Dr. Arie

Assistant Coach: Yoshida, Toshiaki

Manager: Becker, Ruth

Water Polo

Dorst, Christopher T. Also member of 1984 U.S. Olympic team

Figueroa, Gary Lee Also member of 1984 U.S. Olympic team

Hamann, Stephen W.

Lindroth, Eric Emil Also member of 1972 U.S. Olympic team

McDonald, Andrew John Also member of 1984 U.S. Olympic team

Robertson, Kevin George Also member of 1984, 1988 U.S. Olympic team

Schnugg, Peter Hayden

Schroeder, Terry Alan Also member of 1984, 1988, 1992 U.S. Olympic team

Siman, John O'Connell Also member of 1984 U.S. Olympic team

Svendsen, Jon Howard Also member of 1984 U.S. Olympic team

Vargas, Joseph Michael Also member of 1984 U.S. Olympic team

Coach: Nitzkowski, Monte

Assistant Coach: Lindgren, Kenneth

Manager: Sayring, Terry

Weightlifting

Cameron, Mark Also member of 1976 U.S. Olympic team

Carlton, Guy Albert Also member of 1984 U.S. Olympic team

Cohen, Michael M.

Curry Jr., James

Derwin, Brian P.

Giordano, Robert J.

Hannan, Jerome

Karchut, Michael Also member of 1972 U.S. Olympic team

Klaja, Luke David

Puleo, Joseph Robert Also member of 1968 U.S. Olympic team

Schake, Callen N.

Setterburg, Kurt Nils

Stock, Thomas David

Head Coach: Schmitz, James

Manager: Smith, Richard

Wrestling

Azevedo, John

Blatnick, Jeffrey C. Also member of 1984 U.S. Olympic team

Campbell, Christopher L. Also member of 1992 U.S. Olympic team

Chandler, Daniel C. Also member of 1976, 1984 U.S. Olympic team

Fuller, Mark A. Also member of 1984, 1988, 1992 U.S. Olympic team

Gust, Brian B.

Hellickson, Russell O. Also member of 1976 U.S. Olympic team

Johnson, Mark A.

Kemp Jr., Leroy P.

Lewis, Randall S. Also member of 1984 U.S. Olympic team

Matthews, John K. Also member of 1976 U.S. Olympic team

Mello, Daniel A.

Mills, Gene

Minkel, Thomas A.

Peterson, Benjamin L. Also member of 1972, 1976 U.S. Olympic team

Rheingans, Brad B. Also member of 1976 U.S. Olympic team

Thompson, Bruce J. Also member of 1976 U.S. Olympic team

Weaver, Robert B. Also member of 1984 U.S. Olympic team

Wojciechowski, Gregory M.

Yagla, Charles E.

Coach/Manager: Dziedzic, Stan

Coach: Allen, Lee

Assistant Coaches: Baughman, Maj. Wayne
Gable, Dan

Yachting

Anderson, Ron

Benjamin, Stephen D. Also member of 1984 U.S.
Olympic team

Bertrand, John (Joseph) Also member of 1984 U.S.
Olympic team

Bossett, Henry Peter

Buchan, William E. Also member of 1984 U.S.
Olympic team

Davis, Roderick Hopkins Also member of 1984 U.S.
Olympic team

Duane III, John Marshall

Fowler, Neal Lawrence

Haines Jr., Robert Bentley Also member of 1976, 1984
U.S. Olympic team

Kent, Jeff

Loeb, Michael Leshine

Trevelyan, Edward N. Also member of 1984 U.S.
Olympic team

Manager: Merrick, Sam

Assistant Manager: Kober, Chuck

Boatwright: Eichenstein, Carl

Meteorologist: Mairs, Robert

Coach: Arnold, Dr. Homer

Sources

1. Galster, Steve, The National Security Archive; *Volume II: Lessons from the Last War; AFGHANISTAN: THE MAKING OF U.S. POLICY, 1973-1990;* October 9, 2001

2. MacEachin, Doug, and Nolan, Janne E., Kristine Tockman; *The Soviet Invasion of Afghanistan in 1979: Failure of Intelligence or of the Policy Process?* Institute for the Study of Diplomacy Edmund A. Walsh School of Foreign Service GEORGE-TOWN UNIVERSITY; Working Group Report, No. III, September 26, 2005

3. Galster, Steve, The National Security Archive; Volume II: Lessons from the Last War; AFGHANISTAN: THE MAKING OF U.S. POLICY, 1973-1990; October 9, 2001

    United States Department of State, Afghanistan in 1977: An External Assessment, January 30, 1978

4. Galster, Steve, The National Security Archive; Volume II: Lessons from the Last War; AFGHANISTAN: THE MAKING OF U.S. POLICY, 1973-1990; October 9, 2001

    United States Department of State, The Afghan Coup, April 30, 1988

5. Storage Center for Contemporary Documentation (TsKhSD), Moscow: Fond 89, Perchen 25, Document 1, List 1, 12-25; Meeting of the Politburo of the Central Committee of the Communist Party of the Soviet Union, March 17, 1979

6. Storage Center for Contemporary Documentation (TsKhSD), Moscow: Fond 89, Perchen 25, Document 1, List 1, 12-25; Meeting of the Politburo of the Central Committee of the Communist Party of the Soviet Union, March 17, 1979

7. *Le Nouvel Observateur*, Paris, January 15-21, 1998. Translated from French by Bill Blum

8. MacEachin, Doug and Janne E. Nolan, Kristine Tockman; *The Soviet Invasion of Afghanistan in 1979: Failure of Intelligence or of the Policy Process?* Institute for the Study of Diplomacy Edmund A. Walsh School of Foreign Service GEORGETOWN UNIVERSITY; Working Group Report, No. III, September 26, 2005

9. Lyakhovsky, Alexander, *The Tragedy and Valor of Afghan*, GPI Iskon, Moscow, 1995, pp. 109-112

10. MacEachin, Doug and Janne E. Nolan, Kristine Tockman; *The Soviet Invasion of Afghanistan in 1979: Failure of Intelligence or of the Policy Process?* Institute for the Study of Diplomacy Edmund A. Walsh School of Foreign Service GEORGE-TOWN UNIVERSITY; Working Group Report, No. III, September 26, 2005

11. Miller Center of Public Affairs, University of Virginia; Jimmy Carter Speeches; *Address to the Nation on Afghanistan*, January 4, 1980

    http://millercenter.virginia.edu/scripps/digitalarchive/speeches/spe_1980_0104_carter

12. Carter, Jimmy, *State of the Union Address 1980*, January 23, 1980

    http://jimmycarterlibrary.org/documents/speeches/su80jec.phtml

13. Galster, Steve, The National Security Archive; *Volume II: Lessons from the Last War; AFGHANISTAN: THE MAKING OF U.S. POLICY, 1973-1990;* October 9, 2001

    United States Department of State, Afghanistan and Pakistan, March 1978

14. *U.S. Committee backs President: Votes to seek transfer or postponement of Games; The Newark Star-Ledger,* January 27, 1980

15. *U.S. Olympic Committee backs President: Votes to seek transfer or postponement of Games; The Newark Star-Ledger,* January 27, 1980

16. The American Presidency Project; Jimmy Carter, The President's News Conference of February 13, 1980

    http://www.presidency.ucsb.edu

17. The American Presidency Project; Jimmy Carter, The President's News Conference of February 13, 1980

    http://www.presidency.ucsb.edu

18. Gallup, George, *Olympic snub favored by the majority; The Newark Star-Ledger,* March 16, 1980

19. Gallup, George, *Olympic snub favored by the majority; The Newark Star-Ledger,* March 16, 1980

20. Apple, Jr., R.W., *British Olympic Committee, Rejecting Mrs. Thatcher's Pleas, Votes to Go to Moscow Games; The New York Times,* March 26, 1980

21. Associated Press, *Carter Gets Word: 'Try and Stop Us'; The Washington Post*, March 31, 1980

22. Lorge, Barry, *White House Clout Could Make Moscow Boycott Stick*; *The Washington Post*, April 4, 1980

23. Seppy, Tom, Associated Press, *President: Our security at stake*; *The Trenton Times*, April 4, 1980

24. Weisman, Steven R., *Carter Aides Press Athletes on Boycott; The New York Times*, April 4, 1980

25. *Sears, Under Pressure, Defers Olympic Pledge; The Washington Post*, April 4, 1980

26. *Sears to Withhold Olympic Pledge; The New York Times*, April 5, 1980

27. Mondale, Walter F., speech to the USOC House of Delegates; *Address to U.S. Olympic Committee House of Delegates*, Colorado Springs, Colo., April 12, 1980. Walter F. Mondale Papers: Vice President office; Speech texts. Minnesota Historical Society

28. Weisman, Steven R., *U.S. OLYMPIC GROUP VOTES TO BOYCOTT THE MOSCOW GAMES; The New York Times*, April 13, 1980

29. From brief presented in the United States District of Columbia, Civil Action No. 80-1013, *Anita DeFRANTZ v. UNITED STATES OLYMPIC COMMITTEE*; April 23, 1980; pps. 5-10; provided by Edward R. Mackiewicz and Robert B. Zagoria

30. From brief presented in the United States District of Columbia, Civil Action No. 80-1013, *Anita DeFRANTZ v. UNITED STATES OLYMPIC COMMITTEE*; April 23, 1980; pps. 10-11; provided by Edward R. Mackiewicz and Robert B. Zagoria

31. From brief presented in the United States District of Columbia, Civil Action No. 80-1013, *Anita DeFRANTZ v. UNITED STATES OLYMPIC COMMITTEE*; April 23, 1980; provided by Edward R. Mackiewicz and Robert B. Zagoria

32. From brief presented in the United States District of Columbia, Civil Action No. 80-1013, *Anita DeFRANTZ v. UNITED STATES OLYMPIC COMMITTEE*; April 23, 1980; pps. 15; provided by Edward R. Mackiewicz and Robert B. Zagoria

33. From brief presented in the United States District of Columbia, Civil Action No. 80-1013, *Anita DeFRANTZ v. UNITED STATES OLYMPIC COMMITTEE*; April 23, 1980; pps. 16; provided by Edward R. Mackiewicz and Robert B. Zagoria

34. From brief presented in the United States District of Columbia, Civil Action No. 80-1013, *Anita DeFRANTZ v. UNITED STATES OLYMPIC COMMITTEE*; April 23, 1980; pps. 16; provided by Edward R. Mackiewicz and Robert B. Zagoria

35. From brief presented in the United States District of Columbia, Civil Action No. 80-1013, *Anita DeFRANTZ v. UNITED STATES OLYMPIC COMMITTEE*; April 23, 1980; pps. 17; provided by Edward R. Mackiewicz and Robert B. Zagoria

36. From brief presented in the United States District of Columbia, Civil Action No. 80-1013, *Anita DeFRANTZ v. UNITED STATES OLYMPIC COMMITTEE*; April 23, 1980; pps. 18; provided by Edward R. Mackiewicz and Robert B. Zagoria

37. Op-Ed; *Olympian Hubris; The New York Times*, April 11, 1980

38. Povich, Shirley, *Olympic 'Heroes' Deserve Nothing; The Washington Post*, April 25, 1980

39. United States District of Columbia, Civil Action No. 80-1013, *Anita DeFRANTZ v. UNITED STATES OLYMPIC COMMITTEE*; April 23, 1980

Additional Sources
   http://www.Olympic.org
   Amateur Sports Act of 1978
   www.Olympic.org

Index

Bernlohr, Barbara (volleyball coach)
asked Debbie Landreth to attend volleyball camp, 234
Blackman, Rolando (basketball), 94
Blazejowski, Carol (basketball), 126
career: encouraged by Cranford school teachers to take up basketball, 127; persuaded athletic director to have a girls' roundball team, 128; moved to Montclair State College, became the women basketball player of the year in 1978, 128; cut from '76 Olympic team, 129; reputation grew, 129; encouraged to participate in the '77 World University Games by Kyvallos, 130; gold in '79 World University Games, 130; difficult two years before 1980, 130; captain of the 1980 U.S. Olympic women's basketball team, 130
disappointed again, 131; physically ill, 131; stripped of amateur status, 131; 1984 Olympic dream ended, 131
former tomboy, 127; pre-Title IX, 127
general manager of WNBA New York Liberty, 132; grow the sport, 132
inducted into the Naismith Memorial Basketball Hall of Fame, 132
photo with President Carter and family, 132
Boone, Rosemary (swimmer)
one of Lisa Buese' inspiration, 191
Brezhnev, Leonid I. (Soviet President)
agreed to provide Afghanistan with economic and military assistance, 37
greeted the athletes at the Olympic Games, 179
greetings from Amin to, 33
meeting with Politburo members, 40
personal memorandum from Andropov, 39
Brink, Patricia (rower)
plaintiff, 135, 137
Brown, Carol (rower)
plaintiff, 135, 136
Brown, Chris (baseball)
attended Crenshaw High School, 46
Brown, Harold (defense secretary), 86
Bruner, Mike (swimmer), 176
Brzezinski, Zbigniew (U.S. National Security Advisor)
to fund, arm, and train Afghan insurgents, 37-38
"watershed had been crossed," 42

Buese, Lisa (swimmer), 188
"...think through the decision...," 218
bittersweet memories of the 1980 Olympics, 193; moved on after 1980, 193; spectator at the 1996 Summer Games in Atlanta, 193
career: started swimming at a young age, 190; dramatic improvement, 190; peaked at the right time, 191; moved to Cincinnati, 192; boarded with the Caseys of Cincinnati, 192; Olympic Trials, Ronald Reagan presented the award, 192;
experienced sudden cardiac death at age 28, 189; congenital condition, 189; appreciates the quarter found in the cab to take her to hospital, 194
rise up to the challenge, 194
Bush, George W. (U.S. President), 239

Carr, Mel (gymnast from the Temple University team)
inspiration to Ron Galimore, 226
Carter, Amy (President Carter's daughter), 127
Carter, President James "Jimmy"
Carter Doctrine: response to the Soviet invasion of Afghanistan 57; State of the Union address on Jan. 21, 1980, 57; create instability and upset peace in the region, as a stepping-stone to control the world's oil supply, 58; Soviet Union must pay a concrete price for their aggression, 58; no Olympic team sent to Moscow, 59; so close to the Straits of Hormuz, poses a threat to the free movement of Middle East oil, 59; Feb. 13 news conference, President Carter continued to assert the gravity of the crisis in Afghanistan, not obligated to send athletes to Moscow, 65; Feb. 20 deadline passes and hopes fade for competing in the 1980 Olympic Games in Moscow, 67
Cold War: put the world on alert, 60; president asked the world to join the U.S. in boycotting the Summer Olympics in Moscow, Soviet troops to withdraw from Afghanistan by Feb 20, 1980, 60; Russian political-show: Soviet government had a different view, difficult to reach an agreement with the United States, do what we want to do, 61; no one supported diplomacy as a means of resolution, 61

ALSO FROM THE AUTHORS

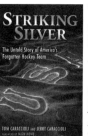

Tom Caraccioli and Jerry Caraccioli also chronicled the silver medal-winning 1972 U.S. Olympic Hockey Team in their first book—*Striking Silver: The Untold Story of America's Forgotten Hockey Team*.

Striking Silver tells the story of that forgotten team and its members which included players that were plucked from the jungles of Vietnam, schoolboy heroes, and college All-Americans: Ahearn, Bader, Boucha, Brown, Christiansen, Curran, Ftorek, Howe, Irving, McElmury, McGlynn, McIntosh, Mellor, Naslund, Olds, Regan, Sanders, Sarner, Sheehy, and Sears—the Silver Medal-winning 1972 United States Olympic hockey team.

ALSO FROM NEW CHAPTER PRESS

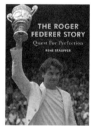

The Roger Federer Story, Quest For Perfection—By Rene Stauffer

Regarded by many as the greatest tennis player in the history of the sport, this authoritative biography is based on many exclusive interviews with Federer and his family as well as the author's experience covering the international tennis circuit for many years. Completely comprehensive, it provides an informed account of the Swiss tennis star from his early days as a temperamental player on the junior circuit, through his early professional career, to his winning major tennis tournaments, including the U.S. Open and Wimbledon. Readers will appreciate the anecdotes about his early years, revel in the insider's view of the professional tennis circuit, and be inspired by this champion's rise to the top of his game.

The Bud Collins History of Tennis—By Bud Collins

Compiled by the most famous tennis journalist and historian in the world, this book is the ultimate compilation of historical tennis information, including year-by-year recaps of every tennis season, biographical sketches of every major tennis personality, as well as stats, records, and championship rolls for all the major events. The author's personal relationships with major tennis stars offer insights into the world of professional tennis found nowhere else.

For more information—including information on how to order these and other New Chapter Press titles—go to www.newchapterpressmedia.com.